From our kitchens to yours

Our global family cookbook

Recipes from our travelers, Tour Directors, and experts around the globe

Food is a powerful thing

It can bring people together.

It can transport you to faraway places.

It can remind you of shared meals
with loved ones.

A taste of the world

Many of my most meaningful travel memories have taken place around a table—tasting local specialties, sipping regional wines, learning unique culinary traditions, and creating close friendships in far-off countries. Every trip I go on, I seek out a cookbook to bring home, so I can try to recreate my favorite dishes for friends and family. My kitchen counter reads like a passport, indexing my past travels from Venice to Vietnam.

As part of our EF Go Ahead Tours community, your mealtime stories and recommendations have inspired me and other travelers to discover new places with all five senses. A few experiences that stick out in my own mind are the smell of wild rosemary in the breeze in Provence, the chatter of local vendors at a farmers' market in Peru, and the taste of generations-old recipes at a Tuscan villa.

Years after you've visited a destination, these colors, smells, and tastes can instantly take you back—at least for the time you're sitting at the table. So if you're prepping for an upcoming adventure or remembering one from long ago, we hope the global dishes recommended by our travelers, Tour Directors, and global staff in this book will help you bring the magic of travel right into your kitchen.

Happy cooking!

Heidi Durflinger
President, EF Go Ahead Tours

Here's to
your adventures!

This cookbook is dedicated to our community of curious travelers. Your enthusiasm for the world around you inspires us each and every day.

....

The photos on this page were shared by Go Ahead travelers like you. Want to see more snapshots from adventures around the globe?

Visit **instagram.com/goaheadtours**

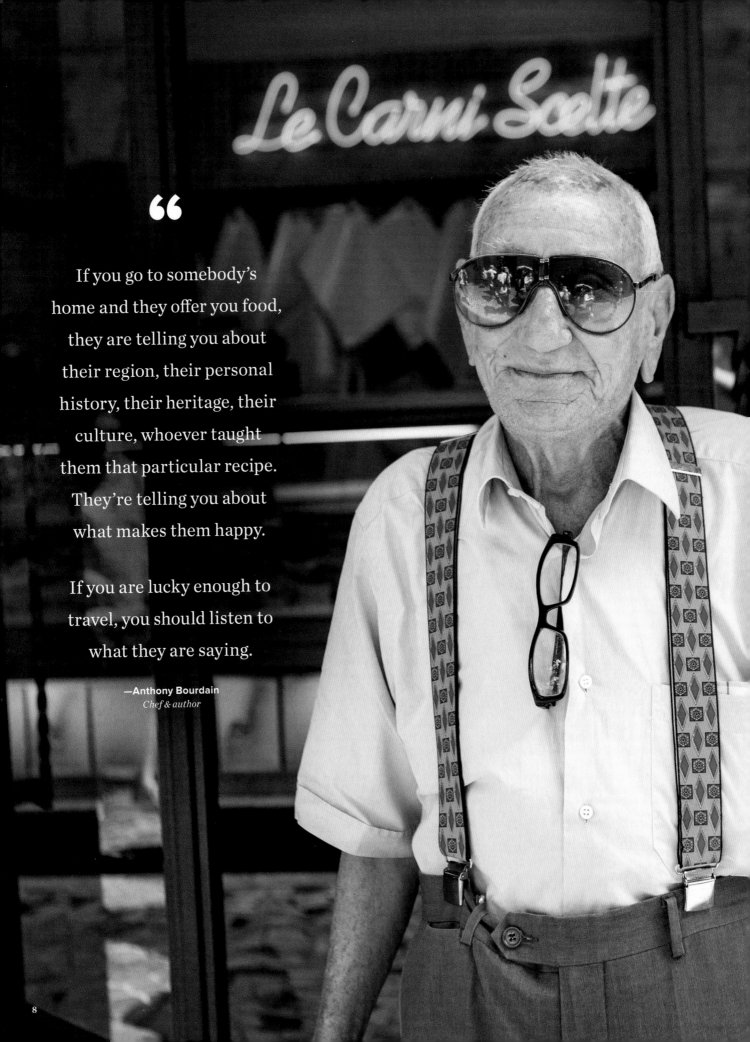

> If you go to somebody's home and they offer you food, they are telling you about their region, their personal history, their heritage, their culture, whoever taught them that particular recipe. They're telling you about what makes them happy.
>
> If you are lucky enough to travel, you should listen to what they are saying.

—**Anthony Bourdain**
Chef & author

Global recipes

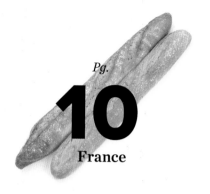

Pg.
10
France

Pg.
48
Great Britain & Ireland

Pg.
72
Italy & Greece

Pg.
122
Spain & Portugal

Pg.
164
Central Europe & beyond

Pg.
190
Nordic countries

Pg.
206
U.S. & Canada

Pg.
222
Latin America

Pg.
252
Asia

Pg.
276
Australia & New Zealand

Pg.
290
Africa & the Middle East

Want to see them all?

Full recipe index
Pg. 316

"

When I think of France, I envision quaint medieval villages with cobblestone streets, small squares for markets, and rustic architecture. Saint-Émilion in Bordeaux fits that image perfectly with its magnificent vineyard views. Here, we had the opportunity to try the original macarons, crafted from a recipe dating back to 1620!

—Scott
5th-time traveler
Food & Wine: France through Bordeaux & the Loire Valley

Baguettes, brasseries & Burgundy wine

———

France

In France, there's a beauty to dining that makes mealtimes so special.

Here, cooking—and eating!—is an art form. Thanks to the precise techniques of haute cuisine, French cooking can feel daunting to home cooks (Julia Child was not the first or last among that set), but there's so much more to it than that. From traditional peasant dishes to modern Parisian bistros to gastronomic masterpieces in Châteaux Country, the theme that runs through French cooking is a celebration of local, seasonal foods—accompanied by a delicious dose of cheese and wine, of course.

Top foodie regions

Normandy in the Northwest

The culinary traditions of the region match the cool, salty climate of its coastal location: think fresh seafood, hearty stews, and crisp apples.

Alsace in the Northeast

Bordering Germany and Switzerland, the cuisine here takes on an Alpine twist with lots of apples, quiches, game, nutty cheeses, and sausages.

Burgundy in central France

The capital of the Burgundy region is Dijon—as in the mustard—and the hometown culinary favorites all seem to complement the namesake condiment: cheeses, meats, and breads.

Bordeaux in the Southwest

Decadent, earthy foods call this region home, like foie gras, duck, farmhouse cheeses, and truffles, along with some of the most revered red wine blends in the world.

Provence in the Southeast

Everything gets lighter, brighter, and more relaxed as you travel through the Provençal countryside. Staples here include vegetables, fruits, eggs, and goat cheese.

The Riviera on the Mediterranean

The cuisine and culture along the Riviera reflect its prime location on the Mediterranean coast. Aromatic herbs, olives, zesty citrus, fresh seafood, and produce of every color make their way into most meals.

Eateries 101

BRASSERIE
Bustling and casual, this is the French take on a classic pub, and remains open from morning till night.

BISTRO
Usually only open during mealtimes, these small eateries keep things simple with a limited menu of crowd favorites written on a chalkboard.

BOUCHON
Found specifically in Lyon, these are the go-to spots for the region's hearty, meat-filled meals.

CRÊPERIE
Cozy eateries specializing in—you guessed it—crêpes, as well as their savory buckwheat cousin, the *galette*.

Pass the butter

Croissants, escargot, hollandaise—if these French favorites have one thing to credit for their rich flavor, it's the generous amount of butter rolled into the recipe. Normandy is the place to go to try the cream of the crop—the region's dairy cows are some of France's best.

Herbes de Provence

Provence is famous for its many markets, overflowing with fresh produce, honey, cheese, flowers, and herbs. The signature herb of the region is a blend called *Herbes de Provence*. While the specifics vary from purveyor to purveyor, it typically includes dried, native oregano, rosemary, thyme, savory, and marjoram.

French bread, the French way

Crusty baguettes are a must-have for dinner (and popular with lunch or as an afternoon snack, too). Stop by the boulangerie right before your meal to pick up a fresh loaf, and eat it right off the table sans butter.

Ordering your oysters

In France, you'll notice numbers next to each oyster on the menu, ranging from 0–6 for flat oysters (*huîtres plates*) and 0–5 for rock oysters (*huîtres creuses*). The key to this code? The larger the number, the smaller the shell.

A course on courses

While this breakdown can be exponentially expanded, this four-course meal is the basis for a formal French dinner.

Hors d'oeuvres
Hors d'oeuvres = starters

Plat principal
Plat principal = main course

Le fromage
Le fromage = cheese course

Le dessert
Le dessert = sweets

13

To the vineyard, s'il vous plaît!

All about French wine

First introduced by the Romans in the middle of the first century, wine has become as much a part of French cuisine as fresh-baked baguettes and coq au vin, and a good glass of rouge, blanc, or rosé is never hard to find.

Drink Pinot Noir
in Burgundy

"Burgundies" refer to the region's dry reds, usually Pinot Noir and Chardonnay. Known for their earthiness, these Pinots are a safe bet for food pairings, ranging from duck to salmon. Burgundy is also the go-to source for fruity Gamay.

Drink Cabernet Sauvignon
in Bordeaux

Perfect with rich cheese or decadent beef dishes, some of the world's most expensive Cabernet Sauvignons and Merlots hail from Bordeaux. While these two varieties are found in Bordeaux blends, which make up 90 percent of the region's output, aficionados can't overlook the flavors of Cabernet Franc, Petit Verdot, and Malbec.

Drink Rosé
in Provence

Wine lovers in North America are finally catching on to France's sophisticated, pink-hued favorite. Typically made using grapes such as Syrah, Grenache, and Mourvedre, French rosés are dry, crisp, and refreshing with flavors that range from strawberry, raspberry, and cherry to ginger, orange peel, and flowers.

TIP:
If you're drinking a Provençal rosé, pair it with light vegetable and fish dishes native to the region.

Drink Champagne
in Champagne

While bubbly wine is found around the globe, it must be made in Champagne, France, to be called Champagne. To the dismay of early vintners here, the region's grapes produced acidic, unexpectedly fizzy wine. By the 1600s, Madame Clicquot and other winemakers added sweetness and embraced the happy accident.

TIP:
Set your flutes to the side. Marie Antoinette glasses were the original vessel of choice for Champagne.

Drink crisp whites
in the Loire Valley

Châteaux Country, just a few hours outside Paris, is home to picturesque villages, vineyards, fruit farms, and grand castles. Here, Muscadet and Sauvignon Blanc from Sancerre and Pouilly-Fumé reign supreme.

TOTAL TIME:

1 hour, 30 minutes

SERVINGS:
4

RECIPE ORIGIN:
France

INGREDIENTS:

1 cup walnuts

10 oz frozen, all-butter puff pastry, thawed and chilled

3 Tbsp unsalted butter

2 onions, thinly sliced

Salt and pepper, to taste

3/4 lb porcini mushrooms, trimmed

1 Tbsp extra-virgin olive oil

A few sprigs of thyme, to serve

Porcini mushroom tartlets

DIRECTIONS:

Preheat oven to 350°F. Place walnuts in a pie plate and bake for about 8 minutes, or until lightly browned. Remove walnuts from the oven and coarsely chop once cooled.

Line a baking sheet with parchment paper. Unfold the puff pastry and cut out 4-in rounds. Transfer rounds to the lined baking sheet and prick generously with a fork. Cover the cutout pastry with more parchment paper and place another baking sheet on top. Bake for 25 minutes, or until golden brown. Remove the pastry from the oven and increase the oven temperature to 400°F.

While the pastry is baking, melt the butter in a large skillet. Add the onions and sauté on medium-high heat for 4 minutes, stirring frequently. Reduce to low heat and continue to cook, stirring often until soft and caramelized, about 50 minutes. Remove from heat and let cool.

Coarsely purée the walnuts and onions in a food processor. Season with salt and pepper and set aside.

Add mushrooms to a medium saucepan of boiling water and blanch until just tender, about 2 minutes. Drain, pat dry, and slice into 1/4 in-thick pieces. Spread baked pastry rounds with the walnut and onion purée, then arrange the mushrooms on top. Brush with oil and bake for 10 minutes, or until hot. Garnish with thyme and serve.

RECIPE RECOMMENDED BY

Philip
Traveler

Did you know?

Porcini mushrooms, or *cèpes* to the French, grow wild in the forest, where they're foraged and brought to local farmers' markets. The best time to have a taste? June and September, especially a week or so after a big rainfall.

TOTAL TIME:

45 minutes

SERVINGS:
4

RECIPE ORIGIN:
France

INGREDIENTS:

Flour, for work surface

1 sheet frozen puff pastry

2 cups gruyère cheese, shredded

1 1/2 lbs asparagus

1 Tbsp capers

1 Tbsp olive oil

Salt and pepper, to taste

Asparagus & gruyère tart

DIRECTIONS:

Preheat oven to 400°F. Flour the work surface, then roll out the puff pastry into
a 16x10-in rectangle and trim any uneven edges. Place the rolled-out pastry on a
baking sheet and lightly score the dough 1 inch in from the edges all the way around,
to mark a rectangle. With a fork, pierce the pastry inside the markings in 1/2-in
intervals. Bake until golden, about 15 minutes.

Remove the pastry from the oven and top with gruyère. Trim the bottoms of the
asparagus spears to fit across the inside of the tart shell. Lay the trimmed spears
crosswise in a single layer on top of the gruyère, alternating ends and tips. Sprinkle
capers on top. Brush with oil and season with salt and pepper. Bake for 20 to 25
minutes, or until the asparagus is tender.

Drizzle with balsamic vinegar for a sweet touch!

Did you know?

Celebrity chef Anthony Bourdain's
career and worldwide culinary quest
can be traced back to this cold soup. He
credits vichyssoise as the first food he
ever really noticed.

TOTAL TIME:

1 hour, 30 minutes

SERVINGS:

6

RECIPE ORIGIN:

Vichy, France

INGREDIENTS:

4 Tbsp butter

8 leeks, white parts only, thinly sliced

2 potatoes, cubed

2 cups chicken stock

2 cups heavy cream

A pinch of nutmeg

Salt and pepper to taste

4 fresh chives, chopped, to serve

Vichyssoise

Chilled potato cream soup

DIRECTIONS:

On medium-low heat, melt butter in a stock pot. Add leeks and allow to sweat for 5 minutes. Add potatoes and cook for 2 minutes, stirring occasionally. Pour in chicken stock and bring to a boil.

Reduce heat and simmer on low until both potatoes and leeks are soft, about 35 minutes. Remove from heat and let cool for 3 to 4 minutes.

In small amounts, add soup to a blender and purée on high speed—making sure the lid is on and secure. Once the entire batch is blended, return to the pot.

Whisk in cream and nutmeg, then season with salt and pepper. Increase heat and bring to a boil, then reduce heat and simmer for 5 minutes. Add more broth if needed.

Pour soup into a mixing bowl and chill in an ice bath until it reaches room temperature. Cover with plastic wrap and finish chilling in the refrigerator. Once soup is completely cold, top with chives and serve.

RECIPE RECOMMENDED BY

Tristan
Tour Director

TOTAL TIME:

45 minutes

SERVINGS:
2

RECIPE ORIGIN:
Nice, France

INGREDIENTS:

1 garlic clove, halved

1 small cucumber, peeled, seeded, and sliced

2 spring onions, thinly sliced

1/2 cup peeled fava beans

1/3 cup niçoise olives, pitted

3 to 4 cups of mixed greens

2 tomatoes or a handful of grape tomatoes

Salt and pepper, to taste

6 Tbsp extra-virgin olive oil

2 Tbsp fresh parsley, chopped

3 hard-boiled eggs

3 to 4 anchovy filets (or substitute
a 6-oz can of tuna)

Salade niçoise

DIRECTIONS:

Start by rubbing the inside of a large salad bowl with a clove of garlic. Add the cucumber, onions, fava beans, olives, and greens to the bowl and set aside.

Slice the tomatoes into wedges and sprinkle with salt. While you finish assembling the salad, let tomatoes drain in a colander.

To make the dressing, mix together oil, parsley, salt, and pepper. Add the tomatoes to the salad bowl, top with most of the dressing, and toss. Note: If substituting tuna for anchovies, toss this with the rest of the salad.

Peel the eggs, cut into wedges, and place on the tossed salad. Finish with anchovies and drizzle the remaining dressing over the top.

Did you know?

While North Americans often consider boiled potatoes and haricot verts critical ingredients of this classic salad, the true southern French way calls for only raw vegetables. Just ask acclaimed cookbook writer and controversial politician Jacques Médecin, who has very strong (and influential) opinions on the matter.

Nice, France

Au marché Français

At the French market

In France, the local markets are more than just places to shop. For many, visits here are just as much about stopping for a chat with friends or soaking in the sunshine as they are about stocking up on daily essentials. Want to join in on the fun? Here are a few pointers for navigating the stalls like the French do.

Making the most of the market

1

Get there early

Typically, vendors will be set up and ready for business by 8:30 or 9 in the morning. Take advantage of the quiet hours before the crowds arrive to enjoy a leisurely stroll through the marketplace and get your hands on the best-quality goods.

2

Look to the locals

Not sure where the line starts or whether or not it's ok to touch those peaches you have your eye on? Pay attention to what others around you are doing and take your cues from them. If you see people picking out their own items, it's generally safe to do the same.

3

Seek out seasonal goods

One of the best parts about a trip to the market is all the ripe, local produce you can fill your bags with. Before your visit, do some research to find out which fruits and vegetables are in season and stock up on those—they'll be the freshest and most flavorful of the bunch.

Best places to picnic

Even better than a market trip? The picnic that comes afterward! Here are our favorite Parisian spots to lunch *en plein air.*

LUXEMBOURG GARDENS
With beautifully manicured flower beds, lavish lawns, and tree-lined avenues, the Luxembourg Gardens serve as a lush escape from the bustling Paris streets.

PARC MONCEAU
Originally planned and built as an English garden in 1778, Parc Monceau is a local favorite, and is considered one of the most elegant gardens in the city.

THE BOTANICAL GARDENS
These sprawling gardens (initially grown as a royal collection of medicinal plants) are spread over 68 acres and feature more than 23,000 plant species.

THE TUILERIES GARDEN
Although the Tuileries Garden was initially reserved for royalty, it is now a well-traveled gathering place and recognized as the oldest public park in Paris.

CHAMP DE MARS
Located directly in the shadow of the Eiffel Tower, this open green space boasts one of the city's most iconic (and sought-after) views.

Learn the lingo

Planning a morning at the market? We've got you covered with these handy phrases to help you cross everything off your shopping list.

In English:	In French:	Pronunciation:
How much?	Combien?	*KOM-bee-en*
I'd like...	Je voudrais...	*ZHE VOO-dray*
That one.	Celui-là.	*SE-loowee lah*
Yes, please.	Oui, s'il vous plaît.	*wee, seel-voo-PLEH*
That will be all, thank you.	Ça sera tout, merci.	*sa seh-RAH too, mer-SEE*
No thank you, I'm just looking.	Non merci, je ne fais que regarder.	*no mer-SEE, ZHE ne fay CUH ruh-GAR-day*

TOTAL TIME:

1 hour

SERVINGS:
2–4

RECIPE ORIGIN:
France

INGREDIENTS:

5 Tbsp butter

2 yellow onions, thinly sliced

2 fresh parsley sprigs, plus more to garnish

2 fresh thyme sprigs

1 bay leaf

1 fresh rosemary sprig

1 cup hard cider, divided

1/4 cup all-purpose flour

2 3/4 cups chicken stock

Kosher salt and pepper, to taste

Baguette, thinly sliced diagonally

1/3 cup gruyère cheese, grated

1/4 cup heavy cream

French onion soup

DIRECTIONS:

In a sauté pan, melt 3 Tbsp of butter on medium-high heat. Add onions and cook until golden brown, about 7 minutes, stirring continuously. Using kitchen twine, tie together the sprigs of parsley, thyme, bay leaf, and rosemary, and add the bundle to the pan along with 1/2 cup plus 2 Tbsp of cider. Bring cider to a boil, then reduce heat and simmer for 5 minutes. Remove from burner.

Melt the remaining butter in a medium saucepan over medium heat. Add flour and cook for 2 minutes, stirring continuously. Whisk in the stock, pouring slowly, and bring to a boil. Turn down heat and simmer for 15 minutes to slightly reduce the broth. Add the onion and cider mixture and cook for 15 more minutes. Remove the herb bundle and discard. Season with salt and pepper.

While the soup is simmering, turn on the broiler. Place sliced baguette onto a baking sheet and broil until golden, about 2 minutes on each side. Divide the rest of the cider evenly between oven-safe serving bowls and ladle soup on top. Place toasted baguette slices on top of each portion of soup, then cover with shredded cheese and a sprinkling of chopped parsley. Drizzle with cream, then broil until cheese is browned and bubbling, about 2 minutes. Serve immediately.

TOTAL TIME:

50 minutes

SERVINGS:

2

RECIPE ORIGIN:

France

INGREDIENTS:

For the béchamel sauce

1 Tbsp butter

1 Tbsp flour

2/3 cup milk

Salt and nutmeg, to taste

For the sandwiches

4 slices sourdough bread

4 thin slices ham

2 Tbsp gruyère cheese, grated

2 eggs

Croque-madame

DIRECTIONS:

To make the béchamel sauce, melt butter in a small saucepan on medium heat. Once butter is completely melted, add flour. Whisk vigorously for 1 minute. Then, slowly add milk and whisk until smooth. Increase heat, bring to a boil, and cook until the sauce reaches a thick consistency. Remove from heat and season with salt and nutmeg.

Preheat oven to 400°F. For the 2 sandwiches, lightly toast the bread, and butter each slice on 1 side. Spread sauce generously over the unbuttered side of 2 of the bread slices, then layer 2 slices of ham on top of each and sprinkle with a small amount of cheese. Spread more sauce onto the 2 remaining slices of bread and close both sandwiches, with the buttered sides facing up. Top sandwiches with a thin layer of béchamel, then cover with the desired amount of cheese.

Place both sandwiches in the oven and bake until golden brown, about 7 minutes. Meanwhile, melt a small amount of butter in a frying pan and fry eggs sunny-side up.

Once sandwiches are cooked through, remove from oven and top with fried eggs. Serve hot.

The only difference from a croque-monsieur? The fried egg!

TOTAL TIME:

1 hour

SERVINGS:

6

RECIPE ORIGIN:

Lorraine, France

INGREDIENTS:

1 pre-made pie crust (or substitute your favorite homemade recipe)

6 strips bacon, cooked and crumbled

4 eggs

1 cup half-and-half

1/4 tsp salt

1/8 tsp white pepper

1/8 tsp nutmeg

1 cup gruyère cheese, grated

Quiche Lorraine

DIRECTIONS:

Preheat oven to 375°F. Lightly grease a deep-dish pie pan and line with crust. Place the pan in the refrigerator to let dough rest for 30 minutes.

Remove the pan from the refrigerator and sprinkle bacon evenly across the bottom. In a mixing bowl, beat the eggs, half-and-half, salt, pepper, and nutmeg together until well combined. Pour the egg mixture into the pie pan over the bacon, and top with cheese.

Bake until eggs are set in the middle, about 45 to 50 minutes. Remove from the oven and let cool before serving.

Eggs aren't just for breakfast! Serve with greens for lunch.

Cooking tip

Once taken out of the oven, quiches continue to cook as they cool. That's why you want yours to have a just-set consistency directly after baking.

TOTAL TIME:

3 hours

SERVINGS:

6

RECIPE ORIGIN:

Gap, a city in the former province of Dauphiné

INGREDIENTS:

Butter, as needed

1 garlic clove

2 lbs Russet potatoes, peeled and thinly sliced

1 1/4 cups whole milk

1 1/4 cups heavy cream

Salt, pepper, and nutmeg, to taste

Gratin Dauphinois

Potatoes baked in milk & cream

DIRECTIONS:

Preheat oven to 275°F. Coat an 8-in baking dish with butter. Cut the garlic clove in half and rub over the inside of the dish. In the prepped dish, arrange potatoes in just-overlapping layers. Mix milk and cream in a bowl, then pour over potatoes until just covered. Bake for 1 hour.

Remove potatoes from the oven and sprinkle with desired amount of salt, pepper, and nutmeg. Return to the oven and continue baking until golden brown and bubbling, about 60 to 90 minutes.

TOTAL TIME:

2 hours

SERVINGS:
8

RECIPE ORIGIN:
Marseille, France

INGREDIENTS:

For the rouille

A pinch of saffron threads

2 garlic cloves

1 red pepper, roasted, peeled, and seeded

1 egg yolk

Juice from half a lemon

1 tsp salt

1/2 cup olive oil

For the stew

3 Tbsp extra-virgin olive oil

2 leeks, white parts only, thinly sliced

1 onion, diced

1 fennel bulb, cored and diced

4 garlic cloves, 3 chopped

2 tomatoes, chopped

2 bay leaves

A pinch of saffron threads

2 Tbsp Pernod or pastis

5 cups fish stock

8 baguette slices

1 1/2 lbs potatoes, peeled and cubed

1/4 tsp cayenne pepper

Salt and black pepper, to taste

2 dozen littleneck clams, scrubbed

3 lbs white fish filets, cut into bite-size pieces

1/2 lb mussels, scrubbed and debearded

1/2 lb large shrimp in shells

Bouillabaisse

Fish stew

DIRECTIONS:

Start by making the *rouille* (or sauce). In the bowl of a food processor, combine all ingredients for the rouille except the oil. Pulse until smooth. Slowly pour in the oil and continue to blend until the mixture thickens. Transfer to a bowl and place in the refrigerator.

For the stew, heat oil in a pot and add leeks, onion, fennel, and chopped garlic. Cook on medium heat until soft and translucent, about 5 minutes. Add tomatoes and cook for an additional 5 minutes. Add in bay leaves, saffron, and Pernod. Bring to a boil, then add fish stock and simmer. Cook on low heat for 20 minutes or until all vegetables are soft. Remove bay leaves and discard.

Pour all contents of the pot into a food processor. Pulse until the consistency is a coarse purée. Place a fine sieve over the pot and strain the purée through.

Meanwhile, turn on your broiler. Place sliced baguette pieces on a baking sheet and broil until golden around the edges, about 1 minute per side. Slice the last garlic clove in half, then rub each piece of bread with the halves. Drizzle with oil.

Add potatoes and cayenne pepper to the puréed broth and simmer. Cook on medium-high heat for 10 minutes or until the potatoes are just tender. Season with salt and pepper. Add clams and thicker pieces of fish, then cover and cook on medium heat until they begin to open, about 3 minutes. Add in the rest of the fish, mussels, and shrimp. Cover the pot and continue to simmer until all clams and mussels are completely open and the fish is fully cooked, about 5 minutes.

To serve, place a piece of baguette at the bottom of each serving bowl. Ladle stew over the bread and top each serving with 1 Tbsp of rouille. Serve hot.

Cooking tip

Part of why French fish stews are so delicious is their use of local, fresh ingredients. This recipe traditionally calls for a pound each of monkfish, halibut, and red snapper, but feel free to substitute any fresh options that are available.

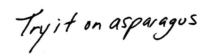

Sauces & vinaigrettes

TOTAL TIME:

15 minutes each

RECIPE ORIGIN:
France

Hollandaise sauce

SERVINGS:
1 1/2 cups

INGREDIENTS:
3 egg yolks
1 Tbsp water
Juice of half a lemon
6 to 8 oz unsalted butter, softened
Salt and white pepper, to taste
A pinch of cayenne pepper

DIRECTIONS:

In a saucepan, completely whisk together egg yolks, water, and lemon juice. Turn heat to low and continue whisking, paying special attention to the bottom and sides of the pan. If eggs are cooking too fast, briefly move the saucepan off the burner, then return to heat, whisking continuously. Remove from heat once eggs have reached a thick, smooth consistency and you can see the bottom of the pan through whisk streaks.

Add the butter, 1 spoonful at a time, whisking continuously. Continue to add butter until the sauce reaches desired consistency. Season the sauce with salt, white pepper, cayenne pepper, and lemon juice. Serve lukewarm.

Try it on asparagus

Did you know?

A hallmark of the country's classic cuisine, the French have a penchant for sauces. In fact, there are five Mother Sauces, including béchamel and hollandaise.

Béchamel sauce

SERVINGS:

3 cups

INGREDIENTS:

2 Tbsp butter

4 1/2 Tbsp flour

3 cups milk

1 tsp salt

A pinch of nutmeg

DIRECTIONS:

In a medium saucepan, melt butter on medium-low heat. Add flour and whisk until no lumps remain. Cook for 3 minutes.

Pour in milk and continue to whisk, bringing mixture to a boil. Season with salt and nutmeg. Turn heat down and let simmer until sauce is able to stick to the back of a spoon.

Try it on a croque-madame on pg. 25

French vinaigrette

SERVINGS:

1 1/2 cups

INGREDIENTS:

1/2 cup red wine vinegar

2 tsp sugar

1 Tbsp Dijon mustard

1 tsp salt

1 1/2 tsp pepper

1 tsp dried tarragon

1 cup olive oil

DIRECTIONS:

Whisk vinegar, sugar, mustard, and seasonings together in a small bowl. Slowly add oil and continue stirring until the mixture begins to thicken.

Try it on simple greens

Courtney
Go Ahead Tours

TOTAL TIME:

2 hours

SERVINGS:
6

RECIPE ORIGIN:
France

INGREDIENTS:

6 chicken thighs, bone-in and skin-on

Salt and pepper, to taste

8 strips bacon, sliced in 1/2-in pieces

10 button mushrooms, sliced

1/2 yellow onion, diced

2 shallots, diced

2 tsp flour

2 tsp butter

1 1/2 cups red wine

6 sprigs fresh thyme

1 cup chicken stock

Coq au vin

DIRECTIONS:

Preheat oven to 375°F. Season chicken with salt and pepper and set aside.

Cook bacon in an oven-safe pot or Dutch oven on medium-high heat until brown. Remove from the pot and set aside on a paper towel to drain and cool.

Turn burner heat up to high and place the chicken, skin-side down, in the pot used to brown the bacon. Cook for 2 to 4 minutes on each side. Remove chicken from pan and set aside. Discard all but 1 Tbsp of drippings from the pot.

Reduce heat to medium-high and sauté mushrooms, onions, and shallots until soft and translucent, about 5 minutes, seasoning with salt as the mixture cooks. Add flour and butter, stirring until flour is absorbed.

Add the red wine and boil while stirring with a wooden spoon. Stir in bacon and thyme, and simmer the mixture until wine is reduced by about 1/3. Add in chicken stock and place chicken in the pot. Bring to a simmer.

Remove the pot from heat and place in the oven. Cook for 30 minutes. After the first 30 minutes, open the oven and baste. Continue cooking for another 30 minutes, or until no pink is showing. Take the pot out of the oven and transfer the chicken to a platter.

Reduce pan juices on high heat until thick. Add salt and pepper to taste and discard thyme. Pour sauce over chicken and serve.

I enjoy cooking with wine, sometimes I even put it in the food...

—**Julia Child**, *Chef & TV personality*

Did you know?

This dish was a noted favorite of TV chef Julia Child. "The French Chef" host prepared it enough times over the life of her show that she is credited with increasing its popularity in North America.

Patrick
Tour Director

TOTAL TIME:

1 hour, 30 minutes

SERVINGS:
4–6

RECIPE ORIGIN:
Nice, France

INGREDIENTS:

6 oz tomato paste

1/4 cup garlic, minced

1/2 onion, chopped

3 Tbsp olive oil

3/4 cup water

Salt and pepper, to taste

1 eggplant, thinly sliced

1 zucchini, thinly sliced

1 summer squash, thinly sliced

1 red bell pepper, cored and thinly sliced

1 yellow bell pepper, cored and thinly sliced

1 tsp fresh thyme leaves

Ratatouille

DIRECTIONS:

Preheat oven to 375°F. Add tomato paste to a 10x10-in baking dish. Top with garlic and onions, then pour in oil and water, stirring until well combined. Season with salt and pepper.

On top of the tomato paste mixture, arrange the vegetable slices in concentric circles working toward the middle of the dish. Alternate between eggplant, zucchini, summer squash, red pepper, and yellow pepper.

Sprinkle oil over the vegetables and top off with salt, pepper, and thyme. Cover the dish with parchment paper and bake for 45 minutes or until vegetables are cooked through.

Sliced veggies look pretty but chopped are just as tasty!

Did you know?

There are two schools of thought around ratatouille. Some people believe it's best prepared with all the ingredients stewed together (like this recipe), while others argue that cooking each vegetable on its own before mixing together preserves the unique flavors.

35

An ode to French oysters

When it comes to enjoying great food, the French most certainly have it down pat—and the country's culinary love affair doesn't end with mouthwatering wine and cheese. Of all the delicious bites to try, fresh oysters, or *huîtres*, have a special place on the gastronomic list. Whether you order *demi-douzaine* on the half shell from a Parisian oyster bar, or a local fisherman shucks you some famous Belon oysters in the Brittany region, these bivalves are a French favorite you don't want to miss.

1

To rinse or not to rinse?

If you wish to wash off any extra grit, using a scrub brush and running your oysters under cold water will do the trick. Or, do as the French do and opt out of rinsing to preserve even more fresh, ocean flavor. No matter what, be sure your oysters are well-chilled before shucking and serving.

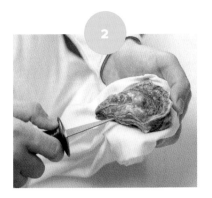

2

Hold it steady

Locate the pointy hinge of the shell, which clamps the top and bottom halves together. With the larger, bottom shell facing down, hold the oyster in place using a kitchen towel, and gently press the blunt tip of the knife into the hinge. (Pro tip: Try not to tilt the oyster while opening it; the juice inside packs a ton of flavor!)

3

Twist the blade

Once you've pressed your blade into the hinge, slowly twist the knife until the shell pops open slightly. Then, run your knife along the inside of the shell from the hinge to the rounded end of the oyster to cut the bivalve's muscle.

4

Give it a nudge

Using your knife, gently scrape the underside of the oyster to free it from the shell, and place it (shell and all) on a bed of crushed ice.

5

Mix up a mignonette

While horseradish, cocktail sauce, or fresh lemon juice are common condiments, a mignonette is the classic French accompaniment. Make your own by whisking together 1 finely minced shallot, 2 cups of red wine vinegar, and freshly ground pepper.

6

Pour an ideal pairing

When it comes to the best oyster pairings, crisp or bubbly wines are the way to go. Pour a glass of Champagne, dry Muscadet, citrusy Sancerre, or Chablis. Both the bubbles and bright flavors are the perfect contrast to an oyster's smooth consistency and briny taste.

7

Enjoy!

The best way to eat raw oysters is straight from the half shell. Top each off with your condiment of choice or savor it plain and simply tilt the shell sideways—no special utensils needed.

TOTAL TIME:

5 hours
+ overnight soaking

SERVINGS:
6–8

RECIPE ORIGIN:
Toulouse, France

INGREDIENTS:

1 lb dried cannellini beans

7 1/2 cups water

10 Tbsp olive oil, divided

2 onions, chopped and divided

2 carrots, chopped and divided

16 garlic cloves, smashed and divided

2 large ham hocks

1 lb pork shoulder, cut into 1-in pieces

1/2 lb pancetta, cubed

4 sprigs oregano

4 sprigs thyme

3 bay leaves

1 cup whole, peeled, canned tomatoes

1 cup white wine

2 cups chicken stock

4 confit duck legs

1 lb pork sausages

Cassoulet

White bean & meat casserole

DIRECTIONS:

Soak beans in water overnight.

In a large pot, warm 2 Tbsp of oil on medium-high heat. Add half the onions, half the carrots, and 8 garlic cloves, and cook until just brown. Then, add the ham hocks, beans, and water, and bring to a boil. Lower heat to a simmer and cook for 90 minutes, or until beans are soft. Remove ham hocks and place on a plate to cool. Debone, chop meat, and add to the pot.

Add 2 Tbsp of oil to a Dutch oven. Brown the pork on medium-high heat for about 8 minutes. Add pancetta and cook for another 5 minutes. Add the rest of the garlic, onions, and carrots, and continue to cook for another 10 minutes.

Using kitchen twine, bundle together oregano, thyme, and bay leaves. Add the bundle to the Dutch oven along with tomatoes and cook until the liquid inside begins to thicken. Then, add wine and cook until reduced by half. Pour in chicken stock and bring to a boil. Once boiling, turn heat to medium-low and cook uncovered for about 1 hour, or until the liquid reaches a thick consistency. Remove the herb bundle.

While the contents of the Dutch oven are cooking, heat a large skillet on medium-high heat and sear duck legs for 8 minutes in 2 Tbsp of oil. Brown sausages in the same skillet for 8 minutes. Remove from heat and cut into 1/2-in slices. Debone the duck legs. Add both duck meat and sausages to the pork mixture.

Preheat oven to 300˚F. Combine the contents of the Dutch oven and the pot in an earthenware casserole dish and drizzle the rest of the olive oil over the top. Bake for 3 hours, uncovered.

Cooking tip

This meat-filled favorite is named after the cooking vessel it's made in: a cassole. A *cassole* is a terra-cotta dish made in a rural village outside of Castelnaudary, a town that shares Toulouse's and Carcassonne's title as the homeland of cassoulet. To present your finished dish like a true French chef, serve it right in the dish you cooked it in.

For the love of fromage

At a formal French meal, a cheese course will be served before dessert, but a selection of fromage is also often enjoyed as a picnic during the day or a starter to a more casual meal. Putting together a cheese plate at home? Here are a few tips to keep in mind.

For a special touch, dress up your cheese with a sprinkling of nuts and herbs.

▼

Pick your cheese

Choose three to five types of cheese to offer a variety of textures, starting with one soft, one hard, and one blue. We suggest Camembert, similar to brie but a bit stronger, for your soft cheese—it's a signature French flavor and a crowd-pleaser. To play off the creaminess of the Camembert, choose a hard cheese that's tangy or nutty like Comté, which hints at the flavors of the Alps. For the always-controversial blue cheese, Roquefort from the Pyrenees is a classic pick.

Add the extras

Skip crackers in favor of a sliced baguette. On the side, add in something sweet, like in-season fruit, fresh fig jam, or local honey, and something savory, like mustards or pickles. Don't go overboard with the accoutrements— the star of the plate should definitely be the cheese.

Serve it up

Let your cheeses come to room temperature before serving. For serious taste-testing, try your selections from the mildest cheese to the strongest. Looking for a wine pairing? If your cheeses are all from a certain area, opt for a bottle with the same origin. If not, a fruity Beaujolais is a universal pick that works well with most flavors.

Encourage a sweet-and-savory combo of rich blue cheese and local honey.

▼

▲

Give each kind of cheese its own knife.

41

TOTAL TIME:

25 minutes

SERVINGS:
17–22 crêpes

RECIPE ORIGIN:
France

INGREDIENTS:

2 eggs

3/4 cup milk

1/2 cup water

1 cup flour

3 Tbsp butter, melted

2 1/2 Tbsp sugar

1 tsp vanilla

Crêpes

DIRECTIONS:

Add all ingredients to a blender and blend on the "pulse" setting for 10 seconds. Refrigerate batter for 1 hour.

Heat a small, nonstick frying pan, and coat with extra butter. Pour 1/8 cup of batter into the middle of the pan and swirl to spread evenly over the surface. Flip the crêpe over after 30 seconds and continue to cook for an additional 10 seconds.

Remove from the pan and let cool. Repeat until batter is gone.

no crêpe maker needed

RECIPE RECOMMENDED BY
Michelle
Go Ahead Tours

Going to the source

The northern commune of Chantilly has a few claims to fame, including its extravagant Château de Chantilly and the town's intricate namesake lace, but the most delicious of its calling cards is definitely Chantilly cream. Go Ahead Tours staffer Michelle recently visited the historic area on our culinary tour, *Food & Wine: France through Burgundy & Champagne*, and tasted the fluffy topper for herself.

Tastes from tour

"We saw a lot of really beautiful villages as we made our way around eastern France, but Chantilly stands out as one of the most elegant. After visiting the massive château and equestrian center, we went to the downtown area for lunch at a local crêperie called La Cour Pavée. For the main course, I had a melty ham-and-cheese crêpe, followed by a sweet dessert crêpe topped with chocolate and the town's famous Chantilly cream, which is basically a really delicious version of whipped cream. The opportunity to taste Chantilly's signature sweet right in Chantilly was such a treat!"

Experience this on tour:
Food & Wine: France through Burgundy & Champagne
goaheadtours.com/tof

Michelle
Go Ahead Tours

A trip
to Chantilly, France

RECIPE FROM TOUR:

Chantilly cream

INGREDIENTS:

1 cup heavy cream

1 Tbsp granulated sugar

1/2 tsp vanilla extract

DIRECTIONS:

In a bowl, combine the cream and sugar. Using a whisk or electric mixer, beat until you get fluffy peaks. Add in the vanilla and beat the mixture for another 30 seconds or so.

TOTAL TIME:

50 minutes

SERVINGS:

1 tart

RECIPE ORIGIN:

France

INGREDIENTS:

3 Tbsp butter

3/4 cup sugar

3 granny smith apples, peeled, cored, and sliced

1 Tbsp flour

9-in pre-made pie crust (or substitute your favorite homemade recipe)

Tarte Tatin

Caramelized apple pastry

DIRECTIONS:

Preheat oven to 425°F. Coat the inside of a 10-in skillet with butter, then evenly distribute sugar over the bottom of the pan.

Add apple slices to the skillet, arranging in a circular design on top of the butter and sugar.

On medium-high heat, cook apples until butter is melted and the sugar starts to caramelize. Once caramelized apples soften and begin to brown, remove skillet from the heat.

Flour your work surface and roll pie crust out to 11 inches in diameter. Lay the crust on top of the apples and tuck excess dough into the skillet.

Bake for 20 minutes, or until crust is golden in color. Remove from the oven and let cool for about 5 minutes. Invert the pie by placing a plate over the pan and flipping over. Release the tart from the skillet. Serve warm.

RECIPE RECOMMENDED BY

Maryanne
Traveler

Did you know?

A delicious accident, this upside-down pastry was made by mistake when the owner of the Hôtel Tatin in Lamotte-Beuvron, France, forgot about her apple pie halfway through baking. This sweet treat was created in an attempt to save the remnants and became the hotel's signature dessert.

Laura
Go Ahead Tours

TOTAL TIME:

1 hour

SERVINGS:

4

RECIPE ORIGIN:

France

INGREDIENTS:

Baking spray

1 stick butter

2 oz bittersweet chocolate

2 oz semi-sweet chocolate

1 1/4 cups confectioners' sugar

2 eggs

3 egg yolks

1 tsp vanilla

1/2 cup flour

Chocolate lava cake

DIRECTIONS:

Preheat oven to 425°F. Spray the insides of 4 ramekins with baking spray and set aside.

Melt the butter and all chocolate in a double boiler, stirring until chocolate is completely melted and the mixture is smooth. Add the sugar and stir until well mixed. Whisk in the eggs, egg yolks, and vanilla. Add the flour and stir until combined. Pour batter into ramekins in equal portions.

Place the ramekins on a baking sheet and bake for 13 minutes, or until the sides have firmed but the centers remain soft.

Remove from the oven and let cool for about 1 minute before serving.

Did you know?

While the rainbow-colored cookies are associated with the French, they originated in Italy and were brought over when the Italian aristocrat Catherine de Medici married France's King Henry II in 1533. A few centuries later, the French left their mark by making them into double-decker cookies filled with jam or buttercream.

"

Our pastry experience, making macarons, was a tasty delight.

—Becky,
7th-time traveler
Food & Wine: France through
Burgundy & Champagne

TOTAL TIME:

2 hours, 30 minutes

SERVINGS:
36 macarons

RECIPE ORIGIN:
France

INGREDIENTS:

For the buttercream filling

6 Tbsp plus 1 tsp granulated sugar, divided

3 egg yolks

1/4 cup plus 2 1/4 tsp whole milk

1 cup unsalted butter, room temperature, cut into 1/2-in pieces

1/2 tsp vanilla extract

For the cookies

1 3/4 cups confectioners' sugar

1 cup almond flour

3 egg whites, room temperature

1/4 tsp cream of tartar

A pinch of salt

1/4 cup superfine sugar

1/2 tsp almond extract

2 to 3 drops pink food coloring

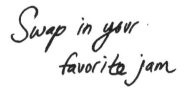

Swap in your favorite jam

Macarons with vanilla buttercream

DIRECTIONS:

Start by making the buttercream filling. Whisk half of the sugar with the egg yolks and set aside. Combine the second half of the sugar with the milk in a saucepan. Warm over medium heat, stirring to dissolve sugar. Just before the milk starts to simmer, give it a quick whisk, remove from heat, and pour into the egg mixture. Return the combined mixture to the pan over medium heat, whisking constantly. Simmer for 1 minute so that the consistency becomes thick. Strain through a fine-mesh strainer into a mixing bowl. Using a stand mixer fit with a whisk attachment, whisk for about 8 minutes on medium, letting the mixture cool. Add the butter in small batches, whisking continuously until the buttercream is light and fluffy. Mix in the vanilla extract.

Preheat oven to 300°F and prep 3 baking sheets by topping them with silicone mats. Whisk together confectioners' sugar and almond flour in a mixing bowl until completely combined. Pass mixture through a fine-mesh sieve, and discard anything left over.

In a metal or glass bowl, beat egg whites, cream of tartar, and salt on medium speed until frothy. Turn speed up to medium-high and gradually add in superfine sugar. Beat until the whites form stiff peaks. Using a rubber spatula, fold whipped egg whites into the almond flour and confectioners' sugar mixture, turning the bowl in quarter turns after each fold. Continue until the whites are completely mixed in. Add almond extract and food coloring and continue folding, scraping down the sides of the bowl as you go. Stop once the batter reaches a smooth consistency and runs off your spatula in a thin ribbon.

Put batter into a pastry bag that has a 1/4-in round tip attached. Pipe 1 1/4-in round circles onto the prepared baking sheets. To release any air bubbles that may have formed during piping, lightly hit the trays against the counter before baking. Allow macaron shells to rest at room temperature until the tops are no longer sticky to the touch. Bake for 20 minutes, or until shells are shiny and have risen about 1/8 in. Remove from the oven and let cool completely.

Create finished macarons by sandwiching a layer of vanilla buttercream between two shells.

"

From the Irish pubs in Galway to Dublin, there
was so much local music, great beer, and Irish
whiskey to be tried. The regional cuisine was
delicious—the seafood chowder, salmon, and
fish and chips were all yummy.

—Kathryn
2nd-time traveler
A Week in Ireland: Galway, Cork & Dublin

Pints, potatoes & pub fare

Great Britain & Ireland

Here's to the best bites from the brisk British Isles.

Comfort and simplicity are the hallmarks of British and Irish cuisine. Hearty stews and homemade meat pies are fitting complements to the region's often cool and cloudy days. This temperate climate is great for raising sheep and pigs, and growing root vegetables and resilient greens like kale and cabbages. The seemingly endless green pastures in the countryside make happy homes for cows, so dairy is a key part of diets—think remarkably tasty butters and cheeses.

Pull up a stool

One of the first things travelers mention after a trip to the UK or Ireland is how much they loved the warm and welcoming pub culture. The perfect spot to chat with locals, relax after sightseeing, and sample the region's signature dishes, these cozy watering holes have long been an important part of the culture. Here are a few of our favorites.

DUBLIN'S BRAZEN HEAD

At over 800 years old, it's Ireland's oldest pub, and home to a knowledgeable staff and nightly live music.

GALWAY'S TIG CÓILÍ

A favorite for both visitors and locals, this cozy bar is the perfect spot for cheerful conversation, or *craic* to the Irish.

EDINBURGH'S ENSIGN EWART

Lively, picturesque, and inviting, this spot is located right on the Royal Mile near Edinburgh Castle.

LONDON'S NAGS HEAD

Overflowing with knickknacks, paintings, and old photos, this Holloway pub has a wonderfully quirky, neighborhood feel.

THE NAME GAME:

Fish & chips

FISH SUPPER
A more homey name for the classic fried combination.

ONE AND ONE
The story of this nickname goes back to an Italian immigrant working at a pub. She would ask patrons if they wanted one of this and one of the other (as in fish and chips) and the expression took hold in Irish vernacular.

CHIPPY
Chip shops are eateries or take-away stands specializing in fish and chips, though locals often just refer to them as chippies or chippers.

DEEP ROOTS:

The history of the Irish potato

The potato made its way to Ireland thanks to Spanish conquistadors. They brought the root vegetable across the Atlantic from the Andes Mountains in South America, where it had been cultivated for thousands of years. While many European countries were instantly smitten, the British were suspicious of the crop's subterranean—and therefore possibly Satanic—origin, so they passed the potato on to Ireland to test out.

Ireland's cloudy climate mirrored the Andes and the crop flourished, breathing new life into the country. The population surged and the country's poor relied so heavily on the energizing veggie that experts estimate a typical farmer would eat a diet of almost entirely potatoes, around nine pounds a day. This reliance made the potato blight of the mid-19th century particularly devastating for Ireland. "The Great Hunger" lasted from 1845 to 1852. During the famine, approximately one million Irish died and one million emigrated, causing the Irish population to fall 20–25 percent.

Clotted cream

This much-loved scone topper, made from heated cow's milk, is like a cross between butter and whipped cream.

Get full on a full breakfast

The Brits and Irish are famous for their "full breakfast" with fruit, cereal, bacon and eggs, sausages, black pudding, fish, grilled tomatoes, and toast with marmalade. Each region has its own twist: haggis (a savory breakfast pudding encased in a sheep's stomach) in Scotland, soda bread in Ireland, and laverbread in Wales.

A complement to cloudy weather

◀ Is there anything better than hot soup on a chilly day? It's no wonder that British and Irish cuisine has so many types of warming vegetable soups.

Head to pg. 54, 56, and 61 for a few favorites.

All in for ale

Out of the many different beers made in England, ale holds a particularly special place on the list. Over the centuries, the country has earned a reputation as a premier brewer of top fermented cask beer, or "real ale."

Not sure which one to try first? Here's a guide to the most widely recognized kinds.

1 Porter

A substantial, bitter beer characterized by its dark color

TASTING NOTES:
chocolate, coffee

VARIETIES:
brown (between 4 and 6% alcohol by volume, or ABV), robust (between 5 and 7% ABV), Baltic (up to 10% ABV)

PAIRING:
Pairs best with roasted meats

2 Bitter

A kind of pale ale, ranging in color from gold to amber

TASTING NOTES:
hops, butterscotch, fruit

VARIETIES:
standard or ordinary (between 3 and 4% ABV); best, special, or premium (around 4% ABV); extra special or strong (around 5% ABV)

PAIRING:
Pairs best with fish and chips

3 Brown

A mild ale with a rich chocolate color

TASTING NOTES:
malt and nuts for northern brews, caramel and dark fruit for southern blends

VARIETIES:
northern (Newcastle), southern (Manns)

PAIRING:
Pairs best with smoked sausages

Fancy a cocktail?

Ale isn't the only thing that puts Britain on the map. The Isles also have a noteworthy menu of traditional spirits that'll quench your thirst if you're looking for something a little stronger.

Scotch

What exactly sets Scotch apart from other whiskies? In addition to a strict set of laws set forth by the Scotch Whisky Regulations that protect the production process, it must be crafted in Scotland.

Pimm's

This spiced liqueur is a longstanding staple of an English summer. Not only is it a featured cocktail at Wimbledon and the Chelsea Flower Show, but remains a time-honored favorite of the university garden party circuit.

Gin

Today, gin brings images of London to mind. This juniper berry-based liquor first rose to popularity in Great Britain when William of Orange took the throne in the late 17th century.

3 gin drinks to try in London

GIMLET

This limey cocktail got its start aboard British Navy ships, where sailors cut their scurvy-fighting lime juice with the juniper-infused liquor.

VESPER MARTINI

Gin, vodka, Blanc Lillet, and a garnish of lemon—though 007 made this martini famous, it's actually traditionally stirred, not shaken.

GIN & DUBONNET

Made with one part gin and two parts Dubonnet Rouge (an aperitif made with fortified wine and herbs), this is a favorite of Queen Elizabeth II.

Warm up & perk up

Like many recipes, the tale behind Irish coffee's origin is somewhat murky. Legend holds that it was invented in the 1940s at the Foynes airbase near Limerick, a popular port of call for seaplanes. As passengers arrived from chilly, wet transatlantic flights, a boozy coffee was just the thing to warm them up! The basics of this recipe? Coffee, Irish whiskey, sugar, and cream.

Brittany
Traveler

TOTAL TIME:

2 hours, 20 minutes

SERVINGS:
6–8

RECIPE ORIGIN:
Ireland

INGREDIENTS:

2 Tbsp olive oil, divided

3 lbs beef chuck roast, trimmed of excess fat, cut into bite-size pieces, and divided

Kosher salt and pepper, to taste

1 large white or yellow onion, diced

4 garlic cloves, minced

1/3 cup flour

12-oz bottle of Guinness® (or substitute stout beer of choice)

4 cups beef stock

3 large carrots, peeled and diagonally sliced into bite-size pieces

2 Yukon Gold potatoes, cut into bite-size pieces

3 Tbsp tomato paste

1 bay leaf

1/2 tsp dried thyme

Fresh parsley, chopped, to garnish

Beef stew with stout

DIRECTIONS:

Heat 1 Tbsp of oil in a large stockpot over medium-high heat. Add half of the beef and season with salt and pepper. Turning the meat often, sear until all sides are browned.

Remove beef from the pot and transfer to a clean plate. Add an additional 1 Tbsp of oil to the stockpot, and sear the remaining beef. Once browned, remove from heat and set aside with the rest of the beef.

Add the onion to the stockpot and sauté until it's soft and translucent, about 5 minutes. Add garlic and sauté for 1 minute. Stir in the flour to coat the onions, and cook for 1 minute. Gradually stir in beer, using a wooden spoon to scrape the bottom and sides of the pot. Stir in the beef stock, carrots, potatoes, tomato paste, bay leaf, thyme, and cooked beef. Bring to a simmer and cover. Reduce heat to low and simmer for 90 minutes, stirring occasionally. You'll know it's done when the beef is tender and the potatoes are soft.

Remove bay leaf, season as needed, and garnish with chopped parsley.

My favorite night in Dublin took place in a little pub in the heart of the old town overlooking the main square. Live music was playing, there was a big bowl of Irish stew in front of me, and I just sat back and soaked in the picture-perfect setting.

—Brittany,
5th-time traveler
Grand Tour of Ireland

RECIPE RECOMMENDED BY

Alaina
Go Ahead Tours

TOTAL TIME:

1 hour

SERVINGS:
4–6

RECIPE ORIGIN:
County Clare, Ireland

INGREDIENTS:

2 Tbsp olive oil

1 Tbsp butter

5 potatoes, peeled and chopped

2 leeks (white part only), sliced

1 onion, chopped

4 cups vegetable stock

2 sprigs of fresh thyme

1 cup whipping cream

Salt and pepper, to taste

2 pieces of bacon, cooked and crumbled

Chives, chopped, to garnish

Potato leek soup

DIRECTIONS:

In a large saucepan, heat oil and butter over medium heat. Add potatoes, leeks, and onion, and sauté until leeks are translucent, about 8 minutes. Add stock and thyme and cover. Simmer until potatoes are soft, stirring occasionally, about 30 minutes.

Remove the thyme sprigs. In a blender, purée the soup in batches. Return soup to the saucepan. Stir in the cream and season with salt and pepper. Garnish with crumbled bacon and chives to serve.

There's nothing better than settling into a warm pub on a chilly, rainy day with a warm bowl of soup, bread, and a pint of beer. The soup in Ireland is creamy and hearty and warms you from the inside out. The best part? Meeting the friendly locals while you soak up the broth with your bread!

—**Alaina**, *Go Ahead Tours*

TOTAL TIME:

1 hour

SERVINGS:

1 loaf

RECIPE ORIGIN:

Dublin, Ireland

INGREDIENTS:

5 cups whole-grain flour

1 1/4 cups plain flour

3/4 cup rolled oats

2 1/2 tsp baking soda

1 tsp salt

2 1/2 Tbsp brown sugar

3 Tbsp butter

2 cups whole milk

3/4 cup black molasses

8 oz of Guinness®

Guinness bread

DIRECTIONS:

Preheat oven to 350°F and grease a loaf tin. In a mixing bowl, combine dry ingredients with butter to create a crumbly dough. Add the milk, molasses, and Guinness. Mix until you have a wet dough. Bake for 40 to 45 minutes.

Did you know?

More than just a beverage, Guinness has become a cultural institution in Ireland and the UK. After Prince Albert died in 1861, Londoners started adding the stout to darken their Champagne, reflecting the country's state of mourning. This marks the arrival of the cocktail, the Black Velvet.

Time for afternoon tea

Miniature sweets:
Favorites include scones with jam and clotted cream, mini cakes, fruit tarts, and mini buns with icing called fancies.

What's in a name?

Afternoon tea, which is served at 3 or 4pm, is also called "low tea," named for the low settees and arm chairs where the 19th-century aristocrats would enjoy it. "High tea" was more of a working-class meal of heartier dishes like meat pies and puddings at the end of a workday, served on higher dining tables.

Queen of the tea party

Anna Russell, Duchess of Bedford, is credited with creating afternoon tea in the mid-1800s. Originally served to her privately in her chamber, she began inviting friends over for tea and a walk, and the trend caught on among aristocrats.

The earl of Earl Grey

This bergamot blend was named for Charles Grey, the 2nd Earl Grey, by a Chinese trader whose son nearly drowned and was saved by one of the earl's men.

Traditional teas:
Darjeeling, Earl Grey, and
lapsang souchong are
authentic picks.

**Dainty finger
sandwiches:**
Classic combos include
cucumber and butter,
egg salad and watercress,
and ham and mustard.

59

TOTAL TIME:

50 minutes

SERVINGS:

8

RECIPE ORIGIN:

England

INGREDIENTS:

10 large eggs, divided

8 sausages

Half a bunch of fresh chives

Half a bunch of fresh parsley

2 tsp nutmeg, grated

1 tsp English mustard

A pinch of salt

A pinch of pepper

A handful of plain flour

1 cup fresh white breadcrumbs

8 1/2 cups vegetable oil

Scotch eggs

DIRECTIONS:

Place 8 eggs in a pan of cold water and bring to a boil. Boil for 3 to 4 minutes, then immediately cool the eggs completely in cold water. Peel.

Prep the sausage mixture by removing the sausage skins and combining meat, herbs, nutmeg, mustard, salt, and pepper in a large bowl. Mix thoroughly and divide into 8 sections. Roll out 8 balls.

Set up an assembly line of three dishes: one with flour, one with the remaining eggs, and one with breadcrumbs. Flour your hands and flatten one of your sausage balls between your hands to create an oval patty. Dust one of the boiled eggs in flour and place it at the center of the patty. Mold the sausage patty around the egg to cover it completely. Roll the meat-wrapped egg in the flour, dip in the egg, and roll in the breadcrumbs. For a thicker coating, dip in the egg and breadcrumbs a second time. Repeat the whole process with the other 7 patties and eggs.

In a deep pan, heat oil to about 300°F and then gently place the meat-wrapped eggs in the pan. Cook for 4 minutes until golden, turning them periodically. Using a slotted spoon, remove the balls and let them dry on a paper towel.

RECIPE RECOMMENDED BY

Bryant
Go Ahead Tours

Did you know?

Contrary to what the name may lead you to believe, this popular picnic dish is English, not Scottish. In fact, it was invented at Fortnum's in Piccadilly, London.

TOTAL TIME:

2 hours

SERVINGS:
4

RECIPE ORIGIN:
England with Indian roots

INGREDIENTS:

1/2 tsp whole mustard seeds

1/2 tsp whole cumin seeds

1/2 tsp whole coriander seeds

2 Tbsp vegetable oil

3 large chicken thighs

Kosher salt and pepper, to taste

1 onion, finely chopped

1 carrot, finely chopped

1 celery rib, finely chopped

1 Tbsp curry powder

3 garlic cloves, finely chopped

1-in piece fresh ginger, grated

1 sweet potato, peeled and cut into 1/4-in pieces

1 apple, peeled and cut into 1/4-in pieces

1 plum tomato, cut into 1/4-in pieces

1/2 cup dry red lentils

6 cups chicken broth

Fresh thyme, to garnish

Greek yogurt, to garnish

Mulligatawny soup

DIRECTIONS:

In a skillet, toast mustard seeds, cumin seeds, and coriander seeds over high heat until spices get aromatic, about 3 minutes. Set aside to cool, then ground down using a mortar and pestle or spice grinder.

Coat a large skillet in oil and place over medium heat. Season chicken thighs with salt and pepper, and place in the skillet with the skin side down. Cook until skin is golden brown, about 5 minutes, and then flip to cook the reverse side for another 4 to 5 minutes.

Remove chicken from the pot and add onion, carrot, and celery. Cook until onions are soft and translucent, about 5 minutes. Add curry powder and stir to coat vegetables. Add garlic, ginger, sweet potato, apple, and tomato, and mix thoroughly.

Add lentils and chicken thighs to the pot. Pour in broth and bring to a simmer. Let the soup cook for about 1 hour, until potatoes and lentils are soft and you've reached your desired thickness.

Remove thighs from the soup and, using two forks, shred the meat and skin. Return the meat to the soup and season with salt and pepper. Garnish with thyme and a dollop of yogurt.

Did you know?

Along with the likes of Champagne from Champagne, France, and Parma ham from Parma, Italy, Scottish-farmed salmon has been awarded the Protected Geographical Indication status by the European Commission.

TOTAL TIME:

20 minutes

SERVINGS:
4

RECIPE ORIGIN:
Scotland

INGREDIENTS:

Four 6-oz Scottish salmon fillets

2 Tbsp olive oil

Salt, to taste

2 Tbsp unsalted butter

1 garlic clove

Juice of 1 lemon

Sugar, to taste

A bunch of fresh thyme or dill, to garnish

Pan-seared salmon

with garlic & dill

DIRECTIONS:

Rub salmon with oil and salt. Warm a nonstick pan over medium-high heat. Add salmon skin-side up to the pan and turn heat to high. Pan-sear until the color turns opaque and a golden-brown crust appears at sides, about 4 minutes. Turn over and cook until the fish is firm to the touch, about 3 more minutes. Remove from heat.

For the sauce, melt butter in a saucepan over low heat. Add the garlic and cook until fragrant and light brown, about 3 minutes. Add lemon juice and sugar to taste. Remove from heat, allowing the sauce to cool for 1 minute. Stir in herbs and spoon sauce over salmon.

Spoon juices over salmon while cooking to keep it moist

TOTAL TIME:

45 minutes
+ overnight marinating

SERVINGS:
4–6

RECIPE ORIGIN:
United Kingdom

INGREDIENTS:

For the marinade

1 tsp paprika

1 1/2 tsp cumin seeds

1 tsp red chili powder

1/2 tsp garam masala

1/2 tsp ground coriander

3-cm piece of fresh ginger

6 garlic cloves

Juice of 1 lemon

2 Tbsp yogurt

2 Tbsp oil

For the chicken tikka masala

1 1/3 lbs chicken thigh fillets, cut into cubes

Salt, to taste

2 Tbsp oil

1 large onion, chopped

1 tsp ginger, minced

1/2 tsp ground turmeric

2 tsp ground coriander

1 tsp paprika

1 tsp red chili powder

1 Tbsp tomato paste

1/4 cup canned tomatoes

Juice of half a lemon

3/4 cup fresh cream

1/4 tsp garam masala

A handful of fresh cilantro leaves, to garnish

Chicken tikka masala

DIRECTIONS:

Rub chicken with salt, and cut into cubes. In a mixing bowl, combine all marinade ingredients and mix thoroughly. Add chicken and mix to coat the pieces. Cover the dish and refrigerate overnight.

Preheat grill. Place marinated chicken pieces onto skewers. Grill for 15 to 20 minutes or until cooked through. Remove chicken from skewers and set aside.

In a large pan, heat oil over medium heat. Add onions and sauté for 2 to 3 minutes. Add ginger and sauté until aromatic. Add turmeric, coriander, paprika, and red chili powder, and sauté for 1 minute. Add tomato paste and let sizzle for a few seconds before adding in the tomatoes. Bring everything to a boil, then reduce heat and simmer for 2 to 3 minutes. Add lemon juice and cream, and stir. If needed, add water to create your desired thickness. Season with salt and let simmer for 3 to 4 minutes. Add garam masala and grilled chicken, and stir to heat evenly. Garnish with cilantro.

Indian food is incredible in England. Sample freshly baked naan bread and chicken tikka masala, which has a creamy, yogurt-based sauce with Indian spices, at one of the many Indian restaurants on Brick Lane in the East End.

—**Charlotte**,
1st-time traveler
London: The City Experience

Did you know?

While a few spots claim this globally adored dish as their own—including India and the British cities of London and Birmingham—experts believe it was in a Bangladesh restaurant in Glasgow, Scotland, where chicken tikka evolved into its creamy cousin, chicken tikka masala.

It's what's inside that counts

Skip the apples or cherries here—when it comes to pies in the UK, savory meat pies are the go-to. Various versions of this pastry-based dish were first eaten in Egypt, Greece, and ancient Rome, but the meat pies we associate with Great Britain and Ireland evolved in the Middle Ages.

Originally, the pie's lidded crust was more of a long-lasting container than the yummy, buttery pastry we enjoy now. The functional pastry was created to easily carry and store food for long periods, and sometimes wasn't eaten at all. The good stuff was all housed inside: meat, vegetables, gravy—pretty much whatever food was readily available. In fact, the name "pie" likely comes from a nickname for the magpie, which is known to collect lots of little scraps in its nest.

Modern-day iterations

Chicken & leek pie
Savory chicken, fresh herbs, vegetables, and creamy gravy make this the ultimate in comfort food.

Steak & kidney pie
A true British classic, this beef and kidney combination is sometimes called a Kate and Sidney pie or a snake and kiddy pie.

Beef Wellington
Forgoing the traditional pie plate, this dish is a stand-alone piece of beef, wrapped in pastry.

Cornish pasty
A personal take on meat pies, this version comes from Cornwall, where miners would bring the handheld lunch to work.

TOTAL TIME:

1 hour, 45 minutes

SERVINGS:
6–8

RECIPE ORIGIN:
Wales

INGREDIENTS:

6 to 8 Yukon Gold potatoes, peeled and cut into cubes

4 Tbsp butter, softened

1/4 cup milk

Salt and pepper, to taste

1 Tbsp vegetable oil

1 1/2 lbs ground lamb

1 medium onion, chopped

2 garlic cloves, minced

1 tsp fresh thyme

3 Tbsp tomato paste

6 to 8 carrots, diced

3 parsnips, diced

1 cup peas

1 cup beef stock

3/4 cup (6 oz) of Guinness® (or substitute more beef stock)

2 tsp Worcestershire sauce

A sprig of parsley, to garnish

Shepherd's pie

DIRECTIONS:

Start by preparing the mashed potato topping. Add the potatoes to a large pot and cover with cold water. Bring to a boil and cook on a low boil until potatoes are fork-tender, about 20 minutes. Transfer potatoes to a mixing bowl and add the butter, milk, salt, and pepper, and mash until smooth. Set aside.

Preheat oven to 350°F. Coat a cast-iron skillet in oil and place on stovetop over medium-high heat. Add the ground lamb, season with salt and pepper, and brown the meat, breaking it up as it cooks.

Transfer the cooked lamb to a bowl, leaving enough meat drippings to coat the skillet. Add the onions and sauté over medium heat until soft and translucent, about 5 minutes. Add the garlic and thyme, and cook for 3 minutes. Mix in the tomato paste. Add the remaining vegetables, beef stock, beer, and Worcestershire sauce, and simmer until the carrots and parsnips are tender, about 20 to 25 minutes. Season if necessary and remove from heat.

In a baking dish, combine the lamb and vegetable mixture. Top with the potatoes, spreading evenly. Place the dish on a baking sheet in the oven and bake until the top is golden brown, about 25 minutes. Let rest for 10 minutes or so, and garnish with parsley before serving.

Did you know?

Originally made with leftovers from a roast dinner, shepherd's pie is made with lamb (that's where the name comes in!), and in Wales, sheep outnumber people four to one. In North America, we often sub in ground beef, but that's called cottage pie in the UK.

Not that kind of pudding!

TOTAL TIME:

1 hour

SERVINGS:
12 muffin-sized pastries

RECIPE ORIGIN:
England

INGREDIENTS:

1 1/4 cups flour

1/2 tsp salt

4 large eggs

1 1/2 cups whole milk

4 Tbsp vegetable oil (or substitute beef drippings)

Yorkshire pudding

Dinner pastry

DIRECTIONS:

Sift flour and salt in a bowl. In a second mixing bowl, combine the eggs and milk. Add in the dry ingredients and whisk until a smooth batter forms. Set aside and allow mixture to rest at room temperature for 30 minutes.

Preheat oven to 450°F with the oven rack placed at the center position. Using a Yorkshire muffin tray or standard 12-hole muffin tray, add 1 tsp of oil or beef drippings in each well. Place the tray in the oven until it's sizzling (almost smoking) hot, about 10 minutes.

Remove the tray from the oven and quickly add the batter, filling up each well 1/2 to 3/4 full. Immediately return the tray to the oven and bake for about 15 minutes. You'll know the pastries are done when they've quadrupled in size and formed a brown top that sounds hollow when tapped. Serve hot filled with gravy alongside roast meat.

TOTAL TIME:

10 minutes
+ 2 hours chilling

SERVINGS:
4

RECIPE ORIGIN:
England

INGREDIENTS:

2 1/2 cups strawberries

1/3 cup Cointreau or ginger cordial (optional)

2 1/2 cups double cream

6 meringues

Eton mess

DIRECTIONS:

Set a few strawberries aside for garnish, and cut the rest of the strawberries into bite-size pieces. Place the cut strawberries in a bowl and pour in liquor, if desired. Cover and chill in the refrigerator for 2 hours.

Whip the cream until soft peaks form. Fold in the strawberry mixture. Crush the meringues and fold into the strawberry and cream mixture. Delicately spoon the mixture into individual serving dishes and top with strawberries.

This strawberry dessert is supposedly really popular with the royals—and it's delicious and easy to make!

—**Pascal**, *Tour Director*

Did you know?

While there are various tales about how this fruit-filled dessert was invented, they all involve Eton College, an English boarding school with famous graduates like Princes William and Harry. The most charming theory? A frisky labrador sat on a picnic basket containing strawberry pavlova at Eton's opening day picnic.

RECIPE RECOMMENDED BY

Laura
Go Ahead Tours

TOTAL TIME:

1 hour, 30 minutes

SERVINGS:
6–8

RECIPE ORIGIN:
England

INGREDIENTS:

For the pudding

1 cup plus 1 Tbsp all-purpose flour

1 tsp baking powder

3/4 cup pitted dates

1 1/4 cups boiling water

1 tsp baking soda

1/4 cup unsalted butter, softened

3/4 cup sugar

1 large egg, lightly beaten

1 tsp vanilla

For the toffee sauce

1/2 cup unsalted butter

1/2 cup heavy cream

1 cup packed light brown sugar

Chocolate shavings, to garnish (optional)

Sticky toffee pudding

DIRECTIONS:

To make the pudding, preheat oven to 350°F. Butter a 10-in round or square baking dish. Sift the flour and baking powder onto a sheet of waxed paper. Finely chop the dates. Place in a small bowl and add the boiling water and baking soda; set aside. In a mixing bowl, beat the butter and sugar until light and fluffy. Add the egg and vanilla; beat until blended. Gradually beat in the flour mixture. Add the date mixture to the batter and fold with a rubber spatula until blended. Pour into the prepared baking dish. Bake until pudding is set and firm on top, about 35 minutes. Remove from the oven and place on a wire rack to cool.

To make the toffee sauce, combine the butter, heavy cream, and brown sugar in a small saucepan; bring to a boil, stirring constantly. Boil gently over medium-low heat until mixture is thickened, about 8 minutes. Preheat broiler. Spoon about 1/3 cup of the sauce over the pudding. Spread evenly on top. Place pudding under the broiler until the topping is bubbly, about 1 minute. Serve immediately in dessert bowls. Drizzle with toffee sauce and top with chocolate shavings if desired.

My brother moved to Scotland and got married. This recipe is from his wife's family and it's delicious!

—**Laura**, *Go Ahead Tours*

Did you know?

While this date-topped dessert is famously British, the recipe is believed to have originated in Canada and been brought to the English countryside by Canadian troops during WWII.

"

Our Tour Director took my husband and me to a *ristorante* in Florence, Italy. I ordered cheese ravioli with a light white wine, lemon, and sage sauce—I can still taste it if I close my eyes and dream. For dessert, I had a cup of vanilla gelato topped with a double espresso. It was an incredible, unforgettable lunch in the city.

—Sharon
6th-time traveler
Grand Tour of Italy

Lemons, tomatoes & Mediterranean sunshine

Italy & Greece

Unforgettable flavors shine in Italy and Greece.

Pull up a seat to any table in either country and you're guaranteed to be greeted by the same thing: a dish made with equal parts local ingredients and love. In both destinations, a homemade meal is synonymous with a warm welcome, and time-honored cooking traditions bring seasonal Mediterranean flavors to the forefront. Here are some of the renowned products each country is known for and where to go for a taste of the best.

For the love of lemons

That brightness that shines through in so many Greek and Italian dishes? It's the citrusy kick of lemon, a culinary star along the Mediterranean coast. Some of Greece's best dishes include a trifecta of lemon, olive oil, and oregano. And in Italy, limoncello liqueur is just the start.

Some of our favorite dishes:

1

Lemon & shrimp risotto

This delicious take on Italy's most famous rice dish is a mainstay along the Amalfi Coast, where lemons grow abundantly.

2

Lemon chicken & rice soup

Simple ingredients make this classic Greek dish, also called *kotosoupa avgolemono*, a hearty go-to on cold days.

3

Lemon potatoes

This flavorful side dish, called *ellinikos lemoni patatas*, is a culinary staple across Greece. The potatoes are soft on the inside and crispy on the outside, and pair perfectly with roasted lamb, chicken, and even fish.

4

Lemon granita

This semi-frozen dessert was first created in Sicily but can be found all throughout Italy. With a consistency somewhere between sorbet and Italian ice, it's a tart, refreshing bite on summer days.

Extra-virgin olive oil

Olive oil production in Italy and Greece goes back thousands of years (as Greece's fossilized, 50,000-year-old olive leaves can attest). While the Ancient Greeks are to thank for bringing olive trees to Italy, the Italians are credited with perfecting oil production—and it's a toss-up as to who makes the best today. Whether you cook with it or simply drizzle it over the top of a dish, extra-virgin olive oil serves as one of the most distinctive Mediterranean flavors.

WHERE TO GO FOR THE BEST:

Catch a ferry to Corfu or Crete, where olive trees grow abundantly. When on Italian soil, opt for peppery olive oil in Tuscany or head south to Puglia, the country's olive oil capital.

Seafood

With country borders bounded by more water than land, Italy and Greece are the places to savor delicious seafood. Their prime coastal locations and deeply ingrained fishing traditions are reflected in countless dishes, in which simple preparation highlights fresh flavors.

WHERE TO GO FOR THE BEST:

Taste coastal favorites in Liguria, a region better known as the Italian Riviera. It's here that anchovies, mussels sourced from "the Gulf of Poets," and a mixed seafood stew called *ciuppin* are standouts. In Greece, an extensive seafaring history is evident in dishes like grilled octopus, lobster, and fried squid. Make your way from Mykonos to Santorini to Crete, popping into a few of the country's countless *psarotavérnes*, or fish taverns, along the way.

Cheese

When it comes to delicious *formaggio*, Italy and Greece set the bar high. From feta and Graviera in Greece to Pecorino Toscano, Parmigiano-Reggiano, and Mozzarella di Bufala in Italy, you really can't go wrong with any type.

WHAT TO TRY:

Dig in to a *horiatiki*, or Greek salad, in Athens, Mykonos, and beyond. Nothing beats fresh feta straight from the place it was produced, layered on top of locally grown veggies. In Italy, a DOP seal stands for *Denominazione di Origine Protetta*, or Protected Designation of Origin, and is the grade reserved for the best-of-the-best. For example, the cheeses from Parma and Campania spring to mind.

At the market

Markets play a key role in both Italian and Greek cultures. Here are a few of the most famous.

LA PESCHERIA

Pay a visit to this famous Catanian fish market in Sicily to watch cleaver-wielding fishermen fillet the day's freshest catch.

SANT'AMBROGIO

Want to walk in step with locals who are doing their food shopping in Florence? Head to this small market in Piazza Lorenzo Ghiberti, which offers up an authentic look at daily life.

VARVAKIOS AGORA

This bustling marketplace in central Athens has been around since 1878, and strolling through is a multi-sensory experience. After eyeing the fare at the meat, fish, and vegetable markets, sit down in one of the bazaar's many authentic tavernas to try some for yourself.

LAIKI AGORA

Meaning "the people's market," these bustling farmers' markets can be found almost every day of the week throughout Greece. They're important social institutions and the places to go to pick up fresh, locally grown items.

Vying for the best vino

All about Italian wine

Producing and drinking some of the world's best vino is serious business throughout Italy. While there are countless varieties to try, we've rounded up some of the best from the country's most beloved wine regions.

Drink Prosecco
in Veneto

Italy's crisp, fizzy favorite is an aromatic white most often found as a sparkling wine (*spumante*), but can also be semi-sparkling (*frizzante*) or still (*tranquillo*).

Drink Marsala
in Sicily

Sicily's wines have their own feel and flavors. Winemaking grapes such as Nero d'Avola and Aglianico grow abundantly in the rich, volcanic soil. The island's specialty? Marsala, a sweet red that's often served as a dessert wine.

Drink Brunello di Montalcino
in Tuscany

Tuscany is known around the world as a region that has perfected the art of making good wine. Here, Sangiovese grapes are crushed down to create shining wines like Brunello di Montalcino, a bold, tannic vino that just gets better with age.

Drink Lambrusco
in Emilia-Romagna

Along with full-bodied reds and whites that can hold their own next to hearty pasta and meat dishes, this region has another unique standout: Lambrusco. The fizzy red is a great lunchtime or appetizer wine thanks to its moderate alcohol content and bright bubbles.

Drink Barolo
in Piedmont

Barolo is referred to as "The King of Wines," and sits distinguished as Piedmont's sweetheart. This prized red produced from Nebbiolo grapes is known for its earthy, rosy flavor and sparked the "Barolo Wars"— a dispute between traditionalists and modernists about the method and length of Barolo winemaking. Barbaresco and Moscato are other Piedmont favorites.

"The King of Wines"

A nod to Greek wine

Greece may not immediately come to mind when thinking of the world's most well-known varietals, but there's certainly something to be said for the country's wines. Greece is home to a proud grape-growing tradition—and has been making wine longer than anyone else in Europe. Here are four of the top types to try.

Assyrtiko

This grape was first grown in Santorini but has become such a favorite that its cultivation has spread to other parts of the country. It's often planted in the volcanic soil of oceanside vineyards and produces a light, dry, citrusy white.

Retsina

Once considered out of style, this unique white wine is making a comeback. What makes the age-old style so unusual? It's fermented with pine resin for an earthy, unexpected flavor profile.

Agiorgitiko

This grape is the most widely grown in Greece and is used to produce a red that's tannic, fruity, and so bold that it's often called "the blood of Hercules."

Xinomavro

Northern Greece is the top producer of this complex, highly acidic red, which is often compared to renowned northern Italian wines such as Barolo.

Did you know?

If you want to whip up a truly authentic salad, don't crumble the feta! Eat like the Greeks and leave it as large blocks.

TOTAL TIME:

10 minutes

SERVINGS:
4

RECIPE ORIGIN:
Greece

INGREDIENTS:

4 tomatoes

1 cucumber

1 green bell pepper

1 red onion

1 cup pitted Kalamata olives

Salt, to taste

4 Tbsp extra-virgin olive oil

1 to 2 Tbsp red wine vinegar

8 oz feta cheese, left in large blocks

1/2 tbsp dried oregano

Horiatiki

Classic Greek salad

DIRECTIONS:

Cut the tomatoes into wedges, slice the cucumber into circles, and core the bell pepper and slice. Cut the onion in half and thinly slice. Place everything on a large salad dish and add the olives. Season with a pinch of salt.

Drizzle oil and vinegar over the top and give everything a very gentle toss (be careful not to over-mix). Top with feta blocks and a sprinkle of dried oregano.

For the food lover, dine on traditional Greek cuisine at an outdoor cafe overlooking the Aegean Sea, or drink the famous Vinsanto wine in Santorini.

—**Erin**,
3rd-time traveler
The Greek Islands: Mykonos, Santorini & Crete

Cooking tip

Classic bruschetta is made with ripe tomatoes and torn basil, but the best part of this fresh-flavored appetizer? Its flexibility. Add pesto, sun-dried tomatoes, your favorite cheese, or even seasonal fruit like grilled peaches.

Two twists on bruschetta

TOTAL TIME:

45 minutes
+ 2 hours resting

SERVINGS:
10

RECIPE ORIGIN:
Italy

Bruschetta ai peperoni

Bruschetta with bell pepper

INGREDIENTS:

1 red bell pepper

1 yellow bell pepper

1 garlic clove, crushed

2 Tbsp black olives, roughly chopped

A few leaves of fresh basil, roughly chopped

Salt and pepper, to taste

3 Tbsp extra-virgin olive oil

1 baguette, thinly sliced for crostini

DIRECTIONS:

Bring grill to medium-high heat, and grill whole peppers until softened and browned, about 6 to 8 minutes. Turn with tongs every few minutes until lightly charred on all sides. Remove peppers from heat and let cool. Once cool, carefully peel and discard skins. Cut off stems, seed peppers, and cut them into thin strips. In a medium bowl, combine peppers, garlic, olives, and basil. Season with salt and pepper, drizzle with oil, and mix. Let the mixture rest about 2 hours.

Preheat oven to 350°F. Brush bread slices with oil, place on a baking sheet, and toast in the oven until golden brown, about 5 to 7 minutes. Lay bell pepper strips on toasted bread and serve.

Bruschetta ai fagioli cannellini

Bruschetta with white beans

INGREDIENTS:

4 garlic cloves, minced

8 cups mixed leafy greens like kale or baby spinach, roughly chopped

3 Tbsp extra-virgin olive oil

2 Tbsp balsamic vinegar

1/2 tsp kosher salt, to taste

1/2 tsp pepper

1/2 large red onion, diced

2 cups cooked white beans

2 tsp dried oregano (or substitute 4 tsp fresh oregano, chopped)

1 cup vegetable or chicken stock

1 baguette, thinly sliced for crostini

DIRECTIONS:

Place a large skillet over medium heat and sauté garlic and greens in 1/2 Tbsp oil until tender, about 5 minutes. In a separate bowl, mix cooked garlic and greens with vinegar, salt, and pepper.

Add oil to the same skillet used to sauté garlic and greens and place over medium heat, saving some oil for bread slices. Sauté onions until soft and translucent, about 5 minutes. Mix in beans, oregano, and stock, and thicken by simmering over medium heat for about 10 minutes. Lightly mash the bean mixture to your desired consistency and stir well.

Preheat oven to 350°F. Brush the bread slices with oil, place on a baking sheet, and toast in the oven until golden brown, about 5 to 7 minutes. Top with sautéed greens, finish with a layer of the bean mixture, and serve warm.

Meze essentials

TOTAL TIME:

1–3 hours
for all three dips

SERVINGS:
4–5

RECIPE ORIGIN:
Greece & throughout the Mediterranean

Tzatziki

INGREDIENTS:

1/2 cucumber

1/2 tsp salt

2 garlic cloves

1 Tbsp white vinegar

2 Tbsp extra-virgin olive oil, plus more for serving

1 1/2 cups plain Greek yogurt

1 Tbsp dill, minced

DIRECTIONS:

In a food processor, grate the cucumber. Toss with 1/2 tsp salt, then transfer to a mesh strainer to drain. Spoon cucumber meat onto a cheesecloth or thick napkin and squeeze to dry.

Wipe the food processor clean and add in garlic cloves, remaining salt, vinegar, and oil. Once a wet paste forms, spoon contents into a large bowl. Add in the cucumber and yogurt and stir to mix thoroughly. Cover mixture and chill in the refrigerator for at least 2 hours. When ready to serve, add fresh dill and drizzle oil on top.

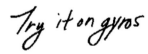

Try it on gyros

Did you know?

Meze is a selection of small bites to enjoy before dinner. Popular snacks include bread and dips, nuts, stuffed grape leaves, cheeses, olives, and more. One thing that's always a must-have? Good conversation. Meze is meant to be shared among friends and family over drinks (traditionally the Greek aperitif of ouzo).

Eggplant mousse

INGREDIENTS:

3 large purple or white eggplants

7 Tbsp extra-virgin olive oil, plus more for serving

1 large garlic clove, mashed

Juice of 1 lemon

Salt and pepper, to taste

Fresh herbs like flat-leaf parsley or thyme, to garnish (optional)

DIRECTIONS:

Char eggplants using your preferred method, and allow them to cool for 10 to 15 minutes. Cut eggplants in half lengthwise and scoop out the flesh with a spoon, placing innards in a colander.

Allow flesh to drain for 10 to 15 minutes, and then place it in a medium bowl. Using a fork, mash it roughly until you've created your desired texture. Add oil, garlic, and lemon juice, and season with salt and pepper. Mash again, and then drizzle with oil and garnish with herbs if desired.

Try it on pita bread

Beet dipping sauce

INGREDIENTS:

2 beets, scrubbed and trimmed

2 Tbsp extra-virgin olive oil, plus more for roasting beets

3 Tbsp water

1/2 cup walnuts

1 large garlic clove

1 tsp kosher salt, plus more to taste

1 cup Greek yogurt

Juice of 1 lemon, plus more to taste

2 tsp fresh dill, chopped

1 1/2 tsp prepared horseradish

Toasted sesame seeds, to garnish (optional)

DIRECTIONS:

Drizzle beets with oil and place in a dish that has 3 Tbsp of water at the bottom. Tightly cover with foil and roast at 375°F until tender, about 1 to 1 1/2 hours, turning beets after 45 minutes. Let cool, then peel.

Grind walnuts, garlic, and salt in a food processor until finely ground. Add the peeled beets, oil, yogurt, lemon juice, dill, and horseradish, then pulse until relatively smooth. Add more lemon and/or salt to taste, and garnish with sesame seeds if desired.

Try it on carrot sticks

What makes buffalo mozzarella the best?

A visit to the farm

Used to make favorites like margherita pizza, caprese salad, antipasto, and more, mozzarella is a true staple in Southern Italy. The reason creamy mozzarella here stands out from the pack? The region's species of water buffalo. The center of buffalo mozzarella production is in Salerno in the region of Campania. On our Amalfi Coast Walking Tour, Go Ahead Tours staffer Brittany recently visited one of the region's organic buffalo farms to taste the gooey mozzarella—and so much more—right at the source.

Brittany
Go Ahead Tours

Tastes from tour

We visited Tenuta Vannulo, a beautiful farm in the Paestum countryside. We toured the stables and grounds, made friends with some buffaloes, and then all sat down to taste the farm's beloved cheese. I was surprised to learn they make more than the revered mozzarella. We tried three kinds of buffalo cheeses—my favorite was ricotta—served simply with fresh bread, the farm's own veggies, and local wine. For dessert, we had peach yogurt and gelato made with buffalo milk—so creamy and delicious.

All the farm's cheese is handmade, and you could taste the care that goes into it with every bite. In fact, we learned that mozzarella gets its name from the Italian word *mozzare*, which translates to "cutting by hand," so it was neat to see the artisans pulling and shaping the mozzarella.

Experience this on tour:
Amalfi Coast Walking Tour
goaheadtours.com/wam

Neapolitan pizza margherita

TOTAL TIME:

3 hours, 30 minutes

SERVINGS:

8

RECIPE ORIGIN:

Naples, Italy

INGREDIENTS:

For the dough

1 1/2 tsp active dry yeast

1 1/2 cups warm water (110°F), divided

1/2 tsp salt

3 1/2 to 3 3/4 cups unbleached all-purpose flour

1 tsp extra-virgin olive oil

For the topping

3 Tbsp extra-virgin olive oil

1/2 cup tomato sauce

One 8-oz ball fresh buffalo mozzarella cheese, cut into small pieces

12 fresh basil leaves

1/2 tsp fine sea salt

Skip the slices — in italy you use a fork and knife

DIRECTIONS:

In a large mixing bowl, combine yeast and 1/2 cup warm water. Allow yeast to dissolve and let it sit to proof for about 10 minutes. Thoroughly combine remaining cup of warm water with yeast, then add the salt and 3 cups of flour. Using either a mixer with a dough hook or your hands, mix the dough. If needed, add remaining flour to ensure the dough stays together.

Knead dough on a floured surface until it's soft rather than sticky, about 10 minutes. Grease a large mixing bowl with 1 Tbsp oil and coat the dough by turning it a few times in the bowl. Using plastic wrap, tightly cover the bowl and let dough rise in a warm spot for about 2 hours.

Preheat oven to 425°F. Remove dough from the bowl, knead it on a lightly floured surface for a couple of minutes, and cut it in half. Using your fingers on a floured surface, stretch and flatten each piece into a 12-in round. Lay each round on an oiled, 13-in pizza pan, and form a rim by turning the dough edges in about 1/2 in.

Using a basting brush, coat each dough round with 1 Tbsp oil. Cover each with 1/4 cup of tomato sauce, sprinkle on cheese, and garnish with basil leaves. Add salt and remaining 1 Tbsp oil. Bake pizzas until crust is browned, about 25 to 30 minutes.

Paula
Go Ahead Tours

TOTAL TIME:

3 hours

SERVINGS:
4

RECIPE ORIGIN:
Milan, Italy

INGREDIENTS:

For the broth

A piece of boiled beef

1 carrot

1 onion

1 celery stalk

1 parsley stalk

2 to 3 peppercorns

Sea salt, to taste

For the risotto

2 Tbsp butter, divided

1/2 onion, finely chopped

1 2/3 cups rice, preferably Carnaroli

1/2 cup white wine

Saffron, to taste

Sea salt and pepper, to taste

1/2 cup Parmigiano-Reggiano cheese, grated

Balsamic vinegar, to taste (optional)

Risotto allo zafferano

Saffron risotto

DIRECTIONS:

In a medium pot, combine all broth ingredients and cover with cold water. Bring the mixture to a boil until the beef is tender, about 2 hours. Season with salt and allow broth to simmer on low heat.

Place a medium saucepan over medium-high heat, warm up 1 Tbsp butter, and sauté onion until it's soft and translucent, about 5 minutes. Toast rice in the pan for about 4 minutes, stirring continuously. Stir in wine until it's absorbed and rice is translucent.

Stir in 1 ladle of broth at a time until each is absorbed, taking care to mix in any grains that may be stuck to the side of the pan to ensure evenly cooked risotto. Taste the dish before adding each scoop of broth to prevent adding too much liquid and overcooking. While adding the broth, remember that stirring slowly and continuously is key.

Place a small pan over low heat and toast the saffron. Release more saffron flavor by crumbling the threads, then mix in a small portion of broth. Cook rice until it's al dente, add the saffron-flavored broth, and season with salt and pepper. Remove mixture from heat and stir in cheese and butter. Serve each portion topped with a generous drizzle of balsamic vinegar if desired.

This dish is super creamy and comforting— I tried it in San Gimignano, where saffron is a specialty, and it was by far my favorite dish in Italy! It's also pretty easy and very rewarding to make at home.

—**Paula**, *Go Ahead Tours*

Did you know?

According to legend, this dish came to be in 1574. A glassmaking apprentice who used saffron to color the stained glass of Milan's duomo decided to sprinkle some in a batch of wedding rice, and this culinary staple, also called *risotto alla Milanese*, was born.

TOTAL TIME:

1 hour, 15 minutes

SERVINGS:
20 arancini

RECIPE ORIGIN:
Sicily, Italy

INGREDIENTS:

10 cups water, lightly salted

4 oz yellow onion, finely diced

2 cups Carnaroli or Arborio rice

6 Tbsp unsalted butter, cubed

Zest of 1 lemon

3/4 cup Parmigiano-Reggiano cheese, grated

Salt, to taste

2 oz fresh mozzarella, cut into 1/2-in pieces

1 cup peas

1 cup flour

1 egg, beaten

1/4 cup panko breadcrumbs, passed through a sieve

1 cup extra-virgin olive oil

Arancini

Fried risotto balls

DIRECTIONS:

Bring 10 cups of water to a boil. Then, place a saucepan over medium heat and sauté onions in a splash of oil until they're soft and translucent, about 5 minutes. Add rice to the pan and toast for about 5 minutes before covering with 1 cup of hot water and stirring while you bring it to a boil. Once most of the water has been absorbed and is just above the surface of the rice, add a second cup of water. Repeat with the remaining cups of water until rice is al dente.

Incorporate butter, lemon zest, cheese, and a pinch of salt, and remove the pan from heat. Spread the risotto on a parchment-lined baking sheet and set it aside to cool. Then, use your hands to roll the risotto into 4-oz balls stuffed with a piece of mozzarella and a few peas. Be sure to seal any holes.

Fill three separate bowls with flour, beaten egg, and breadcrumbs. Cover the risotto balls with flour, then egg, then breadcrumbs. Then, place a large skillet over medium heat and warm 1 cup oil until it's almost smoking. Gently place each breaded risotto ball into the hot oil and cook until golden brown, turning occasionally to brown all sides. Place each ball onto a paper towel-lined plate, sprinkle with cheese, and serve.

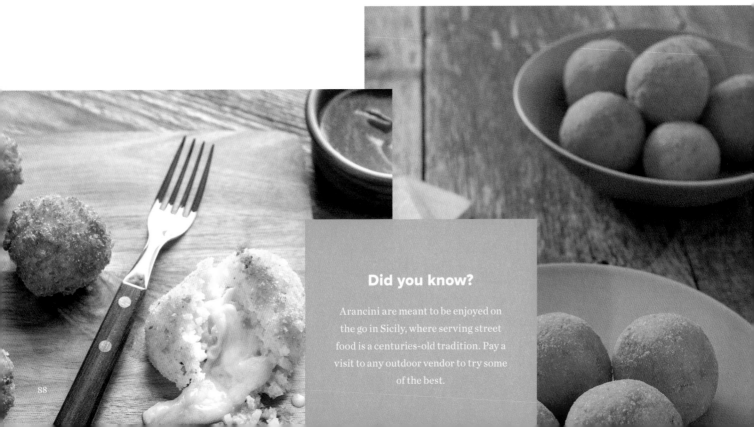

Did you know?

Arancini are meant to be enjoyed on the go in Sicily, where serving street food is a centuries-old tradition. Pay a visit to any outdoor vendor to try some of the best.

TOTAL TIME:

20 minutes

SERVINGS:

6

RECIPE ORIGIN:

Sicily, Italy

INGREDIENTS:

6 oranges, peeled and sliced

1 fennel bulb, chopped

1 oz anchovies, stored in oil, roughly chopped (optional)

2 Tbsp capers, rinsed

1 small shallot or large spring onion, finely chopped

2 Tbsp extra-virgin olive oil

1 tsp sherry or white wine vinegar

Sicilian orange & caper salad

DIRECTIONS:

In a medium dish, combine oranges and fennel bulb, and add anchovies if desired. In a separate bowl, whisk together capers, shallots or onion, oil, and sherry or vinegar. Toss with the orange and fennel mixture and serve.

I loved tasting this salad! The colors and farm-fresh flavors are so bright and bold.

—**Heidi**, *Go Ahead Tours President*

Meet Federica

*Bolognese foodie &
farm-to-table aficionado*

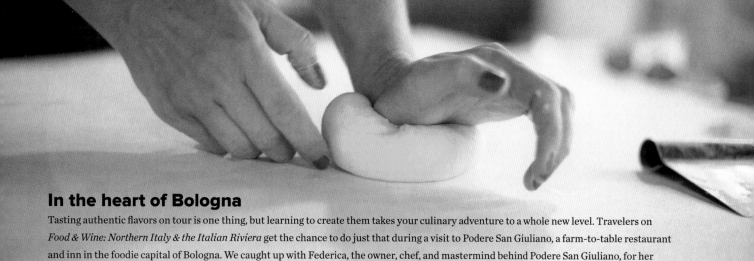

In the heart of Bologna

Tasting authentic flavors on tour is one thing, but learning to create them takes your culinary adventure to a whole new level. Travelers on *Food & Wine: Northern Italy & the Italian Riviera* get the chance to do just that during a visit to Podere San Giuliano, a farm-to-table restaurant and inn in the foodie capital of Bologna. We caught up with Federica, the owner, chef, and mastermind behind Podere San Giuliano, for her insider perspective on Italian food and hospitality.

Go Ahead: Podere San Giuliano was once your family farm. What sparked the transformation?

Federica: During my university time, my parents told me that I could reinvent our family farm. They said, "This could be a big opportunity for your life and for our farm. You could create an *agriturismo*!" An agriturismo is a farm with a restaurant and rooms. In the beginning I was unsure, but day by day, I began to imagine the renaissance of our old country house. My grandmother was a very important person to me. One of her life desires was to open a restaurant. So together, we opened our restaurant in 2002.

Go Ahead: Where do the recipes come from?

Federica: My grandmother taught me everything about the traditions and cuisine of Bologna. When we got started, we only used our family recipes. We're a real family from Bologna, which means we spend nearly all of our time cooking—or thinking about what to cook next, so there are many recipes!

Go Ahead: Podere San Giuliano uses local vegetables and modern techniques. Why's that so important to you?

Federica: I am a creative person and I wanted to discover new types of cooking. I studied with important Italian chefs, and I decided I needed to have a farm next to my restaurant. This farming project was so perfect that other restaurants asked us to grow vegetables for them too. Now the cooking of Podere San Giuliano is locally made, farm-to-table food right from our own garden.

Go Ahead: What are some of your favorite vegetables to grow and cook with?

Federica: I love all vegetables because of their colors and their ability to combine with meat or fish or cheese to create really interesting food that's not too heavy. In particular, zucchini flowers and tomatoes are my favorites. They're simple, but with them, my creativity is free!

Go Ahead: What can travelers expect from your cooking lesson?

Federica: It's wonderful to have the travelers come by because they are so curious—they want to know everything about ingredients, their origins, sometimes technical information too. But what they really prefer is to live the real experience—using their hands to craft pasta, tasting truly local food.

Go Ahead: You and your husband are such wonderful hosts! Any advice for making guests feel welcome for a dinner in our own homes?

Federica: Choose the best ingredients, and know where they're grown. Don't ruin them by adding many sauces or spices. When we're hosting, we ask ourselves, if we were visiting Podere San Giuliano, what would we want to find there? It's our goal to do whatever our guests desire!

Federica
Owner and chef of Podere San Giuliano in Bologna

Inspired?

Flip to the next page for Federica's Bolognese ragù recipe!

RECIPE RECOMMENDED BY

Federica
Local expert

TOTAL TIME:

2 hours, 30 minutes

SERVINGS:

6

RECIPE ORIGIN:

Bologna, Italy

INGREDIENTS:

1/2 lb pancetta, cubed

2 yellow carrots, finely chopped

1 celery stalk, finely chopped

1/2 onion, finely chopped

Salt and pepper, to taste

2/3 lb beef

1 lb pork

17 oz tomato sauce

Half a glass of dry white wine

FROM AN EXPERT'S KITCHEN:

Federica's Bolognese ragù

Bolognese meat sauce

DIRECTIONS:

In a large ceramic or iron pot, sauté the pancetta over medium heat. Add the vegetables and season with salt and pepper. Sauté until the pancetta has lightly crisped and the vegetables have softened, about 10 to 15 minutes.

Turn the heat up to high, add in the beef and pork, and stir thoroughly—you should hear a sizzle. Pour in the wine and cook until it evaporates. Add in the tomato sauce with a few splashes of water. Turn the heat down to low and simmer for about 2 hours. Serve over tagliatelle or your choice of pasta.

Want to sound like a true Italian? Don't ask for spaghetti with Bolognese sauce. It doesn't exist! It's a bad copy of tagliatelle with Bologna's ragù! And after my cooking lesson, you'll know how to cook it yourself.

—**Federica**, *Owner and chef of Podere San Giuliano in Bologna*

Cooking tip

The best way to finish off a plate of *tagliatelle alla Bolognese*? With a generous sprinkling of freshly grated Parmigiano-Reggiano. This renowned cheese is a culinary staple in the Emilia-Romagna region, and always bears a coveted DOP stamp—a sure sign of its quality.

Experience this on tour:

Food & Wine: Northern Italy & the Italian Riviera

goaheadtours.com/tir

RECIPE RECOMMENDED BY

Emmie
Tour Director

TOTAL TIME:

1 hour, 30 minutes

SERVINGS:
6

RECIPE ORIGIN:
Peloponnese Region, Greece

INGREDIENTS:

6 small eggplants (about 1 lb each)

3/4 cup extra-virgin olive oil, divided

7 garlic cloves, minced

1 yellow onion, minced

3/4 lb ground beef (pork or lamb work too)

Kosher salt and pepper, to taste

2 cups crushed tomatoes

3/4 cup dry red wine

2 Tbsp dried oregano

1/4 tsp ground cinnamon

1/8 tsp ground cloves

4 Tbsp unsalted butter

1/2 cup flour

2 cups milk

1 1/2 cups Parmigiano-Reggiano, grated

2 egg yolks, beaten

Freshly grated nutmeg, to taste

Papoutsakia

Beef-stuffed eggplant

DIRECTIONS:

Cut each eggplant in half lengthwise. Using a spoon, scoop out most of the flesh to create a bowl with the skin, leaving a 1/2 in-thick wall. Chop the eggplant flesh and set aside. Working in two batches, panfry the eggplant shells in a splash of oil over medium-high heat for about 5 minutes, turning once, until browned. Transfer eggplant shells to paper towels and set aside.

In a clean skillet, heat 1/4 cup oil over medium-high heat. Add garlic and onions, and cook until soft and translucent, about 5 minutes. Add meat, season with salt and pepper, and cook until browned, about 5 minutes. Stir in eggplant flesh, tomatoes, wine, oregano, cinnamon, and cloves. Season with salt and pepper, and bring to a simmer. Cook, stirring occasionally, until sauce has thickened, about 45 minutes. Remove from heat and set meat sauce aside.

Heat butter in a 4-qt saucepan over medium-high heat. Add flour and cook, whisking constantly, until smooth and slightly toasted, about 2 minutes. Add milk and whisk until sauce coats the back of a spoon, about 8 to 10 minutes. Remove from heat, add 3/4 cup cheese and egg yolks, and season with salt, pepper, and nutmeg. Stir until smooth and then set sauce aside.

Heat oven to 350°F and line a rimmed baking sheet with aluminum foil. Place eggplant boats with the cut side up. Sprinkle shells with half the remaining cheese and fill each with meat sauce. Spoon cheese sauce over the top and sprinkle with remaining cheese. Bake until eggplants are tender, about 20 minutes. Increase heat to broil and cook until the cheesy top is golden brown and bubbly, about 5 more minutes.

SERVINGS:

8

RECIPE ORIGIN:

Greece

INGREDIENTS:

60 to 70 fresh grape leaves
or one 16-oz jar of grape leaves

1 cup extra-virgin olive oil, divided

1 white onion, diced

8 scallions, green stalks only, thinly sliced

1 cup fresh dill, finely chopped

1 cup fresh flat-leaf parsley, finely chopped

1/2 cup fresh mint, finely chopped

1 3/4 cups short-grain rice

Kosher salt and pepper, to taste

1 cup water, plus more as needed

Juice of 2 lemons, divided

Dolmades

Stuffed grape leaves

DIRECTIONS:

If using fresh grape leaves, fill a large pot halfway with cold water and bring to a rolling boil. Blanch the grape leaves in the boiling water until they're soft and pliable, about 2 minutes. Using a slotted spoon, remove the leaves and transfer to a bowl of ice water to cool. When leaves are cool to the touch, remove from water and drain on paper towel. If you're using grape leaves from a jar, remove the stems, rinse, and drain in a colander.

Next, on to the filling. Add 1/3 cup of the oil to a large skillet over medium heat. Once the oil sizzles, add the white onion and sauté until it's soft and translucent, about 5 minutes. Add the scallions and herbs and cook about 3 more minutes. Add the rice, season with a pinch of salt, and stir constantly while toasting for about 2 minutes. Add the water and juice of 1 lemon and cook for 10 minutes, stirring occasionally. Remove from heat, season with salt and pepper, and allow to cool.

Line the bottom of a shallow pan or Dutch oven with 2 or 3 layers of grape leaves, specifically using any torn leaves here as your base. Place the remaining leaves with the glossy side down and the tips pointing toward you to prep the rolling process. Spoon about 1 tsp of cool filling into the center of each leaf. Working one by one, fold the sides of the leaf toward the center, then the tip, and then roll the leaf like a cigar. Be mindful to not overstuff, as the rice will expand in the oven. Tightly line up the rolls in the pan, placed with the seam side down.

Place the pan on the stove, drizzle in 1/2 cup of oil, and add the juice of the second lemon. Add just enough water to cover the stuffed grape leaves and bring to a simmer. Bring the heat down to medium-low, cover the pan, and simmer for 30 to 45 minutes, until the water is absorbed and the leaves are very tender. Remove from heat and cool completely before serving.

Roll these like cigars.

RECIPE RECOMMENDED BY

Giada
Go Ahead Tours

TOTAL TIME:

20 minutes

SERVINGS:

6

RECIPE ORIGIN:

Sicily, Italy

INGREDIENTS:

For the sauce

Juice of 1 lemon

1/4 cup extra-virgin olive oil

1 tsp dried oregano

Red pepper flakes, to taste

2 tsp kosher salt

1 tsp pepper

For the fish

6 swordfish steaks (5 to 6 oz each)

Salt and pepper, to taste

4 oz arugula (optional)

Zest of 1 lemon

A small bunch of fresh mint

Sicilian grilled swordfish

DIRECTIONS:

Whisk together the sauce ingredients and then set aside. Season the swordfish with salt and pepper, and place on the grill. Cook for 2 minutes on each side, until the fish is almost cooked through. Remove from heat and place onto a sheet of foil. Using a fork, prick the filets and pour the sauce to cover the fish. Season with salt and pepper, then wrap the still-hot fish in foil and set aside for 5 minutes. Plate the fish, top with arugula if desired, and pour the leftover sauce on top. Finish with grated lemon zest and mint leaves.

There is a little of everything to be found in Sicilian flavors: the spices and exotic flavors of the Arabs, the creativity of the Spanish, and the rational, elegant combinations of the French. All of these cultures are reflected in Sicilian cuisine, creating a captivating and refined culinary art.

—**Giada**, *Go Ahead Tours*

Cooking tip

This grilled swordfish is best cooked outside on a charcoal grill, but can also be prepared on a gas or stovetop grill over medium-high heat. For a traditional finish, balance out the flavors of your cooked fish with a handful of fresh, peppery arugula.

▲ Tagliatelle

Long and flat, tagliatelle are a type of ribbony pasta hailing from the northern region of Emilia-Romagna. These noodles are traditionally made fresh with an egg-and-flour dough and are the perfect complement to thick sauces like Bolognese ragù—check out our favorite recipe on page 93!

▲ Trofie

These short, rolled noodles hail from the Liguria region, where a mountainous terrain made it necessary to craft noodles from chestnut flour instead of wheat throughout history. Trofie are still crafted with a portion of chestnut flour and tossed with pesto, producing one of Liguria's signature dishes.

◀ Tortellini

The foodie capital of Bologna is the hometown of these ring-shaped noodles. While they are traditionally filled with pork or cheese, you can enjoy a wide range of fillings, from vegetables to herbs to seasonal fruit.

Pasta shapes 101: Know your noodles

Spaghetti, penne, ravioli—plenty of Italy's more than 350 styles of pasta are probably familiar (and may be part of a favorite weeknight meal), but there's a world of shapes, sizes, and styles out there to discover. Learn a little bit about eight special noodles you'll find on dinner plates across *il bel paese*, or the beautiful country.

Ravioli

Dating back to the 14th century, this popular pasta variety is more of a square dumpling than your average noodle. Originally served with broth, and eventually tomato sauce, traditional varieties are stuffed with ricotta and vegetables.

A floured workspace is key

◄ Rotini

This corkscrew-shaped pasta first popped up in Southern Italy. Its tightly wound shape holds onto the region's oily pestos and tomato sauces. The spirals also help catch garlic, pine nuts, olives, and other small but flavorful ingredients.

Sacchettini

The name says it all. Sacchettini, or "little sacks," are small, pouch-shaped noodles, stuffed with cheese and other fillings, and gathered at the top.

99

Cooking tip

To prepare your pasta the way an Italian would, there are a few musts to keep in mind. Season your noodles by adding a pinch of salt to already-boiling water, get the right consistency by mixing a cup of cooking water into your sauce, and remember: When it comes to perfectly cooked pasta, preparing it al dente is key.

Gnocchi

While gnocchi has been made since Roman times with traditional wheat flour, potatoes have become a common ingredient over the past few centuries, especially in central Italy. Today, you can find these pillowy bites with and without potato—and they're both worth a try!

Linguine

A cross between spaghetti and fettuccine, these long noodles get their name from the Italian translation for "little tongues." Originating in the coastal region of Liguria, they're most often served with pesto and seafood dishes, rather than meat sauces.

Basil pesto

INGREDIENTS:

1 to 2 large bunches of fresh basil (leaves only)

1 to 2 garlic cloves

1/3 cup pine nuts, toasted

Salt and pepper, to taste

1/4 to 1/3 cup extra-virgin olive oil

1/3 cup Parmigano-Reggiano cheese, grated

DIRECTIONS:

Add the basil, garlic, pine nuts, and salt and pepper to a food processor; pulse until a thick paste has formed. Drizzle in the oil and add cheese. If the pesto is too thick, add 1 tsp of reserved pasta water (if you're serving with pasta), or add more oil. Remember: The mixture should be smooth, not runny.

Try it with trofie or Linguine pasta

Amatriciana sauce

Spicy tomato sauce

INGREDIENTS:

28-oz can whole, peeled tomatoes

2 Tbsp extra-virgin olive oil

1/4 pound pancetta, diced

3 garlic cloves, chopped

1 red onion, thinly sliced

1 tsp red pepper flakes

A small bunch of fresh basil, chopped

Kosher salt and pepper, to taste

DIRECTIONS:

Using a food processor, purée the tomatoes until smooth and then set aside. In a skillet, warm oil over medium-high heat until simmering. Add the pancetta and sauté until golden brown, about 5 minutes, stirring often. Add garlic, onion, and red pepper flakes and sauté until fragrant, about 1 to 2 minutes. Stir in tomatoes and basil, and season with salt and pepper. Reduce heat to low and simmer uncovered until the sauce thickens, about 15 minutes.

Did you know?

In Italy, traditional spaghetti alla puttanesca (and most other dishes made with fish) is not served with cheese. But you won't miss the Parmigiano-Reggiano—the pasta's capers, anchovies, and olives pack enough of a salty kick.

TOTAL TIME:

15 minutes

SERVINGS:
4

RECIPE ORIGIN:
Naples, Italy

INGREDIENTS:

1/4 cup extra-virgin olive oil

4 large garlic cloves, finely chopped

28-oz can whole, peeled tomatoes in purée

1/2 cup Kalamata olives, halved and pitted

3 anchovy fillets, chopped

1 1/2 Tbsp capers, drained

1 tsp dried oregano

1/2 tsp red pepper flakes

Salt and pepper, to taste

Water (as needed)

3/4 lb spaghetti

2 Tbsp fresh, flat-leaf parsley, chopped (optional)

Top with parsley for extra freshness

Spaghetti alla puttanesca

DIRECTIONS:

Place a large pot over medium heat and warm up olive oil. Sauté garlic for about 1 minute, then mix in tomatoes, olives, anchovies, capers, oregano, and red pepper flakes.

Turn heat to medium-low and break up tomatoes with a spoon as you allow sauce to simmer and thicken, about 8 minutes. Season with salt and pepper.

While sauce simmers, bring a large pot of water to a boil, add a pinch of salt, and cook pasta until it's al dente. Drain cooked pasta, combine it with sauce, and top with parsley if desired.

You really can't get a bad meal in Italy. Everything is so fresh and even though there are a lot of pasta dishes, each was completely different and exquisitely seasoned.

—Sharon,
2nd-time traveler
Grand Tour of Italy

103

Take a seat

Lunch with a Sicilian Contessa

Made with love

On Azienda Casabianca, a sprawling, rustic estate in the Sicilian countryside, Contessa Giovanna Modica Notarbartolo invites our travelers into her home to share a freshly cooked meal that gets to the heart of Italian hospitality. Beyond the generations-old recipes and vibrant flavors, the magic of this meal lies in the preparation. Each dish is made with love and warmth. Here, traveler Rosie shares her experience at the villa.

This was delicious!
See pg. 89 for our take

Rosie
6th-time traveler & former teacher taking students abroad with EF

Rosie's story

I've been traveling with EF for 20 years and I've been fortunate to have some really wonderful adventures around the world, but our meal at the Contessa's villa in Sicily stands out as a truly special experience.

Of course the food was outstanding—nothing beats a home-cooked Italian meal—but looking back on it now, the hospitality is what left the biggest impression on me.

We drove down this long dirt road surrounded by orange orchards dotted with white stucco houses—it was like a countryside scene right out of a movie. The Contessa welcomed us as if it was completely normal for us to stop by for lunch, and it instantly felt like a casual family meal. After walking around the beautiful grounds, we gathered around these big, rustic farm tables and enjoyed a long, lingering, family-style meal.

My own family is Sicilian and the feeling of the day reminded me of my childhood, when the families in our Italian community would get together for weekend meals in the backyard. During our time here, our bus driver's daughters stopped in and our Tour Director's sister came by, and it really felt like a family party. It was truly special. Before we knew it, there was spur-of-the-moment dancing, kids running around in the yard, and dish after dish being passed around the table. I could see my father's face reflected in the men I met there and it felt like I was coming back to my roots. That's the beauty of Italian food—you can feel the care and warmth that goes into each dish, and it's almost like your own family made the meal.

Experience this on tour:
Food & Wine: Southern Italy & Sicily
goaheadtours.com/tsi

Giovanna Modica Notarbartolo
Sicilian Contessa

A culinary chat with the Contessa

The Contessa was kind enough to share some of her culinary expertise with us. When it comes to seasonal Sicilian dishes to serve, she explains that freshness is the most important thing. "We do not use frozen food, rather we choose seasonal products. According to this, during the winter months we offer more caloric and spicy food; in summer we eat light food," she says.

The approach taken in her kitchen is one that focuses on using what is available locally. "Typical ingredients are those cultivated on the farmland," she offers. "We use olive oil—rarely butter and never margarine—with vegetables such as eggplant, asparagus, and pepper, plus tomatoes and zucchini in summer and yellow pumpkin in winter." Familiar seasonings like salt and pepper are often added, as well as aromatics like mint, sage, bay leaves, garlic, basil, parsley, rosemary, and oregano.

Pasta with zucchini, mint & pecorino

INGREDIENTS:

12 oz short curly pasta, such as gemelli or fusilli

Sea salt, to taste

2 Tbsp extra-virgin olive oil, plus more for serving

3 anchovy fillets, rinsed and patted dry

2 garlic cloves, minced

5 small zucchini, shredded with a box grater

1/4 tsp red pepper flakes, plus more for serving

2/3 cup Pecorino Romano, finely grated, plus more for serving

1/4 cup lightly packed fresh mint leaves, chopped, plus more whole leaves for serving

DIRECTIONS:

Cook pasta in a large pot of generously salted boiling water until al dente. Reserve 1 1/2 cups of water; drain pasta.

Heat a large skillet over medium-high heat. Swirl in oil. Add anchovies and garlic; cook, stirring, just until anchovies break down and garlic turns golden, about 30 seconds. Add zucchini; season with salt and pepper flakes. Cook, stirring occasionally, until zucchini is very tender, about 5 minutes. Add pasta and 1 cup reserved pasta water. Simmer, stirring occasionally, until liquid is reduced and slightly thickened, 1 to 2 minutes.

Remove from heat; stir in cheese and mint. Add more pasta water if needed, a few spoonfuls at a time, until sauce evenly coats pasta. Serve drizzled with oil and sprinkled with more mint, pepper flakes, and cheese.

RECIPE RECOMMENDED BY

Jamie
Go Ahead Tours

TOTAL TIME:

2 hours

+ overnight soaking

SERVINGS:

10

RECIPE ORIGIN:

Tuscany, Italy

INGREDIENTS:

16 oz dried white beans, soaked overnight

9 cups water, divided

1 garlic clove, chopped

1 onion, chopped

8 Tbsp extra-virgin olive oil, plus more for serving

2 Tbsp tomato purée

1 carrot, finely chopped

1 celery stalk, finely chopped

1/2 Savoy cabbage, washed and cut into strips

1 red cabbage, washed and cut into strips

1 bunch chard, washed and cut into strips

2 potatoes, peeled and thinly sliced

Salt and pepper, to taste

12 oz stale Italian bread, sliced

Ribollita

Tuscan white bean stew

DIRECTIONS:

Place a medium pan over high heat and boil white beans in 8 cups of water until they're tender, about 45 minutes. Spoon one quarter of the beans out of the pan and put them aside. Purée the remaining three quarters of the beans by rubbing them through a sieve, and put the purée back in the water you cooked them in.

Place a medium pan over medium heat; cook garlic and onion in olive oil until soft and translucent, about 5 minutes. Then, mix tomato purée with 1 cup warm water and add to the pan with sautéed onion and garlic. Mix in carrot, celery, cabbage, chard, and potatoes, and season with salt and pepper. Allow the mixture to cook for a few minutes before adding puréed beans in water, and cook for about 1 hour.

Finally, add bread and whole white beans, mix well, and serve each portion with a generous drizzle of oil.

Sitting down to a bowl of this hearty soup is one of the best ways to warm up on a chilly fall day in Florence. There's something so comforting about the simple, Tuscan flavors.

—**Jamie**, *Go Ahead Tours*

Cooking tip

To make an even more authentic ribollita, do as the Tuscans do and use saltless bread. As the story goes, loaves in the region have been baked without salt since the Middle Ages when Pisa imposed high taxes. Bakers simply opted not to use it, and *pane toscano* came to be.

Jessica
Traveler

TOTAL TIME:

1 hour, 45 minutes

SERVINGS:
6

RECIPE ORIGIN:
Greece

INGREDIENTS:

For the octopus

One 2- to 3-lb octopus, cleaned

6 cups water

2 cups white wine

2 cups red wine

1 large onion, chopped

3 garlic cloves, crushed

1 leek, sliced

2 celery stalks, chopped

Juice of half a lemon

2 bay leaves

1 bunch fresh parsley, whole with stems

1 Tbsp peppercorns

For the marinade

1/2 cup extra-virgin olive oil

1 Tbsp red wine vinegar

Juice of 1 lemon

2 garlic cloves, minced

2 tsp dried oregano

1/4 cup fresh parsley, chopped

Salt and pepper, to taste

Grilled octopus

DIRECTIONS:

In a large pot, combine all the ingredients for cooking the octopus. Bring to a boil and simmer uncovered for 45 minutes to 1 hour or until the octopus is tender. Remove the octopus from liquid and cut into pieces.

While the octopus is cooking, combine all marinade ingredients in a large bowl. Add in the cooked octopus pieces and let sit for 15 to 30 minutes. Grill octopus pieces on high for 4 to 5 minutes, until browned.

The Venetian streets of coastal Chania keep surprises hidden around every corner, like cute cafes, mouthwatering Cretan food, cobblestone alleyways, and shady spots to relax under vibrant *bougainvilleas.*

—Jessica,
2nd-time traveler
The Greek Islands: Mykonos, Santorini & Crete

Cooking tip

Not sure what "tender" means when simmering an octopus? You'll know you're done when the skin at the base of the tentacles yields to a small knife with similar pressure as a potato would.

Jessica's photos from tour!

How to buy the best olive oil

Mix colors for different ripeness flavors

Pick top quality

Always buy extra-virgin olive oil; it's unrefined and the best-quality, least-processed option out there. Specifically look for cold-pressed or cold-extracted (a modern twist on cold-pressed) written on the label.

Don't be fooled by labels

Labels that say "Product of Italy" or "Bottled in Italy" don't necessarily mean the oil is processed there or all the olives are grown there. In order to know your olive oil is truly from a country (as in grown, harvested, and bottled), look for a specific estate name on the label.

Check the hue

Color matters—a little. Foodies used to believe that the greener the oil, the better the quality. That thinking is now considered passé, but a green color does signify younger, often stronger-flavored olives.

Keep it fresh

Unlike a nice bottle of red wine, you don't want to age your olive oil. As soon as you buy your oil, open it and enjoy! And always look for a "best by" date or ideally a harvest date on the label.

Don't buy in bulk

The longer a bottle is open, the more the flavor and aroma will deteriorate, so opt for smaller bottles that you'll go through fairly quickly.

Pick dark bottles

Light causes the oil to oxidize and deteriorate, so go for olive oil packaged in dark glass bottles.

What kind of olive oil to use when

While you really can't go wrong with any type of extra-virgin olive oil, the terroir an olive tree grows in impacts the final flavor. Light fish or vegetable dishes shine with sweet, buttery olive oil from northern Italy. Steak and soups can handle bolder, peppery olive oil from Tuscany and Umbria. And Sicily and Puglia in southern Italy produce bright, crisp olive oils that pair well with tomatoes, eggplant, and grilled fish.

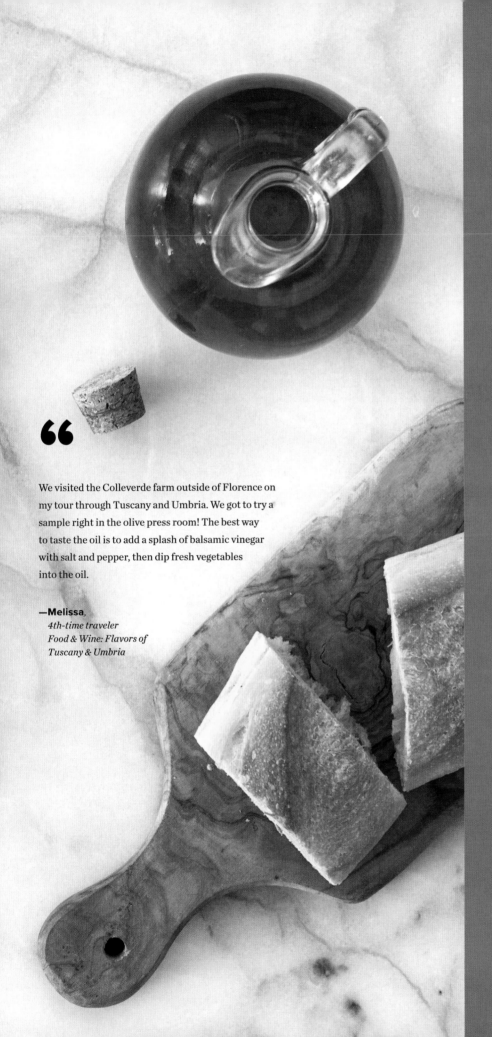

> **"**
>
> We visited the Colleverde farm outside of Florence on my tour through Tuscany and Umbria. We got to try a sample right in the olive press room! The best way to taste the oil is to add a splash of balsamic vinegar with salt and pepper, then dip fresh vegetables into the oil.
>
> **—Melissa**,
> *4th-time traveler*
> *Food & Wine: Flavors of*
> *Tuscany & Umbria*

Make room for
Aceto Balsamico Tradizionale di Modena

If there's any product on par with Italy's renowned extra-virgin olive oil, it's northern Italy's *Balsamico Tradizionale*. This celebrated balsamic vinegar produced only from grapes in Modena and Reggio Emilia is more than worth seeking out—here's why.

It boasts the DOP stamp

Meaning Denominazione di Origine Protetta, or Protected Designation of Origin, this stamp is only awarded to top-quality products made by local producers using traditional methods.

It's aged to perfection

When it comes to this prized balsamic, producing the best of the best is no small—or quick—task. The vinegar picks up hints from the type of wood barrel it's aged in, and aging takes a minimum of 12 years. Anything over 25 years is labeled *extravecchio,* or "very old."

It brings out the best flavors

Adding Balsamico Tradizionale to a hot cooking pan will ruin its well-rounded flavor. The best way to enjoy it? Drizzled on top of your finished dish. Taste some with Parmigiano-Reggiano cheese, swirl a bit onto a risotto, or even savor the concentrated flavor straight from a spoon—it really is that good.

Did you know?

Roasted lamb is the star of every
Greek table on Easter Sunday, when
families mark the occasion by cooking
the whole lamb over charcoal on a
large spit, or *souvla*.

TOTAL TIME:

2 hours

SERVINGS:
8

RECIPE ORIGIN:
Greece

INGREDIENTS:

6 garlic cloves

A bunch of fresh oregano, chopped

Juice and zest of 1 lemon

6 Tbsp extra-virgin olive oil

Salt, to taste

1 large leg of lamb, about 6 lbs 8 oz

3 to 3 1/2 lbs new potatoes

14-oz can of chopped tomato

A large handful of baby Kalamata
olives, pitted

Roasted lamb with potatoes

DIRECTIONS:

Preheat oven to 460°F. Using either a food processor or a mortar and pestle, create an herb paste with the garlic, half the oregano, lemon juice and zest, a splash of oil, and a pinch of salt. Then, use a sharp knife to puncture the meat all over, and stuff the holes with as much herb paste as possible.

In a large roasting pan, add the potatoes and toss with the rest of the oil and any leftover herb paste. Carve out a spot for the lamb in the center of the pan and roast for 20 minutes.

Reduce the temperature to 350°F and roast for an additional 1 hour 15 minutes for medium-rare, or more to fit your preference. During roasting, baste the lamb a few times and toss the potatoes. Once the lamb reaches your desired doneness, remove from the pan and let it rest. Also move the potatoes into a serving dish and add in the other half of oregano.

Leave the juices in the roasting pan and place over medium heat. Add the tomatoes and olives, and simmer for a few minutes to create a sauce to serve alongside the lamb and potatoes.

Greek food has so much to offer in terms of flavor. From the salads dressed in fine olive oil and served with chunks of feta to the savory lamb and pork souvlaki, each meal tasted fresh in its own delicious way.

—**Jay**, *Go Ahead Tours*

RECIPE RECOMMENDED BY

Melissa
Traveler

TOTAL TIME:

45 minutes

+ 2 hours chilling

SERVINGS:

8

RECIPE ORIGIN:

Italy

INGREDIENTS:

Water, as needed

7 egg yolks

1/2 cup sugar

1/3 cup sweet marsala, plus 2 Tbsp

8 oz mascarpone, softened to room temperature

1 cup heavy cream

1 cup brewed espresso coffee

1 oz dark chocolate, roughly chopped

1/4 cup rum or brandy

1 tsp natural vanilla extract

48 ladyfingers

1/4 cup unsweetened cocoa powder

Tiramisu

DIRECTIONS:

Place a heat-proof bowl over a pot of simmering water and cream together egg yolks and sugar. Whisk in 1/3 cup of marsala until the mixture thickens and doubles in volume. Remove mixture from heat and stir in mascarpone. In a chilled bowl, whip heavy cream until soft peaks form. Then, gently fold the whipped cream into the mascarpone mixture.

In a small saucepan, combine the espresso, chocolate, rum, vanilla extract, and remaining 2 Tbsp marsala. Place the pan over low heat and stir the mixture until all chocolate is melted. Then, chill the mixture for about 15 minutes before quickly dipping each ladyfinger in, making sure not to soak the biscuits too much. Arrange dipped ladyfingers in a single layer on a 13x9-in glass baking pan, and use a spatula to evenly cover with 1/2 of mascarpone cream. Repeat with a second layer of dipped ladyfingers and remaining mascarpone cream. Sprinkle cocoa powder on top and refrigerate for 2 hours before serving.

Taking an Italian cooking class was so fun. We made three distinctly Tuscan courses using ingredients that were in season, starting with the tiramisu. Our culinary instructor, Ana, guided us through the process of soaking the ladyfingers in fresh strawberry sauce and maraschino cherry liqueur. Ana mentioned that the tiramisu we typically think of (made with brandy) is usually a fall or winter dessert, while fresh fruit is common in the spring and summer.

—Melissa,
4th-time traveler
Food & Wine: Flavors of Tuscany & Umbria

Did you know?

It's the energy-inducing ingredients in tiramisu—espresso and cocoa—that give it its name, which translates to "pick me up."

RECIPE RECOMMENDED BY

Jessie
Go Ahead Tours

TOTAL TIME:

2 hours, 30 minutes

SERVINGS:

15

RECIPE ORIGIN:

Greece and the Mediterranean

INGREDIENTS:

For the baklava

17 oz walnuts, chopped

2 tsp ground cinnamon

2 tsp ground clove

10 oz butter, melted

25 to 30 sheets of phyllo dough

For the syrup

20 oz sugar

14 oz water

2.8 oz honey

Zest of 1 lemon or orange

1 cinnamon stick

Baklava

DIRECTIONS:

Preheat oven to 300°F and prepare ingredients. In a large bowl, mix nuts, cinnamon, and clove. Melt butter in a saucepan over medium-low heat. Trim your sheets of phyllo dough to the size of your baking dish if necessary (this recipe calls for a large baking pan approximately 16x12 in).

Using a cooking brush, butter the bottom and sides of a baking pan. Layer the pan with sheets of phyllo, topping each with melted butter between layers, until about half the phyllo is used.

Layer the nut filling over the phyllo base. To create the top of the baklava, repeat the same layering process over the nuts with the rest of the phyllo sheets. Brush the top of the baklava with butter.

Chill the baklava in the fridge for 15 minutes. Using a sharp knife, cut the dessert into pieces in a grid shape. Place the baklava on the lower rack and bake until crisp and golden, about 1 1/2 to 2 hours.

While the baklava bakes, prepare the syrup. In a small pot, combine syrup ingredients and bring to a boil for 2 minutes, or until sugar is dissolved. Remove syrup from heat and let cool. When baklava comes out of the oven, drizzle with cold syrup and let it fully soak through.

Panna cotta

TOTAL TIME:

30 minutes

+ 3 hours chilling

SERVINGS:

6

RECIPE ORIGIN:

Italy

INGREDIENTS:

4 gelatin sheets

Water (as needed)

1/2 stick vanilla

2 cups heavy whipping cream

4 oz sugar

Fresh fruit (optional)

DIRECTIONS:

Place gelatin sheets in a bowl of cold water and soak for 10 minutes. Drain and squeeze. Using a paring knife, butterfly the vanilla bean and remove the seeds. Add seeds to a medium saucepan along with cream and sugar, and put on high heat. Whisk the mixture as you bring it to a boil.

Remove mixture from the heat and stir in gelatin sheets until melted and fully combined. Pour mixture into small panna cotta molds and refrigerate until firm, about 3 hours.

Remove molds from the fridge and place them in a pot of hot water for a moment, making sure the water does not go over the top of the mold. Remove panna cotta by turning the mold upside down on a plate. Garnish with fresh fruit, caramel, or your topping of choice.

Try it with your favorite seasonal fruit

RECIPE RECOMMENDED BY

Katie
Go Ahead Tours

RECIPE RECOMMENDED BY

Rosie
Traveler

TOTAL TIME:

1 hour, 30 minutes

SERVINGS:
24 cannoli

RECIPE ORIGIN:
Sicily, Italy

INGREDIENTS:

For the shells

2 cups all-purpose flour

1 egg

1 Tbsp vegetable oil

1 Tbsp sugar

1/4 cup red wine

3 Tbsp milk

1 egg white for sealing edges, beaten

Vegetable oil (as needed)

For the filling

4 cups sheep's milk ricotta, drained

3/4 cup confectioners' sugar, plus more as needed

A dash of cinnamon

Semi-sweet chocolate chips, roughly chopped (optional)

Pistachios, chopped (optional)

Candied fruit (optional)

Try with chopped nuts

Cannoli Siciliani

DIRECTIONS:

Add flour to a large bowl, create a well in the center, and fill the indentation with egg, oil, red wine, and milk. Combine the ingredients in the well, then use your hands to slowly mix them into the flour and knead to create dough.

Use your hands to flatten a small portion of dough before rolling it out to about 1/8 in with a rolling pin or pasta roller. Cut flattened dough into circles with a 4-in diameter and wrap each around wooden or stainless steel dowels or cannoli molds. Press edges together using beaten egg white to seal.

Place a deep pot filled halfway with oil over medium-high heat. Using tongs, drop a few dough-wrapped dowels or molds into hot oil and fry shells until golden, about 2 minutes. Remove from oil and, and taking care not to burn your hands, slide cannoli shells off molds and onto a tray.

In a medium bowl, whisk together ricotta, confectioners' sugar, and cinnamon until completely combined and smooth. Use a pastry bag to pipe the filling into each shell. If you wish, dip each end into pistachios, chocolate, or candied fruit. Dust with confectioners' sugar and serve immediately.

Tasting an authentic cannoli was a must on my tour of Sicily. From the creamy ricotta filling to the crunchy outer shell, there's so much to love about these signature pastries. Be sure to try one with pistachios! The green nut is popular all throughout the region and reflects the area's multicultural cuisine.

—**Emily**, *Go Ahead Tours*

Cooking tip

You can get a jump-start on making this sweet treat by whipping your cannoli filling up to 24 hours before serving. But, hold off on piping it into shells until the cannoli are ready to eat; filling them too early will result in soggy shells.

TOTAL TIME:

2 hours, 15 minutes

+ 3 hours freezing

SERVINGS:
6

RECIPE ORIGIN:
Italy

INGREDIENTS:

1 1/2 cups hazelnuts

1 cup whole milk

2 cups heavy cream

3/4 cup sugar

1/4 tsp coarse salt

4 oz milk chocolate, finely chopped

5 large egg yolks

1/8 tsp vanilla extract

Chocolate & hazelnut gelato

DIRECTIONS:

Start by toasting your hazelnuts. Preheat oven to 350°F, then spread the nuts in an even layer on an ungreased baking sheet. Bake for 10 to 12 minutes, stirring occasionally to keep them toasting evenly, until hazelnuts are golden brown.

Let hazelnuts cool to room temperature and gather them in a kitchen towel. Gently rub hazelnuts with the towel for about 30 seconds to peel off as much of the papery skin as you can. (You don't have to make it perfect—you'll strain these later.) Transfer the peeled hazelnuts to a food processor or blender and finely chop.

In a medium pot, warm the milk, 1 cup of cream, sugar, and salt. Once warm, add the chopped hazelnuts. Remove from heat, cover, and let steep for 1 hour. Strain hazelnut-infused milk over a medium saucepan. Press down on the nuts with a spatula or your hands to get all the liquid out. Discard the hazelnuts.

Begin heating the remaining cup of cream in a medium saucepan until it begins to boil. Place chocolate in a medium bowl and pour the heated cream over the top, stirring until smooth. Set a fine mesh strainer or cheesecloth-lined colander over the top of your bowl.

In a separate small bowl, whisk together egg yolks. Then, re-warm the hazelnut-infused milk until it's just steaming (around 165°F to 170°F on an instant-read thermometer). Temper your eggs by slowly pouring half of the warm milk over the yolks, whisking constantly. (It helps to have a second pair of hands for this part.) Then, return the warmed egg yolks back to the saucepan.

Continue stirring the mixture over medium heat with a spatula. When the mixture thickens and coats the spatula (around 180°F on an instant-read thermometer), pour it through your strainer and stir into the chocolate mixture. Add the vanilla extract and stir until cooled over an ice bath. Chill the mixture in the refrigerator, then freeze in an ice cream maker according to the manufacturer's instructions.

Did you know?

If you've ever been to Italy, you've no doubt noticed that some gelaterias sell puffy gelato that's piled up high in the case. These tourist-friendly treats look appetizing, but they're made from a mix with artificial thickeners and have been whipped up to give the gelato extra height. The taller the gelato, the less authentic it is— the good stuff doesn't need to advertise from afar.

"

I walked charming streets of historic cities such as Granada, Toledo, and Ronda, and soaked up the local culture at a flamenco show and every time we ate. From paella and tapas to decadent desserts and fine wine, each dining experience created fond memories.

—Ralph
5th-time traveler
Grand Tour of Spain

Port wine, paella & patatas bravas

Spain & Portugal

Spain and Portugal practically invite foodies to pull up a chair.

These neighboring destinations share many similarities when it comes to what ends up on the table. Hearty stews, plenty of pork, and fresh seafood like squid and shellfish are popular in both countries, but it's the use of varied spices that sings an ode to individual histories. Spain favors saffron and paprika, while Portugal's cuisine features lots of coriander and a signature North African chili pepper called piri piri whose Portuguese roots trace back to the spice trade.

Eat like the locals

Dig into paella in Valencia

While paella has come to symbolize Spanish cuisine in general, the rice and seafood dish has its roots in the rice country of southeastern Spain. Here, farmers would toss whatever they caught and grew into big pots of rice and seasonings.

Try kebabs in Seville

Spain's southern Andalusia region is heavily influenced by surrounding countries, especially the Arabic and African countries to the south.

Nibble on pa amb tomàquet in Barcelona

Catalan cuisine, which can be found in Barcelona, is markedly different from food in other parts of Spain. Nearly every restaurant will offer this starter of toasted bread with tomato and olive oil.

Drink cider in San Sebastián

With large French and Jewish influences, Basque Country in Northern Spain offers its own version of Spanish cuisine. One can't-miss? Spiked cider. The region is home to countless cider houses, where the fruity beverage flows from big barrels. While you can enjoy this specialty any time of year, the best time to visit is during the apple harvest, which takes place around January in Spain.

Seville, Spain

Small plates, big flavors

Tapas in Spain

Tapas are snacks or small portions that can range from cold and casual bar bites like olives, to more complex dishes fresh from the kitchen like slow-cooked chorizo or fried *croquetas*. Dinner in Spain is served late, so tapas are traditionally enjoyed in the late afternoon after the work day is over, with friends and cocktails. However, it's not uncommon to have tapas any time during the day, or to enjoy a selection of several tapas as your dinner.

Pintxos in Basque Country

A form of tapas eaten in the Basque region of northern Spain, pintxos (pronounced peen-tcho) typically consist of a combination of fish, meats, cheeses, or peppers secured with a toothpick to a small slice of bread. It's the toothpick that sets them apart from traditional tapas as they take their name from the Spanish word *pincho*, or "spike."

Petiscos in Portugal

Petiscos are the Portuguese equivalent of tapas with a particularly heavy dose of seafood. These small bites serve as much (if not more) of a social purpose as they do a culinary one, with friends gathering in blue-and-white tiled taverns for end-of-day snacks and drinks. Though some petisco bars have specialized menus, standbys like snails, squid, and chorizo make their way on to most menus.

Mercado de San Miguel

Located near Madrid's Plaza Mayor, the bustling Market of San Miguel (called *Mercado de San Miguel* by locals) is the perfect place to spend an evening. You can walk around with a local beer or wine in hand as you peruse the various stalls, try lots of unique specialties, and chat with locals at the different counters. Our picks for can't-miss vendors? The Croquetas Cart and Café del Art.

Do get the daily catch

Portugal boasts an extensive coastline and has a deep seafaring past. Local fishermen bring back daily hauls each morning and the plate of the day, or *pratos do dia*, is always a good idea for super-fresh fish and shellfish.

Hello, jamón!

The Spanish take their ham seriously. Learn the basics, like the difference between Jamón Ibérico and Jamón Serrano, in our guide on pg. 156.

Munch on Manchego

Made in Spain's La Mancha region, this distinctive sheep's milk cheese must follow strict regulations for age, size, and even sheep breed in order to get the coveted Manchego-designated mark.

Regal reds to sip & savor

All about Spanish & Portuguese wines

While it's the world's third-largest producer, Spain's winemaking has stayed very traditional. Portuguese viticulture on the other hand developed in relative isolation. The result? Less familiar wines, now getting a lot of buzz.

Drink Port in Porto,
Portugal

The most well-known of Portuguese wines, Ports are produced exclusively in Portugal's Douro Valley. This fortified sweet red wine is often enjoyed with dessert or after dinner. The style got its name as more and more bottles were shipped out of the city of Porto in the early 1700s, when exports spiked because the British were at war with France and their supply of good reds was dwindling.

Drink Douro Reds in the Douro Valley,
Portugal

Reminiscent of the plummy fruits and spices of Port, these non-fortified "Douro Reds" also offer big flavors thanks to Tinta Roriz grapes, blended with native Portuguese varieties. Many critics consider these the most exciting up-and-comers in the biz.

The age-old appeal of wine punch

Versions of sangria were popular around Spain and throughout Europe for centuries, but it wasn't until 1964 at the World Fair in New York City that Americans were introduced to the fruity concoction. The name comes from the Latin word for "blood" and the red wine is usually spiced with cinnamon and cloves. If the whole thing sounds a bit medieval to you, you're not far off. The spiced wine punch was a safe drinking option that stayed flavorful for a while—a win-win in the days when water was iffy. Over the centuries, families created countless fruit-filled versions of the recipe, making it a Spanish standby.

See our favorite recipes on pg. 163

Drink Rioja in La Rioja,
Spain

As Spain's most revered wine-making region, La Rioja produces full-bodied reds that mix earthy, spicy, and fruity flavors. One of the most important grape varieties in Spanish winemaking is Tempranillo, which is found in Rioja wines. For pure Tempranillo wines that become more complex with age, the neighboring region of Ribera del Duero is the spot.

Drink Cava in Catalonia,
Spain

A less expensive (but equally tasty) alternative to Champagne, Spain's signature sparkling wine is usually dry and refreshing, and can be either white or rosé. The perfect place to taste-test the bubbles? One of the many Cava bars in the Catalonian capital of Barcelona.

Drink Albariño in the Rías Baixas,
Spain

While reds take center stage in much of Spain, white Albariño grapes grow beautifully in the Rías Baixas region of Galicia in northwestern Spain. Think of this fruity, acidic wine as the go-to complement to the fresh fish around the Iberian Peninsula.

Did you know?

Love these shriveled peppers? Try
their Japanese counterparts, shishito
peppers, prepared a similar way.

TOTAL TIME:

10 minutes

SERVINGS:
4

RECIPE ORIGIN:
Padrón, Spain

INGREDIENTS:

1 Tbsp vegetable oil

12 oz Padrón peppers

Coarse sea salt, to taste

2 Tbsp extra-virgin olive oil

Pimientos de Padrón

Blistered Padrón peppers

DIRECTIONS:

Heat vegetable oil in a cast-iron skillet over high heat. Once oil starts to sizzle, place peppers along the base of the skillet in a single layer. Let peppers cook until they start to blister, about 30 seconds, and then flip to reverse side. Turning occasionally, cook for about 1 more minute, until the peppers are tender and crisped all over. Remove from heat, drizzle with olive oil, and season with plenty of salt.

About one in ten of these little peppers bring serious heat, so it's like playing Russian roulette with each bite.

—**Brian**, *Go Ahead Tours*

RECIPE RECOMMENDED BY

Diane
Traveler

TOTAL TIME:

15 minutes

SERVINGS:

4

RECIPE ORIGIN:

Spain

INGREDIENTS:

For the dressing

1 1/2 tsp of white wine vinegar

2 Tbsp of extra-virgin olive oil

A pinch of caster sugar

Salt and pepper, to taste

For the salad

2 fennel bulbs

1 cucumber

Half of 1 red onion

A bunch of cilantro

A bunch of parsley

7 oz crumbled feta cheese

Seeds of half a pomegranate

Fennel & pomegranate salad

DIRECTIONS:

Combine all the dressing ingredients in a mixing bowl. Trim the fennel by cutting and setting aside the wispy fronds and discarding any tough outer leaves. Quarter the bulbs, remove the core, and finely slice lengthwise. Add the fronds and sliced fennel to the mixing bowl with the dressing and toss to coat.

Peel the cucumber, cut it in half lengthwise, and slice it into semi-circles. Slice the onion and chop the herbs. Add each of these to the mixing bowl and toss to coat.

Transfer the dressed salad to a serving dish. Sprinkle with feta cheese and pomegranate seeds.

Cooking tip

Collecting a pomegranate's arils, or seeds, is simpler than it seems. Instead of cutting the fruit straight down the middle, start by cutting off the top just below the stem. Then, divide the pomegranate into about five vertical sections by scoring the skin— again, without cutting all the way through the fruit. Pull each segment apart and remove the seeds by bending back the skin over a bowl of water.

TOTAL TIME:

25 minutes

SERVINGS:

1 cup

RECIPE ORIGIN:

Spain

INGREDIENTS:

1 1/4 cups pitted manzanilla olives, rinsed and drained

2 tsp capers, drained

1 garlic clove, minced

1/4 cup extra-virgin olive oil

1 tsp fresh lemon juice

Salt and pepper, to taste

2 Tbsp fresh cilantro, chopped

1 baguette, sliced and toasted

Olive tapenade with crostini

DIRECTIONS:

Combine olives, capers, and garlic in a food processor. Chop until smooth, and then, with the motor running, drizzle in the oil and lemon juice. Process until blended, scraping the sides as needed. Transfer to a serving bowl, season with salt and pepper, and stir in cilantro. Let the tapenade sit for 10 minutes, allowing the flavors to settle. Serve on toasted baguette.

RECIPE RECOMMENDED BY

Richard
Traveler

The ultimate street food in Barcelona

Patatas bravas

Potatoes with spicy aioli

TOTAL TIME:

1 hour, 15 minutes

SERVINGS:
4–6

RECIPE ORIGIN:
Spain

INGREDIENTS:

Olive oil, for frying

1/2 red onion, finely diced

2 garlic cloves, minced

1 Tbsp smoked paprika

3/4 cup mayonnaise

1 plum tomato, halved, seeded, and roasted

A dash of hot sauce

A splash of sherry vinegar

Salt and pepper, to taste

4 Russet potatoes, parboiled, peeled, and cubed

A bunch of fresh parsley, chopped

DIRECTIONS:

Place a baking sheet in the oven and preheat to 375°F. In a small sauté pan, heat 1 Tbsp of oil on medium heat. Add the onion and garlic and cook until soft and translucent, about 5 minutes, then add paprika and cook for an additional 30 seconds. Let cool.

Make the aioli by placing cooked onion mixture, mayonnaise, tomato, hot sauce, and vinegar in a food processor. Blend until smooth. Season with salt and pepper. Transfer processed mixture to a bowl, cover, and let chill in the refrigerator for half an hour.

Fill a heavy-bottomed skillet 2 in deep with oil and heat until it starts to simmer. Add potatoes and season with salt and pepper. Fry until potatoes are an even golden color on all sides. Remove potatoes from oil to drain on a plate lined with paper towels.

Remove the baking sheet from the oven and arrange potatoes in an even layer on top. Return them to the oven and bake until crisp, about 10 minutes. Season cooked potatoes with salt and move to a serving platter. Garnish with aioli and parsley before serving.

Fried eggplant with honey

TOTAL TIME:

30 minutes
+ 2 hours soaking

SERVINGS:
4

RECIPE ORIGIN:
Andalusia, Spain

INGREDIENTS:

2 eggplants

2 cups whole milk

Salt, to taste

1 cup all-purpose flour

Olive oil, for frying

1/4 cup local honey (the runnier, the better)

DIRECTIONS:

Cut the eggplants into round slices. Pour the milk into a bowl, add a pinch of salt, and submerge eggplant pieces in milk for about 2 hours.

After eggplant has soaked, drain the milk. Cover a shallow plate in flour and a pinch of salt. Working in batches, take the eggplant slices out of the milk and dredge in flour on both sides.

Coat a deep pan in oil and place over high heat until oil starts to sizzle. Arrange eggplant slices in the pan in a single layer and brown on each side. Remove from oil, drain on paper towels, and sprinkle with a pinch of salt if desired. Drizzle honey on top and serve immediately.

This dish is traditionally from the Andalusia region of Spain, but I first tried it at a tapas bar in Catalonia. It was the single best thing I ever ate in Europe. The crispness and richness of the fried eggplant with the light sweetness of the honey is a combination to die for! Nothing compares to eating this with a glass of wine on a warm summer night in Barcelona.

—**Salam**, *Go Ahead Tours*

Cod is king in Portugal

With its prime location along the Atlantic and a seafaring history that stretches back hundreds of years, it's no wonder that Portugal boasts an impressive seafood scene. Fishing villages dot the coast from Porto to Lisbon to Cape St. Vincent, where both commemorative monuments and culinary gems sing an ode to the country's maritime discoveries. Of all the delicacies from the sea, bacalhau is the one that truly shines. Here are a few things to know about this dried, salted cod.

It's fondly called *fiel amigo*

In a country with ready access to almost any type of fresh fish, dried cod sourced from far-off waters has still earned the nickname "faithful friend." It's an endearing moniker that alludes to Portugal's love for the culinary staple, which reigns supreme as its national dish.

It's not native to Portugal

It may come as a surprise that a fish so integral to Portugal's cuisine isn't pulled from the country's own coast, but that's where the Age of Discovery comes in. Cod was first introduced into Portuguese cuisine back in the 1500s, when fishermen caught it along Newfoundland, Canada. While Portugal may get most of its sustainable cod from Norway and Iceland today, each dish is inextricably linked to the country's history of maritime exploration.

There's reportedly over 365 recipes

It's been said that Portugal has a cod recipe for each day of the year, and that's not too hard to believe. From *bacalhau à bras* prepared with eggs and potatoes to *bolinhos de bacalhau*, or salt cod fritters, there are countless ways to enjoy it. Want to taste it on its own? Dig in! People have enjoyed the strong, salty taste since the 16th century, when explorers relied on it for long voyages across the sea.

TOTAL TIME:

45 minutes

SERVINGS:
4

RECIPE ORIGIN:
Spain

INGREDIENTS:

1/4 cup olive oil

1 onion, finely chopped

6 garlic cloves, minced

28-oz can of tomatoes, drained and chopped

3 Tbsp fresh parsley, chopped

1/4 tsp dried thyme

1/4 tsp red pepper flakes

4 lbs mussels, scrubbed and debearded

1/8 tsp black pepper

Salt, to taste

A bunch of fresh parsley

One-pot mussels with garlic

DIRECTIONS:

In a large pot, warm oil over low heat. Add onion and garlic and cook until the onion is soft and translucent, about 5 minutes. Create the broth by adding tomatoes, parsley, thyme, and red pepper flakes. Reduce the heat and simmer, partially covered, for 25 minutes. Stir occasionally.

Add mussels to the pot, cover, and bring to a boil. Boil until the mussels open, about 3 minutes. Transfer opened mussels to serving dishes and discard any that don't open.

Stir the black pepper into the pot. Season the broth with salt and ladle spoonfuls over the mussels. Garnish with parsley and serve with crunchy bread.

RECIPE RECOMMENDED BY
Emily
Traveler

Cooking tip

Give mussels a thorough review before cooking. Any with broken shells or that don't clamp shut when tapped should be tossed.

RECIPE RECOMMENDED BY

Lauren
Go Ahead Tours

TOTAL TIME:

35 minutes

SERVINGS:
8–10

RECIPE ORIGIN:
Spain

INGREDIENTS:

6 potatoes, peeled

1 yellow onion

Salt, to taste

2 1/2 cups plus 2 Tbsp olive oil

6 large eggs

Tortilla de patata

Spanish omelette

DIRECTIONS:

Cut potatoes in half lengthwise, slice into 1/8 in-thick pieces, and set aside. Peel onion and chop into 1/4-in pieces. Place both potatoes and onion into a bowl and toss with salt to taste.

Heat 2 1/2 cups oil in a large nonstick frying pan on medium-high. Carefully add potatoes and onions to the pan. The potatoes should be almost covered by the oil. If the potatoes cook too quickly, turn the heat down slightly to avoid burning.

Cook until potatoes can be easily broken with a spatula. Once cooked through, remove both potatoes and onions from the pan and drain on a plate covered with a paper towel. Let cool.

In a large mixing bowl, beat eggs with a whisk then add potato mixture to the bowl. Let stand for 5 minutes.

Add 2 Tbsp of olive oil to a 10-in cast-iron skillet and place over medium heat until hot. Stir the potato and egg mixture, then pour into the pan, making sure it spreads evenly. Cook until it's brown on the bottom and ready to flip.

To flip the tortilla, remove skillet from heat and bring over to the sink. Place a large plate upside down over the top of the pan and secure it with one hand. With the other hand grabbing the skillet handle, turn upside down so that the tortilla comes out of the skillet and sits on the plate.

Return the skillet to the burner and coat with just enough oil to cover the bottom and sides. Let warm for about 30 seconds, then return the tortilla to the pan with the browned side up. Cook for 3 to 4 minutes before turning off the heat. Let sit in the pan for 2 minutes before serving.

Did you know?

Also called *tortilla española*, this versatile Spanish bite is often considered one of the country's national dishes and is commonly eaten as a type of tapa.

TOTAL TIME:

40 minutes
+ 3 hours chilling

SERVINGS:

6

RECIPE ORIGIN:

Spain

INGREDIENTS:

1 Tbsp extra-virgin olive oil

3/4 cup flour

1 cup milk

1/2 cup ham, finely minced

Nutmeg, to taste

Salt and pepper, to taste

2 eggs

3 1/2 oz breadcrumbs

Olive oil, for frying

RECIPE RECOMMENDED BY
Rebecca
Go Ahead Tours

Croquetas de jamón

DIRECTIONS:

Heat 1 Tbsp oil in a frying pan over medium-high heat, and remove the pan from the heat before the oil starts to smoke. Mix flour into the hot oil until it becomes a paste, about 3 minutes. Place the pan over medium-low heat and stir continuously as you slowly add milk. Then, add ham, nutmeg, salt, and pepper, stirring as the mixture thickens. Place the thickened mixture into a bowl and refrigerate until cold, about 3 hours. Once mixture is cool, divide it into 1-in balls, roll into oval shapes, and put aside.

Pour breadcrumbs into a small bowl and whisk eggs together in another. Then, fill a large frying pan with enough oil to cover croquetas and heat to about 355°F. Using one hand, cover each croqueta in egg, roll in breadcrumbs, and carefully place in hot oil. Fry until golden. Remove with a slotted spoon, place on a paper towel to drain, and serve immediately.

Kristen
Traveler

TOTAL TIME:

45 minutes

SERVINGS:
4

RECIPE ORIGIN:
Andalusia, Spain

INGREDIENTS:

2 Tbsp olive oil

1 onion, finely chopped

2 red peppers, finely chopped

2 garlic cloves, finely chopped

2 to 3 tomatoes, chopped

1 Tbsp smoked paprika

8 eggs

8 slices Serrano ham

8 slices chorizo

5 oz peas (fresh or frozen and defrosted)

Salt and pepper, to taste

A bunch of fresh parsley, chopped (optional)

Toasted bread, to serve

Huevos a la flamenca

Flamenco style eggs

DIRECTIONS:

Preheat oven to 400°F. Place a frying pan over medium heat and warm oil. Sauté the onion and peppers in the oil until they are soft and golden, about 7 minutes. Then add the garlic and sauté for about 4 minutes before mixing in the tomatoes and paprika.

Turn heat down to low and cook mixture for 15 minutes. Then divide evenly and place in 4 ramekins. Crack 2 eggs into each ramekin and top with 2 slices of ham, 2 slices of chorizo, and a handful of peas. Place ramekins into the oven and bake for about 10 minutes or until the eggs are cooked to your liking. Season with salt and pepper, garnish with parsley if desired, and serve alongside toasted bread.

Did you know?

While breakfast may seem like the perfect time to serve this dish in the U.S. and Canada, you'd be hard-pressed to find it on any breakfast tables in Spain. Eggs are more commonly enjoyed at lunch or dinner throughout the country.

141

TOTAL TIME:

25 minutes

SERVINGS:
4

RECIPE ORIGIN:
Cordoba, Spain

INGREDIENTS:

8 tomatoes

1 baguette

A splash of Sherry vinegar

Salt, to taste

1 garlic clove

1 cup extra-virgin olive oil

2 hard-boiled eggs

Sliced Serrano ham

Salmorejo cordobés
Puréed tomato & bread soup

DIRECTIONS:

Slice a small cross in the bottom of each tomato and add them to a large pot of boiling, salted water for about 30 to 60 seconds. Remove immediately, place in a large bowl filled with ice water, and peel the skin off each. Cut out the tomato cores and blend the tomatoes on high speed for about 30 seconds.

Next, remove the bread inside the baguette and place about 2 cups of it into the blender. You can add more or less based on your desired consistency. Let the bread soak for about 5 minutes and add vinegar, salt, and garlic. Blend the mixture until smooth and all bread is broken down. Stop the blender, add a small amount of oil, and blend. Repeat until all oil is added. Finally, blend in a hard-boiled egg. To serve, spoon into bowls and top with ham and a diced hard-boiled egg.

This is a very simple summer soup, yet it is so rich and delicious. Every time travelers try it, they fall in love with it.

—**Manuel**, *Tour Director*

TOTAL TIME:

50 minutes

SERVINGS:
6

RECIPE ORIGIN:
Portugal

INGREDIENTS:

A bunch of collard greens, thoroughly washed

1/2 cup extra-virgin olive oil

1 onion, quartered

3 garlic cloves, minced

2 lbs Yukon Gold potatoes, peeled

8 cups chicken or vegetable broth

1 lb sausage (chorizo, linguiça, or kielbasa), thinly sliced

Salt and pepper, to taste

Caldo verde soup

DIRECTIONS:

Remove any rough stems from the collard greens and cut them into strips by stacking a few at a time, rolling them like cigars, and slicing them crosswise. Set aside.

In a heavy-bottomed pot, add oil, onion, and garlic; sauté until fragrant, around 2 to 3 minutes. Add the potatoes and chicken broth and bring broth to a boil over high heat. Lower the heat to medium-low and simmer until potatoes are tender, about 20 minutes.

Scoop the potatoes out of the pot. Mash them with a potato masher or fork and then return them to the pot. Working in batches, blend the soup in a blender until smooth (a hand blender in the pot does the trick, too). Add the collard greens and sausage, stir, and cook for 15 more minutes. Season with salt and pepper.

RECIPE RECOMMENDED BY

Kathy
Traveler

143

A day in the life: Eat like a local

Sampling flavorful dishes, trying delicious wines, and lingering around the table make the experience of dining in Spain an unforgettable part of any visit here. In fact, the pace of life in Spain is dictated by these cultural traditions. The main culinary event of the day is a three-course lunch, followed by a mid-afternoon siesta to recharge. After a few more hours in the workday, the evenings take on a life of their own, moving from tapas to dinner to drinks.

Morning:
breakfast or el desayuno

The Spanish tend to have a small breakfast in the morning of just coffee or juice paired with a pastry or toast. Have a sweet tooth? Decadent *churros con chocolate* are a traditional treat that's definitely worth a try.

Midday:
lunch or el almuerzo

This is the most important and hearty meal of the day and is served around 1pm or later. It can be made up of several courses, starting with soup (*sopa*) or salad (*ensalada*), followed by a meat (*carne*) or fish (*pescado*) dish like savory seafood paella, and ending with fruit or dessert.

Afternoon:
resting time or siesta

Siesta is that sleepy time in the afternoon between 2 and 4pm when many Spanish shops and businesses slow or close down, allowing for people to enjoy a long lunch and unwind for a bit. Bars and restaurants often take siesta later, sometime between 4 and 8pm, after the post-lunch crowd has cleared. There are many reasons behind the siesta—Spain's large lunches, late nights, and midday heat all make an afternoon break appealing—but the long-held tradition is getting less common with today's nonstop lifestyle.

Evening:
dinner or la cena

Usually a lighter meal than lunch, dinner is often not started until 9 or 10pm. In the summertime, it's not out of the ordinary to head out to dinner around midnight!

Nighttime:
drinks

Nightlife is big (and late!) in Spain, and isn't reserved just for the young. People of all ages go out to enjoy drinks, bites, and music, with bars filling up around midnight. Not sure what to sip on? The gin and tonic is hugely popular here and comes in an oversized balon glass. Don't expect the standard lemon or lime though—Spanish G&Ts often come creatively garnished with herbs, spices, or unexpected fruit.

Anytime:
Small bites or tapas

Small bites called tapas (or *pintxos* in Basque Country) can tide you over any time of day, but particularly during that long afternoon stretch between lunch and dinner. Another category you may see on the menu? *Raciónes*, which are similar to tapas but are made in slightly larger portions. While it's traditional to snack on tapas between meals, you can also order a bunch as your dinner and share with friends.

TOTAL TIME:

1 hour
+ 2 hours chilling

SERVINGS:
4

RECIPE ORIGIN:
Portugal

INGREDIENTS:

3 sprigs of thyme

3 garlic cloves, divided

1 shallot, roughly chopped

1 tsp smoked paprika

Salt, to taste

3 Tbsp olive oil, divided

3 to 3 1/2-lb chicken, spatchcocked
(or equivalent weight in bone-in chicken parts)

1 red onion

1 red bell repper

5 piri piri peppers

1/4 cup fresh cilantro leaves

1/2 tsp dried oregano

Juice and zest of 1 lemon

2 tsp red wine vinegar

Piri piri chicken

Chicken with piri chili sauce

DIRECTIONS:

Make the marinade with a mortar and pestle by combining the thyme, 1 chopped garlic clove, shallot, paprika, and a pinch of salt. After a paste has formed, add 2 Tbsp of oil and mix well. Place the chicken in a baking dish and pour the marinade on top—make sure to rub all over to coat. Cover and chill in the refrigerator for at least 2 hours.

To make the piri piri sauce, heat an outdoor grill to medium heat. Cut the unpeeled onion into quarters and remove the bell pepper's stem and seeds. Place onion, bell pepper, piri piri peppers, and remaining unpeeled garlic cloves on the grill. Rotating regularly, grill until charred, about 5 to 10 minutes. Peel the onions and garlic cloves and place all vegetables plus cilantro, oregano, and lemon juice and zest into a food processor. Add 1 Tbsp of oil and the vinegar and pulse until smooth. Add more liquid if needed, and season with salt.

Oil the grill grates and place chicken skin-side down. Ladle some marinade on top and cook until lightly charred on the bottom, about 15 minutes. Flip over, spoon more marinade over the skin, and cook until the chicken reaches 165°F inside, about 15 to 25 more minutes. Allow the chicken to rest for 5 minutes before cutting.

Did you know?

With roots in both South America and Africa, the spicy piri piri—which translates to "pepper pepper" in Swahili—gained popularity in Portugal thanks to the country's worldwide trading routes.

Middle Eastern influences

The Moors from North Africa ruled the Iberian peninsula from the 8th to the 15th century. While their influence can be felt throughout Spain, it's unquestionably strongest in Andalusia, the autonomous community at the southernmost tip of the country that's home to cultural capitals like Málaga and Seville. Traveling through the region, the flavors, colors, and architecture feel reminiscent of North Africa and the Middle East.

Signature spices

Some of Spain's classic herbs, aromatics, and spices traveled up from the country's southern neighbors.

Saffron   **Cumin**   **Coriander**

Nutmeg   **Mint**

Fresh crops

Everyday veggies and perfect-for-paella rice came onto the scene from the Moors.

Eggplant   **Spinach**   **Rice**   **Carrots**

Sweet treats

Desserts got an earthy spin with nuts, dried fruits, and more.

Honey   **Almonds**   **Dried figs**   **Cinnamon**

Easy-to-spot architecture

Repeated patterns, archways, and intricate tilework make Moorish architecture stand out.

The Alhambra in Granada

The Mezquita in Córdoba

The Giralda Tower of the Seville Cathedral

RECIPE RECOMMENDED BY

Kristen
Traveler

TOTAL TIME:

1 hour, 30 minutes

SERVINGS:
4

RECIPE ORIGIN:
Valencia, Spain

INGREDIENTS:

5 Tbsp olive oil

1 onion, chopped

Half of 1 red bell pepper, chopped

2 garlic cloves, minced

2 tomatoes, peeled and chopped

1/2 tsp sugar

Salt, to taste

1 tsp sweet paprika

A pinch of saffron threads

2 cups medium-grain paella rice
or bomba rice

3 cups fish or chicken stock

1 cup dry white wine

1 Tbsp fresh parsley, minced

12 jumbo shrimp in their shells

16 mussels, scrubbed and debearded

Seafood paella

DIRECTIONS:

Coat a 16-in paella pan in oil (use a large, shallow pan if you don't have a paella pan). Cook the onions and pepper until soft, about 5 minutes. Add the garlic and cook until soft but not browned, and then add the tomatoes.

Stir in the sugar, salt, paprika, and saffron, and cook until the tomatoes are reduced to a jammy consistency. Add the rice and stir to coat.

In a saucepan, combine the stock and wine over medium-high heat and bring to a boil. Pour the wine mixture over the rice, bring to a boil in the paella pan, and season with parsley and salt to taste. Stir well to create an even consistency in the pan—this should be the last time you stir the rice! Simmer over low heat for 18 to 20 minutes, occasionally rotating the pan for even cooking.

Cook the shrimp in the same pan by laying them across the top of the rice mixture until they've become pink, about 10 minutes, and then flip them to the reverse side.

Meanwhile, steam the mussels in a covered frying pan with 1 in or so of water for about 5 minutes. You'll know they're done when they open.

While the rice cooks, feel free to add more hot stock to the pan if it makes dry, cracking noises. Arrange the shrimp and mussels around the top and serve right in the paella pan.

The burnt edges are the best part

During our cooking lesson in Barcelona I learned about the steps for preparing paella, ending with delicious results.

—Kristen,
2nd-time traveler
Grand Tour of Spain

Did you know?

Cod—considered a national dish of
Portugal—isn't even native to the
country's coastline. Find out more
about why this fish became so popular
in Portugal on pg. 136.

TOTAL TIME:

1 hour
+ overnight soaking

SERVINGS:
4–6

RECIPE ORIGIN:
Lisbon, Portugal

INGREDIENTS:

12 oz bacalhau (salted cod), soaked overnight

4 potatoes, peeled

1/4 cup olive oil, divided

1 onion, chopped

A pinch of saffron (about 10 threads)

1 garlic clove, minced

8 eggs

1 tsp salt

1 tsp pepper

A bunch of fresh parsley, chopped, to serve

1/3 cup of black olives, chopped, to serve

Bacalhau à Brás

Salted cod with eggs & potatoes

DIRECTIONS:

Start by rehydrating the cod. Rinse the fish and place it in a baking dish or bowl and cover with water. Cover the container and chill overnight, changing the water 2 or 3 times. The next day, drain the fish and place in a saucepan to poach. Cover with water and bring to a boil. Lower the heat to a simmer and cook until the fish easily flakes apart, about 12 to 15 minutes. Remove from the pan, pat dry, and use 2 forks to pull the fish into bite-size pieces.

Meanwhile, peel the potatoes and use either a cheese grater or mandoline to make potato matchsticks. Set potato matchsticks in a bowl of water and let sit for 5 minutes to draw out starch. Drain on paper towels.

Coat a skillet in oil and warm over medium-high heat. Working in batches, cook the potatoes until golden brown, about 5 minutes. Re-coat the pan with oil as needed and set cooked potatoes on paper towels to drain.

Re-coat the pan with oil and add onion, saffron, and garlic. Sauté until the onion is golden brown, about 6 to 8 minutes. Add the fish and an additional 1 1/2 tsp of oil, and cook for 3 minutes, stirring occasionally. Add potatoes and cook for 2 more minutes.

While the fish and vegetables are cooking, combine eggs, salt, and pepper in a mixing bowl. Whisk together and then pour over the fish mixture. Stir occasionally and cook until the eggs are soft-scrambled, about 3 minutes. Sprinkle with parsley and olives to serve.

This is the most common and popular way that the Portuguese people eat their cod—and it's irresistible!

—**Leonor**, *Tour Director*

RECIPE RECOMMENDED BY

Rafael
Tour Director

TOTAL TIME:

1 hour, 30 minutes
+ overnight soaking

SERVINGS:
8

RECIPE ORIGIN:
Portugal

INGREDIENTS:

1 lb dried navy beans or kidney beans

8 oz sliced bacon

1 large yellow onion, chopped

3 garlic cloves, minced

1/4 cup tomato paste

8 oz Portuguese chorizo, cut into 1/4 in-thick slices

4 cups water

28-oz can diced tomatoes

A bunch of fresh parsley

1 bay leaf

1 Tbsp sweet paprika

1/2 tsp red pepper flakes

2 tsp kosher salt, plus more to taste

Feijao a Portuguesa

Sausage & bean stew

DIRECTIONS:

Rinse the dried beans and let soak overnight in a large bowl. After at least 8 hours, drain and set aside. In a large, heavy-bottomed pot, cook bacon over medium heat until browned, about 10 minutes. Transfer the bacon to paper towels to drain. Discard all but 1 Tbsp of the pork fat and add the onion and garlic into the pot. Stir to coat in fat and cook until golden and translucent, about 5 minutes.

Keeping the bacon set to the side, combine all remaining ingredients in the pot and bring to a boil. Reduce the heat to medium-low, cover, and simmer until the dried beans are tender, about 1 hour and 15 minutes. Remove the bay leaf, crumble the bacon into the stew, and season with salt to taste.

If you'd like to grab a bite to eat and people-watch in Lisbon, Rua de Rosa is the place to go. It's a bustling, pedestrian street where you can kick back on the mosaic sidewalks while trying traditional food.

—Rebecca, *Go Ahead Tours*

Cooking tip

If you're using canned instead of dried beans, just rinse and drain the beans, and then allow for less simmering time once all the ingredients are combined.

Jamón to write home about

While there are many delicacies to sample throughout Spain (and trust us, they're all good), one thing foodies should be sure to seek out is *jamón*, or ham. This gastronomic gem sits distinguished as one of the country's most impressive products. Here are the different types to try while exploring the Iberian Peninsula.

1
Jamón Ibérico Puro de Bellota

This pure ham claims the title as some of the best and most expensive in the world. Nutty and sweet, it's sourced from 100% free-range Iberian black pigs. These *Pata Negra* feed on mainly *bellotas*, or acorns, in large oak forests known as *dehesas* for up to four months.

The meat is then air-cured in the mountains for up to five years, tested by eight expert "sniffers" who make sure the aroma is just right, and stamped with the revered distinction known as the *Cinco Jotas* brand.

2
Jamón Ibérico

To the untrained palate, the differences between pure Bellota ham and the other three types of *Jamón Ibérico* may be hard to identify. But in the ham world, the way each pig is raised results in a significantly different flavor and fat content. While Bellota ham comes from 100% free-range Iberian pigs, *Jamón Ibérico de Recebo, de Cebo de Campo*, and *de Cebo*, can come from crossbred pigs that are at least 50% Iberian and don't indulge in as many (or any) acorns.

3
Jamón Serrano

White pigs rather than indigenous Iberian pigs produce this popular ham, which is an everyday go-to for locals and visitors alike. It's still delicious (and the price is right), but don't be fooled by fancy names such as *Jamón Reserva, Jamón Curado*, or *Jamón Extra*. They're all simply ways to say the same thing—Serrano ham—which is a tasty, traditional bite to enjoy in tapas, sandwiches, and more.

A Tour Director's take on a cultural delicacy

After a culinary journey through Spain, blogger Rachelle of *The Travel Bite* sat down for a Q&A with her expert Tour Director, Emilio. Here, both foodies reminisce about the cuisine they enjoyed during their shared adventure on *Food & Wine: A Taste of Spain*.

Rachelle, *Blogger, The Travel Bite*

Emilio, *Tour Director*

Rachelle: I'm here with my friend Emilio in Madrid. We just finished a 12-day Food & Wine Tour in Spain. Let's talk about what kinds of food we've experienced!

Emilio: I think that we cannot divide the ideal food in Spain from the tapas concept. It's very interesting. The idea of tapas started many years ago. It's a wonderful way of eating in general because it can be paired with the new concept of healthy food that suggests we eat several times during the day, but just a small portion of something. You can definitely do this in Spain with the tapas or pintxos—it depends where you are. Just stop and have a small bite of something amazing paired, obviously, with good wine.

R: What are the types of food you think people have to try when they come to Spain?

E: The jamón. They have to—it's amazing.

R: We tried the jamón when we ordered a little fast food, *comida rápida*. We were looking for something quick to go and we ended up getting jamón and chorizo in a cone.

E: For some protein!

R: The three basic food groups in Spain are chocolate, coffee, and jamón. The cone of jamón looks like an ice cream cone except it's filled with meat.

E: You eat also, especially here in Madrid, the fried calamari.

R: Yes! You can do the calamari sandwich.

E: It's really unique. Only in Spain. I've seen that only in Spain.

How to order jamón

AT BREAKFAST

Spring for *la tostada con aceite, tomate, y jamón*. This warm piece of artisanal toast topped with extra-virgin olive oil, vine-ripened tomatoes, a pinch of salt, and thin slices of jamón is the ultimate way to start the day.

ON THE GO

Pop into almost any market and order jamón in a paper cone. It's a popular type of *comida rápida*, or fast food, and the tasty, savory snack will keep you fueled while out exploring.

FOR TAPAS

Opt for a serving of *croquetas de jamón*. These traditional fried bites are stuffed with jamón and béchamel—how can you go wrong?

Jamón Ibérico is amazingly tasty! I tried it for the first time in Barcelona, and I enjoyed watching butchers in markets along Las Ramblas prep it right in front of me. They had some sliced up in little cups and there were uncut pieces on display, and I was able to take a taste with a toothpick before I bought any. Trying it that way was even better than ordering it from a restaurant.

—Harris, *Go Ahead Tours*

TOTAL TIME:

1 hours, 30 minutes
+ 2 hours chilling

SERVINGS:
24 tarts

RECIPE ORIGIN:
Portugal

INGREDIENTS:

For the pastry

2 cups all-purpose flour, plus more for dusting

1/4 tsp salt

3 1/2 Tbsp water

9 oz soft butter, divided

For the filling

2 cups cream

9 egg yolks

10 Tbsp sugar

A pinch of cinnamon, to serve

A pinch of confectioners' sugar, to serve

Pasteis de nata

Egg custard tarts

DIRECTIONS:

In a mixing bowl, combine the flour, salt, and water. Using your spoon and then your hands, make a soft, light dough, adding more water if needed.

Dust a work surface in flour and roll out the dough to create a square. Wrap the pastry in plastic wrap and chill in the fridge for 20 minutes.

Divide the butter into 3 equal portions. Take the chilled dough out of the fridge and roll out again creating a larger square. Leaving the righthand third of dough bare, use a spatula to spread one of the butter portions over the left and middle thirds of the square. Fold the righthand side flat onto the middle third of the dough; then fold the lefthand side onto the middle third, almost like you're folding together a trifold pamphlet. Once both sides are folded in, you'll be left with a rectangle shape where the middle third of the square was, and you shouldn't be able to see any buttered parts of the dough. Chill the dough for about 10 minutes.

Gently roll the dough out to a square again. Repeat this process a second and third time, trying to keep the layers of butter intact inside each time. Add flour liberally to keep the dough intact, and let the dough rest and cool between each round.

After the third round, roll out dough into a rectangle. Spread a thin layer of butter along the whole rectangle, leaving about 1 in bare along the border. Starting on a short side of the rectangle, gently roll the dough into a tight, spiraled log. Cut the log in half, wrap each section in plastic wrap, and refrigerate for at least 2 hours.

Preheat oven to 550°F. After chilling, slice the dough into 3/4-in thick circles. Place each slice into a muffin tin and allow it to soften for about 3 minutes. Dip your fingers in water and gently press the dough into the shape of the tins.

Make the custard in a *bain-marie* by placing a bowl over boiling water. Combine sugar, egg yolks, and cream in the bowl, and whisk continuously until it comes to a boil and thickens. Allow the egg mixture to cool slightly, then pour it into the muffin tins. Bake for 15 minutes. You'll know it's done when the custard gets brown and patchy-looking. Remove from the oven and sprinkle with cinnamon and sugar.

Did you know?

Catholic monasteries used to use large amounts of egg whites to starch clothing (you have to keep those habits looking sharp!), and the leftover egg yolks made their way into savory pastries sold by the monks. That's how these popular eggy pastries got their start in the 18th century. When the monastery closed in 1834, the monks sold their secret recipe to the Fábrica de Pastéis de Belém in Lisbon, which is the only place you can purchase true pasteis de nata to this day.

Taste the real thing!

Pastéis de Belém | Lisbon, Portugal

The flavors of Spain & Portugal

Did you know?

While we usually consider this sweet treat a dessert here in North America, Spaniards traditionally indulge in the fried pastry for breakfast alongside an espresso.

TOTAL TIME:

35 minutes

SERVINGS:
8

RECIPE ORIGIN:
Spain

INGREDIENTS:

For the churros

1 1/4 cups water

Salt, to taste

1 tsp sugar, plus 3 Tbsp for serving (optional)

1/2 cup unsalted butter

1 cup plus 2 Tbsp all-purpose flour

4 eggs

4 cups vegetable oil, for frying

2 Tbsp cinnamon, to serve (optional)

For the dipping chocolate

2 cups milk

7 oz dark chocolate

Churros con chocolate

DIRECTIONS:

In a medium saucepan, heat the water, salt, 1 tsp of sugar, and butter over high heat. In a mixing bowl, sift the flour. When the water boils, add the flour. Using a wooden spoon, stir continuously until the dough comes away from the sides. Transfer the dough to a bowl and let it cool slightly. Beat the eggs into the dough. Spoon the dough into a piping bag with a fluted nozzle.

Fill a high-sided frying pan with enough oil to reach a depth of about 2 1/2 in. Over medium heat, bring the oil to 360°F. Working in batches, squeeze the dough out in strips, leaving room in the pan between each strip. Deep-fry for 1 to 2 minutes, turning once, until golden brown. Use a slotted spoon to remove the churros from the oil and drain on paper towel. If opting for a sweet dusting, pour the cinnamon and the remainder of the sugar in a dish and mix together. Roll the churros in the dish to lightly coat.

While the churros are frying, combine the milk and chocolate in a saucepan over low heat. Cook for about 5 minutes, stirring continuously until chocolate is smooth and drippy. Pour chocolate into a dish for dipping and serve churros immediately.

How could I forget the churros and chocolate? The churros in Spain do not have the sugar and cinnamon that we put on them in the U.S. They're more of a plain, fried donut and there's a really thick chocolate that you dip them in. It's delightful. You need an espresso afterward to kind of cut the sweetness.

—Rachelle,
2nd-time traveler
and blogger behind The Travel Bite
Food & Wine: A Taste of Spain

What's your sangria style?

TOTAL TIME:

10 minutes
+ 2 hours chilling

SERVINGS:
6

RECIPE ORIGIN:
Spain

Red sangria

Red wine punch

....

INGREDIENTS:
2 Tbsp water
1 to 3 Tbsp sugar, depending on
sweetness preference
2 oranges
2 lemons
2 peaches or apricots (optional)
1 1/2 bottles of young Tempranillo or
Garnacha wine
1/2 cup brandy
1 cinnamon stick

DIRECTIONS:
Make a simple syrup by heating the
water over low heat and dissolving the
sugar. Set aside and let cool.

Halve 1 orange and 1 lemon, and
squeeze juice into a pitcher. Wash your
remaining fruit thoroughly, cut into
pieces, and add to the pitcher. Pour in
the wine, simple syrup, and brandy, and
stir well. Add the cinnamon stick and
let the mixture sit at least 2 hours, or
overnight if possible.

Cava sangria

Sparkling white wine punch

....

INGREDIENTS:
1 red apple
2 oranges
1 cup of pineapple, cut in bite-size chunks
2 Tbsp sugar
1/2 cup brandy
1/2 cup orange liqueur
3/4 cup pineapple juice
8 fresh sprigs of mint
2 cinnamon stick
2 bottles of chilled cava brut

DIRECTIONS:
Wash your fruit thoroughly. Slice
oranges into thin rounds and cut apple
into bite-size chunks. Combine orange,
apple, and pineapple in a bowl, cover
with sugar, and let sit for 15 minutes.

In a pitcher, combine the brandy, orange
liqueur, pineapple juice, and mint, and
gently muddle the mint with a wooden
spoon. Add the fruit and cinnamon, and
chill this mixture for about 1 hour. Just
before serving, pop the cava and add to
the punch.

"

Salzburg had the best German food I've ever had.
We arrived in Salzburg just in time for one of
those famous German festivals, complete with a
polka band, and plenty of beer and sausage.

—Janice
6th-time traveler
Budapest, Vienna & Prague

Sausages, schnitzels & seasonal treats

Central Europe & beyond

OKTOBERFEST EATS:

5 foods worth loosening the waistband on your lederhosen

Originally conceived to celebrate the marriage of Crown Prince Ludwig and Princess Therese of Bavaria, early iterations of Oktoberfest culminated in a horse race. Today, festivities include a 12-gun salute, a ceremonial tapping of the first keg, carnival games and rides, and of course plenty of beer. The selected brews are held to strict standards: The beer must be produced within Munich city limits with a minimum of 6% alcohol by volume. Despite the beer-fueled theme, the festival is almost as much about the food as it is about the drinks. Here are 5 must-try bites for the beer hall.

1. Pretzels

2. Spit-roasted chicken

3. Potato dumplings called *knödel*

4. Weisswurst sausage

5. Cheese-covered noodles called *käksespätzle*

Comfort food finds its niche in Central Europe.

As you travel through Europe from west to east, the flavors become richer, the meals become heartier, and the desserts take on decadent sweetness. The landlocked countries at the heart of Central Europe rely heavily on meats, grains, and stews, with seasonings that reflect their individual influences and climates.

Bavaria, Germany

Coffee, please

If a bold-roasted brew is up your alley, Budapest is the place to go. The city is dotted with historic coffeehouses, where you can sip fresh-brewed coffee alongside decadent pastries while admiring Old-World décor.

The crème de la crème: Swiss chocolate

With its temperate climate, Central Europe may seem like an unlikely spot for a chocolate hub, but that's exactly what you'll find in Switzerland. Europeans got their first tastes when Spanish conquistadors brought home liquid chocolate in the 16th century. Within 100 years, the drink had taken hold across Europe. The Swiss leveraged two of their strengths—tech-savvy manufacturing and a plentiful milk supply—to become power players in the world of chocolate. Their speciality? Solid, high-quality milk chocolate.

The name game: sausages

Bratwurst

Arguably the star of German sausages, the bratwurst—or brat for short—is a smoked sausage made from finely shopped veal, pork, or beef. Traditionally, it's a mild sausage flavored with peppers, onions, and sage, and then served in a bun with mustard, but it's not uncommon in Germany to find it topped with curry ketchup for a currywurst.

Bloedworst

In Belgium and the Netherlands, this blood sausage is either served as slices of a large, 4-inch-wide loaf, or individual banana-sized sausages. Its go-to accompaniment? Pan-fried apples or applesauce.

Kielbasa

This smoky variety is usually a mixture of lean pork and beef seasoned with garlic. As a staple of Polish cuisine, it comes in many forms, from stews and casseroles to plain sliced sausage served with fried onions or sauerkraut.

Wiener

Named for the city of Vienna, this sausage is a close cousin to the German frankfurter or American hotdog. The best spot to try these? Sidewalk sausage stands.

Weisswurst

These German sausages hail from Bavaria and are easy to recognize. The distinguishing factor? They're ghostly white—in fact, the name translates simply to "white sausage." Made with minced veal and pork, they're seasoned with parsley, lemon, onions, ginger, and cardamom.

Sauerkraut: a culinary staple

It may be German for "sour cabbage," but don't count sauerkraut out. This fermented dish made from cabbage and salt has made many names for itself in Central Europe (each country has its own take), and it adds a whole new level of flavor to everything from pork and sausages to pierogi and soups.

Shape-shifters:
Your guide to beer glasses

Chalices

GOOD FOR:

Belgian IPAs, German
bocks & more

Perfect for more complex
brews, the shape's large
mouth allows the beer
to keep its foamy head,
while also opening up its
dynamic flavors.

▼

Pilsner glasses

GOOD FOR:

Pilsners, ales & more

The tall, simple shape is
meant to show off the classic
color and carbonation—two
hallmarks of a pilsner beer.

▼

Tulip glasses

GOOD FOR:

Belgian ales, Belgian strongs
& dubbels

The wide, tulip-shaped bowl is
tapered at the top, capturing
the aroma of the beer inside,
making it a great choice for
fruity, aromatic beers.

▼

Pint glasses

GOOD FOR:

Lagers, stouts & dark German ales like dunkel

Pint glasses in their various forms—like simple shaker glasses and notched nitro glasses—are a go-to for uncomplicated beers.

▼

Weizen glasses

GOOD FOR:

Hefeweizens & weizenbiers

These glasses complement the unfiltered qualities of cloudy wheat beers. The curve at the base is designed to trap yeast or sediment at the bottom to give drinkers a nice, clean sip.

▼

German steins

GOOD FOR:

Beer hall brews

Ready for lots of cheers-ing, these hearty glasses have thick walls to keep beer cold, heavy handles to hold on to during toasts, and lids to prevent spills (and to keep out fruit flies back in the day).

▼

Get to know German wine

The thought of classic German drinks may immediately call strong lagers to mind, but don't count the country's wines out. Some truly spectacular varieties are produced in 13 different wine regions, where vineyards find the ideal settings on steep slopes along meandering rivers. And while the country's cool temperatures prevent most red grapes from thriving, they allow white wines like Riesling to shine—and the well-known varietal is certainly in good company.

German words to know about wine

Trocken

This German word means "dry" and is used to classify wines with the least amount of sugar (and surprise, some of the best Rieslings are trocken!). Half-dry wines will be labeled halbtrocken.

Süss

Translating to "sweet," this distinction is used for any wine that has more than 45 grams of residual sugar. It's safe to say a wine is süss if the bottle doesn't specifically label it otherwise.

Eiswein

When it comes to winemaking, letting grapes freeze on the vine may seem strange. But, that's exactly what growers do to create this "ice wine," a refreshing dessert wine with the right amount of sweetness.

Federweisser

Germany's fall season ushers in a short span of time to sip this "feather white" new wine. It's a popular drink that's high-sugar and low-alcohol, and is enjoyed just as it begins to ferment.

Grapes in high places

In southwestern Germany, where vines need more sunshine to balance out the country's chillier temps, a steep vineyard is synonymous with a good vineyard. This ideal grape-growing terrain may make tricky, difficult business for winegrowers, but it's a good trade-off for the best vintages. Here are a few of Germany's most popular wine regions, where terraced vineyards tower over rivers like the Mosel and the Rhine—and yes, it is just as pretty as it sounds.

Mosel: where bright Rieslings reign

Crisp, citrusy Rieslings full of minerality find their niche in this wine region, which is widely considered to be one of the oldest and most famous in Germany. Here, slate soil soaks up warmth from the sun, keeping vines warmer at night for riper, fruitier grapes. One of the region's other impressive attributes? It's home to some of the world's steepest vineyard slopes and the Bremmer Calmont vineyard wins the prize with a staggering 65-degree incline.

Rheingau: a wine center at a bend in the Rhine

With a prime spot between the Rhine River and Taunus Mountains, Rheingau is one of Germany's warmest wine regions. Its winemaking roots date back to the 12th century when monks at the Eberbach Abbey got curious about viticulture. Today, Pinot Noir, Riesling, and other grapes thrive here. The Rieslings are bolder than Mosel's but are still elegant, acidic, and known 'round the world. In fact, the old English nickname for German white wine, "hock," comes from one of Rheingau's main villages, Hochheim.

Rheinhessen: a hub of innovative winemaking

Rheinhessen sits distinguished as Germany's largest wine region, where ancient Romans once planted vineyards and the oldest records of a German vineyard, Glöck, have been found. It's the place to stray from Riesling (although that's great too), and see what curious winemakers have grown in the region's diverse terroir. Some types to sip are light-bodied reds and white varietals made from Silvaner grapes.

Riesling: the darling of the Rhine

Often fruity and always vibrant, Riesling is unquestionably Germany's most well-known wine. This famous varietal found its roots in the Middle Ages (it was first recorded in Germany in the 1400s), and among the varietal's glowing attributes is its adaptability. The grapes thrive in a wide variety of soils and climates, and they're crushed into wines with an acidity that allows them to age well. Have you stayed away from Riesling because you imagine them to be super sweet? That's not always the case! Here's a short guide to Reisling labels, so you can find the perfect finish.

Look at the alcohol percentage
Drier Rieslings have higher alcohol content. If the bottle doesn't specifically say *trocken*, or dry, simply check to see if the alcohol is over 11 percent.

Peek at labels for Pradikatswein or "QmP"
While high-quality Rieslings with these labels traditionally have some sweetness, it varies! The ripeness of the grapes used divides QmP wines into six subcategories, from driest to sweetest: Kabinett, Spätlese, Auslese, Beerenauslese, Trockenbeerenauslese, and Eiswein.

TOTAL TIME:
40 minutes

SERVINGS:
8

RECIPE ORIGIN:
Germany

INGREDIENTS:

2 seedless cucumbers

1 tsp salt

1 Tbsp granulated sugar

3 Tbsp white vinegar

3 Tbsp fresh dill

1 tsp fresh parsley

1/2 red onion, thinly sliced (optional)

Gurkensalat

German cucumber salad

DIRECTIONS:

Slice cucumbers very thinly—it's easiest with a mandoline or the slicer opening on a box grater. Salt the cucumbers and place them in a colander to drain for 20 minutes. Rinse thoroughly and pat dry.

In a large bowl, combine sugar, vinegar, dill, and parsley. Gently fold in cucumber and sliced onion, if desired. Let rest 15 minutes, then serve.

Cooking tip

If you're growing your own herbs, remember that dill's flavor is at its peak just as it starts to flower. Whether homegrown or store-bought, to make the most of it, be sure to rinse and pat dry before chopping the feathery branches.

TOTAL TIME:

20 minutes

SERVINGS:

4

RECIPE ORIGIN:

Belgium

INGREDIENTS:

4 tomatoes

8 oz peeled baby shrimp, precooked

1 egg yolk, room temperature

1 Tbsp mustard

1/2 cup oil

Juice of half a lemon

Salt and pepper, to taste

A small bunch of fresh parsley, chopped

A small bunch of fresh dill, chopped

Salad greens, to serve

Tomate aux crevettes

Shrimp salad in a tomato

DIRECTIONS:

Cut off the tops of the tomatoes and save to use as lids. With a spoon, scoop out as much of the inside of the tomatoes as possible, creating a bowl. Place the tomatoes upside down on a tray and set aside.

In a small bowl, mix the egg yolk with mustard and whisk thoroughly. Add a pinch of salt and pepper, then let rest 3 minutes. Add the oil a little bit at a time, whisking until the dressing thickens and starts to look glossy. Add lemon juice and adjust seasoning to taste.

Combine the dressing with the shrimp and parsley in a large bowl, folding until coated evenly. Spoon the shrimp salad into each of the tomatoes and garnish with dill. Top with the tomato "lid" and serve on a bed of salad greens.

We made this during our cooking class on our tour, *Food & Wine: Beers of Belgium & Germany*. It was delicious—I liked it so much, I ended up ordering it at a restaurant the next day!

—**Miriam**, *Go Ahead Tours*

Did you know?

Obatzda sauce and pretzels make a perfect Bavarian pair for Oktoberfest. But in the beer tents, the cheesy sauce is also often served alongside the *Munchener bier* radish, an heirloom variety that grows in northern Europe.

TOTAL TIME:

1 hour
+ 2 hours chilling

SERVINGS:
8

RECIPE ORIGIN:
Germany

INGREDIENTS:

For the obatzda
1 lb camembert cheese, rind removed

3 Tbsp unsalted butter

3/4 cup mascarpone (or substitute cream cheese)

1/3 cup onion, finely chopped, plus finely sliced rings for garnish

1 to 2 tsp paprika

1/2 tsp caraway seeds

4 to 8 Tbsp wheat beer

Salt and pepper, to taste

2 Tbsp of chives, finely chopped

For the pretzel
12 oz amber beer

1 packet (1/4 oz) dry yeast

2 Tbsp butter, melted

2 Tbsp sugar

1 1/2 tsp salt

4 1/4 cups flour

10 cups water

2/3 cup baking soda

1 egg yolk

1 Tbsp water

Coarse salt, to taste

Pretzels & obatzda

Pretzels with spicy beer cheese

DIRECTIONS:

Start with the obatzda cheese sauce because it needs to chill for 2 hours. Roughly chop the camembert cheese. Combine the chopped camembert, mascarpone, and butter, and mix with a fork until it's mixed, but not overly smooth.

Add the chopped onions, half of the paprika, caraway, salt, and pepper. Adjust for seasonings as desired. Add half the beer and stir until combined. Keep mixing in the remaining beer a little bit at a time until the cheese reaches a scoopable consistency.

Transfer to a sealable container or cover with plastic wrap, then refrigerate for 2 hours. Taste and adjust for seasoning again, if necessary.

Before serving, let the obatzda sit out for a few minutes until it softens a bit. Then, top with sliced onions and chives.

Now on to the pretzels. Pour the beer into a small saucepan and warm to 110°F. Remove the pan from the heat and stir in yeast until dissolved. Combine melted butter, sugar, salt, yeast-and-beer mixture, and 3 cups of flour in a large mixing bowl and beat on medium speed until smooth. Then, stir in the remaining flour until the dough reaches a soft, sticky consistency.

Place the dough onto a floured surface and knead until it becomes smooth and elastic (around 6 to 8 minutes). Place kneaded dough in a greased bowl, turning it over once to coat the top. Cover the bowl with plastic wrap and set it in a warm place. Let rise for 1 hour, or until the dough has doubled in size.

Preheat oven to 425°F. Remove plastic from the bowl and punch down the dough. Place punched-down dough onto a lightly floured surface and divide it into 8 equally-sized balls. Roll each ball into a 24-in rope and twist to form the classic pretzel shape.

In a separate pot, bring water and baking soda to a boil. Dropping them into the pot two at a time, boil pretzels for 30 seconds. Remove, and place on paper towels to absorb excess water.

For the topping, whisk egg yolk and water together in a small bowl. Place boiled pretzels 2 in apart on greased cookie sheets and brush with the egg wash. Sprinkle with coarse salt to taste and bake for 10 to 12 minutes or until golden brown. Cool on a wire rack before serving.

RECIPE RECOMMENDED BY

Courtney
Go Ahead Tours

TOTAL TIME:

35 minutes

SERVINGS:

4–6

RECIPE ORIGIN:

Switzerland

INGREDIENTS:

2 to 3 Russet potatoes, peeled

2 Tbsp unsalted butter

2 Tbsp extra-virgin olive oil

A bunch of parsley, chopped

Salt and pepper, to taste

Rösti

Fried potato pancake

DIRECTIONS:

Using a mandoline slicer or box grater, slice the potatoes into thin matchsticks. Squeeze out the excess liquid. Add salt and pepper to taste.

Melt butter and oil in a 12-inch nonstick skillet over medium heat, then add potatoes. Flatten the potatoes into a pancake in the pan.

Cook until the bottom of the potatoes are golden brown, about 10 minutes.

Flip the potato pancake by sliding it onto a plate, covering it with a second plate, and then turning it over. Return the potato pancake to the pan, browned side up.

Continue cooking on the stove until browned on both sides, another 10 minutes. Garnish with chopped fresh parsley and serve.

Hungarian goulash

TOTAL TIME:

2 hours, 15 minutes

SERVINGS:

4

RECIPE ORIGIN:

Hungary

INGREDIENTS:

2 Tbsp lard or butter

2 onions, finely diced

Salt, to taste

2 Tbsp sweet Hungarian paprika

1 tomato, diced

1 yellow bell peper, diced

1 lb beef shank, cut into 1-in cubes

2 bay leaves

10 black peppercorns

8 cups water

2 carrots, peeled and diced

1 parsnip, peeled and diced

1 tsp ground caraway seeds

1 garlic clove, minced

2 to 3 potatoes, peeled and cubed

DIRECTIONS:

In a large soup pot or Dutch oven, melt the lard or butter over medium heat. Cook the onions until just beginning to brown, about 7 minutes, and add a pinch of salt. Remove from heat and add the paprika, stirring until fragrant and being careful not to burn it. Add the tomatoes, yellow pepper, and beef, then return to heat, cooking for 10 minutes until the beef is browned.

Add bay leaves, peppercorns, water, and salt to taste. Cover the pot and simmer on reduced heat until the beef is tender, about 1 1/2 hours. Then, stir in the carrots, parsnip, caraway, garlic, and more salt to taste. Re-cover and place over high heat. Once the mixture starts to boil, reduce the heat and simmer until the vegetables are partially tender, about 5 minutes. Then, add the potatoes and cook for another 5 to 8 minutes.

TOTAL TIME:

45 minutes

SERVINGS:
4

RECIPE ORIGIN:
Belgium

INGREDIENTS:

For the mussels

2 cups dry white wine

1/2 cup shallots, minced

8 parsley sprigs

1/2 bay leaf

1/4 tsp thyme

1/8 tsp pepper

6 Tbsp butter

1 lb mussels, scrubbed and debearded

1/2 cup parsley, roughly chopped

For the fries

6 Russet potatoes

1/4 cup extra-virgin olive oil

Salt and pepper, to taste

Mayonnaise, for serving (optional)

Fries with mayo is a must!

Moules-frites

Mussels and fries

DIRECTIONS:

Preheat oven to 400°F. Peel the potatoes, or leave the skin on if you prefer. Cut lengthwise into quarters, then cut again lengthwise into half-inch-thick batons. Place into a large pot and cover completely with cold water. Add 1 Tbsp of salt, and bring to a boil. Simmer until the potatoes are easily pierced with a knife, about 5 minutes.

Drain the potatoes and transfer to a bowl. Add oil, salt, and pepper, and toss. Then, lay out in a single layer on a baking sheet and bake until light brown and crispy, turning once, about 20 minutes.

While the potatoes are in the oven, combine wine, shallots, parsley, bay leaf, thyme, pepper, and butter in a Dutch oven or large, lidded saucepan. Bring to a boil and continue cooking for 2 to 3 minutes.

Add the mussels, then cover the pot and continue boiling for about 5 minutes, stirring the mussels halfway through. As the mussels open, remove them from the pan with tongs.

After 5 minutes, remove from heat and discard any mussels that haven't opened. Scoop out the remaining mussels with a slotted spoon. Serve the mussels in bowls, adding a little bit of the cooking liquid on top. Enjoy alongside fries, with mayonnaise if desired.

Did you know?

There are a few different ways to enjoy moules-frites, but the most popular is this recipe: *à la marinière.* That means the mussels are cooked with white wine, shallots, and butter—but *à la crème* (in cream sauce) and *à la bière* (in beer) are two other favorite options.

Did you know?

Even though it's one of Maria's favorite things in *The Sound of Music*, "schnitzel with noodles" is not an actual dish in Austria. Schnitzel is usually served simply with roasted potatoes.

TOTAL TIME:

30 minutes

SERVINGS:

4

RECIPE ORIGIN:

Austria

INGREDIENTS:

4 boneless pork chops

Juice of half a lemon, plus 1 lemon for serving

1/2 tsp salt

1/2 cup flour

3 Tbsp water

1 egg

1 cup breadcrumbs

3 Tbsp butter

3 Tbsp vegetable oil

A bunch of parsley, chopped

Pork schnitzel

DIRECTIONS:

Arrange the pork chops between two sheets of wax paper or plastic wrap. Using a heavy rolling pin or the flat side of a meat tenderizer, pound out the pork chops to 1/4-in thickness. Season both sides with lemon juice, salt, and pepper.

Place three separate shallow bowls on the counter. In the first, combine flour and a pinch of salt. Mix a lightly beaten egg and water in the second and breadcrumbs in the third. Take each pork chop and coat it in flour, dip it in egg, and cover with breadcrumbs. (To reduce mess, use just one hand for this step.) Shake off excess breadcrumbs. Continue with the remaining pork chops.

In a large cast-iron skillet or stainless steel frying pan, heat 1/4 in of oil until it reaches 330°F. Work in batches, frying the schnitzel for about 2 to 3 minutes on each side, until golden brown, and transfer cooked schnitzels to a paper towel-lined plate. While frying, monitor the temperature of the oil with a thermometer, maintaining around 330°F.

Serve immediately, topping with slices of lemon and chopped parsley.

Germany was charming, from Heidelberg's narrow streets to Munich's glockenspiel. The food was different, but delicious—we liked trying new things, like schnitzel!

—**Gail**,
12th-time Traveler
Germany, Switzerland & Austria

RECIPE RECOMMENDED BY

Adam
Go Ahead Tours

TOTAL TIME:

1 hour

SERVINGS:
24 dumplings

RECIPE ORIGIN:
Poland

INGREDIENTS:

For the dough

2 cups all-purpose flour

1 tsp salt

1 egg yolk

1/2 cup sour cream

1 Tbsp extra-virgin olive oil

For the filling

1 lb sauerkraut

2 Tbsp oil

1 white onion, finely diced

1 lb white mushrooms, finely chopped

Salt and pepper, to taste

Herbs for garnish (rosemary or parsley)

Pierogi

Stuffed dumplings

DIRECTIONS:

Start by making the dough, by mixing flour and salt together in a medium bowl. Add egg and stir to combine. Fold in the sour cream and olive oil until the dough becomes a sticky ball, and place the ball of dough under a bowl to rest, about 15 minutes. Then, place the dough on a clean work surface. Very lightly knead until it starts to become smoother and elastic.

Next, make your filling. Squeeze any extra liquid from your sauerkraut, then place it in a medium pot on low heat and cook until soft and lightly browned, about 5 minutes. In a separate pan, warm olive oil and sauté onions until tender. Add heated sauerkraut, mushrooms, and pinches of salt and pepper to the onion pan, and cook on high for about 5 minutes. The filling is ready to go once cooled.

To fill your pierogi, cut the dough into two equal portions and roll out one half to 1/8-in thickness. Use a 2-in round cookie cutter or the bottom of a glass to make circles of dough. Continue with remaining dough.

Place a large pot of water on high heat, add a pinch of salt, and boil. Meanwhile, start filling your pierogi. Fill each round of dough with about 2 tsp of filling. Fold the dough over itself, pinching the edges of the pierogi to seal in the filling. If you're having a hard time getting the dough to stick to itself, use your fingertip or a pastry brush to wet one edge of the dough with a bit of water. Press the sealed edge down with a fork to close tightly.

Working in batches, cook the pierogi in the boiling salted water. After about 5 to 10 minutes, pierogi should be cooked—they will float to the top of the water when done. Scoop out cooked pierogi with a slotted spoon, and continue cooking until all your pierogis are done. Serve with sour cream or applesauce, and garnish with herbs if desired.

Comfort food at its finest!
This dish instantly reminds
me of my grandmother.

—**Adam**, *Go Ahead Tours*

TOTAL TIME:

30 minutes

SERVINGS:

6

RECIPE ORIGIN:

Austria

INGREDIENTS:

1 lb strawberries, quartered

1 1/4 cups granulated sugar, divided

1/8 tsp lemon zest, grated

1 tsp vanilla extract

4 Tbsp unsalted butter

Juice of half a lemon

1 cup milk

1 cup all-purpose flour

4 large eggs, separated

1 tsp lemon zest

Pinch of salt

1/3 cup confectioners' sugar

1 pint raspberries

RECIPE RECOMMENDED BY

Vicky
Traveler

Kaiserschmarrn

Sweet torn pancakes

DIRECTIONS:

In a medium saucepan, combine strawberries, 1 cup of sugar, lemon zest, and vanilla extract. Bring to a boil over high heat, stirring well. Then, reduce heat and simmer for about 10 minutes, or until the mixture thickens. Remove the sauce from heat and place in a bowl, then refrigerate until ready to top off the dish.

Whisk together flour, milk, egg yolks, lemon zest, and 2 Tbsp of sugar until batter is smooth. In the bowl of a stand mixer fitted with the whisk attachment (or in another medium bowl if using an electric mixer), beat the egg whites together with the salt, on high, until soft peaks form. Beat in 1 Tbsp of sugar until the egg whites stiffen and begin to look glossy.

Combine the beaten egg whites and batter by folding gently, careful not to deflate the egg whites too much.

Then, melt 1 Tbsp of butter in your skillet over medium heat. When the butter is melted and pan is hot, add the batter. Lower the heat, cover the pan, and cook until the pancake is golden-brown on the bottom and small bubbles begin to form at the edges, about 5 minutes. Flip the pancake with a large, wide spatula or carefully invert the pancake onto a plate, then return it to the skillet, uncooked side down. Cook until both sides of the pancake are browned, about 3 more minutes.

In the skillet, use a wooden or metal spatula to roughly tear the pancake into 2-in squares. Sprinkle with the remaining butter and confectioners' sugar. Then, add the strawberry sauce and toss, cooking about 5 minutes. Add raspberries and continue cooking about 1 minute until the berries are warmed through. Serve immediately, sprinkling with more confectioners' sugar if desired.

SERVINGS:
1 torte

RECIPE ORIGIN:
Austria

INGREDIENTS:

For the crust

4 1/2 cups walnuts, shelled

3 cups all-purpose flour, divided

2 tsp ground cinnamon

1/4 tsp ground cloves

1/2 tsp salt

2 1/2 sticks unsalted butter, cut into chunks

1 2/3 cups granulated sugar

1 egg plus 2 egg yolks, divided

Zest of 1 lemon

1 tsp water

For the filling

1/4 cup fine, dry breadcrumbs

2 cups seedless raspberry jam

*Perfect for the holidays
and all year long!*

Linzer torte

DIRECTIONS:

Preheat oven to 400°F. Butter a 12-in round cake pan or springform pan and line the bottom with parchment paper.

Combine walnuts and 1/2 cup flour in a food processor, blending for 15 seconds or until the nuts are finely ground. In a large mixing bowl, combine the remaining 2 1/2 cups flour with cinnamon, cloves, and salt. Using your fingertips, work the cold butter chunks into the dry ingredients. Once texture is coarse, add the sugar and walnut-flour mixture.

In a small dish, beat the whole egg, 1 yolk, and lemon zest until combined. Stir into dry ingredients, first mixing and then working with your hands until a soft dough forms. When you can gather the dough into a ball, transfer it to a work surface and divide it in half. Using one half of the dough, line the bottom of your cake pan by flattening the dough and pressing firmly into an even layer. Bake until it begins to brown at the edges, about 15 minutes. Remove the par-baked shell from the oven and let cool. Reduce the oven temperature to 350°F.

Meanwhile, roll out the second half of your dough on a lightly floured surface until it's about 1/4-in thick and slightly larger than your pan. Place on a parchment-lined baking sheet and transfer to the freezer, letting rest for 15 minutes.

Now, make the filling. Pulse your breadcrumbs in a food processor until you have about 1/4 cup of fine powder. Sprinkle the breadcrumbs onto your par-baked shell, then add the raspberry jam on top, spreading out in an even layer.

Cut your remaining dough into 3/4-in strips. Peel the strips off the parchment paper, then arrange them in a lattice pattern over the top of the torte, weaving to create diamond-shaped openings. Pinch the edges of the dough together to seal. Mix egg yolk and water, then brush over the top of the torte. Bake for 45 to 60 minutes, until the filling is bubbling and the crust is golden brown. Set on a wire rack to cool slightly before serving.

Did you know?

According to regional Tour Director
Frank, the secret is *Schwarzwälder
Kirschwasser*—or "Black Forest cherry
water," which is the kirsch liqueur that
gives the cake its signature flavor.

TOTAL TIME:

3 hours

SERVINGS:
1 cake

RECIPE ORIGIN:
Germany

INGREDIENTS:

For the cake

3 Tbsp unsalted butter, melted and cooled, plus more for buttering cake pans

1/2 cup all-purpose flour, plus more for flouring cake pan

1/4 cup Dutch-process cocoa powder

Pinch of salt

6 large eggs, room temperature

3/4 cup superfine sugar

1 tsp vanilla extract

For the syrup

1/2 cup sugar

1/2 cup water

2 Tbsp kirsch (or fruit brandy if unavailable)

For the frosting and layers

4 cups heavy cream

1 cup confectioners' sugar, plus more for dusting

2 tsp vanilla extract

2 cups sour cherries, drained

8 fresh cherries, pitted and stems removed

1/2 cup dark chocolate, ground

Black Forest cake

DIRECTIONS:

Preheat oven to 350°F and place a rack in the center. Butter and flour a 10-in springform pan (or a 10-in cake pan that is at least 3 in deep) and line the base with parchment paper, cut to size.

Spread a sheet of parchment paper out on a clean workspace. Sift the flour, cocoa powder, and salt together over the parchment and set aside. Using a stand mixer fitted with the whisk attachment, beat the eggs, sugar, and vanilla at high speed for about 8 minutes until the mixture thickens and triples in volume.

Lower the mixer speed and carefully transfer the dry ingredients into the bowl, a little at a time. Once all the flour is added, turn off the mixer. Pour in melted butter and, gently folding, finish combining the flour into the batter, mixing as little as possible.

Fill the prepared cake pan, place on a baking sheet, and bake for about 40 minutes. The cake should be springy but firm to the touch, and a tester inserted into the center should come out clean. Let the cake cool in the pan for about 5 minutes, then turn upside down on a rack to finish cooling.

Make the syrup in a small saucepan over medium-high heat. Bring sugar and water to a boil, whisking frequently to dissolve sugar. Once it begins to boil, add the kirsch and immediately remove from heat. Pour into a small glass measuring cup and set aside.

Now on to the frosting. In the bowl of a stand mixer fitted with the whisk attachment, whip the cream, vanilla extract, and sugar on medium-high. Once the mixture forms stiff peaks, it's ready—be careful not to beat beyond that point.

Split the frosting into 4 roughly equal portions, and split the sour cherries into 2 equal halves.

To assemble, flip the cake back over, with its slightly domed top facing up. With a long, serrated knife, work around the edges of the cake, carefully removing any hard crust. Using the same knife, cut the cake horizontally, creating 3 even layers. Set the top layer of your cake on a serving plate, upside down. Brush the cake with kirsch syrup, soaking it. Then, spread on a 1/2-in layer of frosting, smoothing the frosting a little bit over the edge of the cake. Sprinkle sour cherries on top.

Set the middle layer of your cake on top of the cherries, pressing the two layers gently together. Repeat adding syrup, frosting, and the second half of cherries. Add the last layer, cut side up, onto the cake. Press the layers together gently, then brush the last layer with syrup. Spread a thin layer of frosting over the top. Then, frost the sides of the cake with a thicker layer.

Once your cake is frosted, apply the ground chocolate liberally to the sides of the cake. With the remaining frosting, add rosettes around the top of the cake using a pastry bag or sandwich bag with one corner cut out. Add a cherry to the center of each rosette. Sprinkle the top with confectioners' sugar to finish.

A few of our Christmas Market favorites

Europe's winter months bring sparkling Yuletide celebrations, when historic squares come to life with twinkling lights, the jingle of music, and the scents of holiday noshes. For a taste of seasonal flavors, try some of these traditional Christmas sweets—washed down with a warm glass of spiced mulled wine, of course.

The sweet side of Yuletide

Linzer

Two spiced butter cookies, sandwiched together with a dollop of jam, dusted with confectioners' sugar? Yes, please! It's almost impossible to have just one of these Austrian sweets.

Lebkuchen

These giant circles of flourless gingerbread have been baked in Nuremberg, Germany, for hundreds of years; you can practically taste Christmas in every bite of each soft, spiced cookie.

Vanillekipferl

Vanilla dough made from ground walnuts or almonds and a generous sprinkle of powdered sugar make these half-moon-shaped biscuits a special treat in Austria, Bavaria, and beyond.

Dresdner Stollen

This rich, bread-like cake is crafted with nuts, dried fruit, and marzipan, and takes its name from the city it was invented in: Dresden, Germany.

Where to go for the best and brightest

PRAGUE, CZECH REPUBLIC

Prague's markets are the places to taste sugar-coated fried dough called *trdelník* before warming up with Czech *medovina*, a traditional honey wine.

FREIBURG, GERMANY

Pay a visit to any Christmas stall in this city, known as the entry to the Black Forest, to pick up traditional crafts such as cuckoo clocks or handblown glass.

BUDAPEST, HUNGARY

Make your way to Budapest's Vörösmarty Square to try chimney cake, buttery cylinders of dough coated with caramelized sugar, nuts, and cinnamon.

KRAKÓW, POLAND

Stop by the Historical Museum of Kraków to see *szopki*, Nativity scenes resembling small cathedrals, handcrafted for puppet plays.

Age-old celebrations: Germany's festive history

The Late Middle Ages ushered in Europe's very first Christmas markets, which sprung up in the German-speaking part of the continent. Today, Germany alone hosts more than 2,500 holiday markets, and each is truly a sight to behold. These celebratory gatherings bring Old-World traditions of the season to life with festive icons that Germany invented: Christmas trees, tinsel, nutcrackers, and gingerbread houses.

Glühwein
Warm mulled wine

TOTAL TIME:

45 minutes

SERVINGS:
16

RECIPE ORIGIN:
Germany

INGREDIENTS:

2 lemons

2 oranges

10 whole cloves

5 cardamom pods

1 1/4 cups granulated sugar

1 1/4 cups water

Two 3-in cinnamon sticks

Two 750-ml bottles dry red wine, such as Cabernet Sauvignon or Beaujolais Nouveau

1/2 cup brandy

Cheesecloth

Butcher's twine

DIRECTIONS:

Use a vegetable peeler to remove the zest from the lemons and oranges in wide strips, avoiding the white pith, and place the zest in a large saucepan. Juice the peeled citrus fruits and add the juice to the pan.

Add the sugar, water, and cinnamon sticks, and place the pan over high heat. Stir to dissolve the sugar as the mixture comes to a simmer. Reduce the heat to low and continue to simmer for about 20 minutes, stirring occasionally.

When the mixture is reduced by about one-third, stir in the red wine and brandy, and bring to a simmer. Take the pan off the heat right before boiling, remove the spice bundle, and serve!

In Iceland, we opted for smaller meals rather than extravagant sit-down ones and enjoyed simple, fresh foods, rich coffees, and even some local licorice. We had fun making our own kinds of "tastings" with little bits of seafood and other treats.

—Audrey
6th-time traveler
Iceland: Reykjavik & the Golden Circle

Tasty Scandinavian simplicity

Nordic countries

An ode to all things cozy

Land of the hygge

Pronounced "hoo-guh," *hygge* is loosely translated to a state of coziness, comfort, and contentment. Epitomized by an evening curled up with warm tea, homemade cookies, cozy socks, and a crackling fire, this tradition is ideal for the cold winters of Denmark and its Scandinavian neighbors.

Reset over fika

In Sweden, *fika*, or a social coffee break, is an everyday occurrence where you gather with coworkers or friends to catch up over a coffee and pastry. Most offices and establishments partake in either a morning fika or a morning and mid-afternoon fika to break up the day.

Glögg, glögg, glögg

Similar to German *Glühwein*, Scandinavians have a warming mulled wine that's popular during the winter holidays. *Glögg*, the Nordic version, is made with red wine and spiced with cinnamon, cardamom, cloves, and ginger.

Freshness is at the heart of Nordic cuisine.

It shines through when you sit down to any meal in Denmark, Finland, Iceland, Norway, and Sweden—the five nations that make up the Nordic countries. Nestled up near the North Pole, they have a distinctly rugged-meets-refined feel that's all their own. This lifestyle is reflected in the cuisine with earthy, simple, thoughtful foods like healthy grains, plentiful seafood, bright berries, and great cold-weather cookies.

Iceland

In a pickle

Pickling is popular throughout the Nordic countries. Like much of Central Europe, you'll find pickled produce such as beets, cucumbers, cabbage, and capers. But the very best pick for pickled goods here goes to fish, not veggies. Pickled herring and salmon are culinary hallmarks of the region.

Grab a pail

From the beginning of August through mid-September, Icelandic locals head out into the countryside to take part in the longstanding seasonal tradition of *berjamór*, or berry picking. In late summer, the country's fields are abundant with wild bilberries and crowberries, and it isn't uncommon to find groups of people out filling up their pails.

Now trending:
New Nordic cuisine

Copenhagen's groundbreaking restaurant Noma opened in 2003 and was repeatedly been named the world's best restaurant. The chefs behind the iconic eatery have championed a movement call New Nordic cuisine, which has swept the culinary world throughout Europe and beyond. The style is rooted in simplicity and pureness, not unlike the sparse-but-elegant Scandinavian design sense. The movement mixes a return to unfussy, Viking-esque ingredients—think foraged mushrooms, local fish, and hearty grains—with modern and often playful cooking techniques.

Spices

Allspice is a signature seasoning used on everything from herring and sausages to holiday cookies. Cinnamon, cardamom, and fennel are just a few of the many other flavorful spices found in baked goods.

Crayfish

These tasty crustaceans signify the peak of summer. Crayfish parties called *kräftskiva* are an end-of-season tradition where people gather outside for boiled shellfish, drinks, and rowdy sing-a-longs.

Dill

The feathery herb is a staple in Scandinavian foods, used to season everything from veggies and fish to soups and salads.

Root vegetables

The northern location means these countries have a short growing season, so they rely heavily on hearty root vegetables like potatoes, beets, radishes, turnips, and carrots.

Seafood

Unsurprisingly, the extensive coastline makes fish and shellfish mainstays on menus in this region. You can find them raw, roasted, pickled, salted, fried, boiled—you name it!

An unexpected Icelandic favorite

◄ Iceland might be best known for its distinctive and sometimes outrageous cuisine (fermented shark, anyone?), but this Icelandic favorite should be familiar to anyone who's ever been to a ballpark or barbecue. It's the humble hot dog, made here with a mix of lamb, pork, and beef. Icelanders prefer their dogs served with the works: sweet mustard, ketchup, rémoulade, and a mix of raw and fried onions.

Did you know?

Legend has it that this dish was invented by Tore Wretman, a forefather of Swedish cuisine, while he was aboard a ship off the coast of Skagen, Denmark. While the tale is much disputed, the spirit of a thrown-together but fresh snack is true to the appetizer's plucked-from-the-sea taste.

TOTAL TIME:

15 minutes

SERVINGS:
4

RECIPE ORIGIN:
Sweden

INGREDIENTS:

1 cup sour cream

1 cup mayonnaise

2 Tbsp fresh dill, chopped, plus 8 fronds to garnish

2 Tbsp chives, chopped

2 tsp lemon juice

1 lb precooked, shelled prawns or baby shrimp

Salt and pepper, to taste

3 Tbsp butter

8 slices white bread, crusts removed and cut into triangles

1 tsp roe, to serve (optional)

Toast Skagen

Cold prawn salad on toast

DIRECTIONS:

In a large bowl, mix together the sour cream, mayonnaise, dill, and lemon juice. Season with salt and pepper, then fold in the prawns. Adjust for seasoning.

Melt the butter in a large frying pan and toast bread until golden brown on both sides.

To serve, top each slice of toasted bread with a generous spoonful of prawn salad. Garnish each with a frond of dill and roe if desired.

This makes for a perfect light snack to enjoy on a warm day as you watch people stroll by in the Old Town of Gamla Stan in Stockholm.

—**Josh**, *Go Ahead Tours*

TOTAL TIME:

1 hour, 30 minutes
+ overnight chilling

SERVINGS:
16 small or 8 large flatbreads

RECIPE ORIGIN:
Norway

INGREDIENTS:

For the flatbread

1 lb Russet or Yukon Gold potatoes

1/4 cup unsalted butter, room temperature

1/4 cup heavy cream

1/2 tsp salt, plus more to taste

1 to 1 1/2 cups all-purpose flour

For the toppings

Soft goat cheese or cream cheese

Gravlax or smoked salmon

A bunch of fresh dill

Lemon wedges, to serve

Lefse with gravlax

Potato flatbread with salmon

DIRECTIONS:

Peel the potatoes and cut them into large chunks. Place in a small saucepan and cover with cold water, then bring to a gentle boil over medium-high heat. Cook until the potatoes are soft and easily pierced with a fork. Drain and transfer to a large, heatproof mixing bowl.

Mash the potatoes until smooth, eliminating any visible lumps. Cut the butter into small pieces and mix in with potatoes until just combined, then add cream and salt. Continue mixing until the butter is melted and the liquid is absorbed. Taste and adjust with salt as desired. Cover your bowl with plastic wrap or transfer the potatoes to a sealable container, and refrigerate overnight.

After refrigerating, mix the mashed potatoes with 1 cup of flour. Mix until flour and potato come together—it will be dry at first, but keep stirring until the mixture forms a dough. Turn out the dough and knead a couple times to create a smooth ball. Then, roll the dough into a log and divide into 16 equal portions for small lefse, or 8 for large lefse. Clear a large workspace for rolling out the dough. Shape each portion of dough into a small ball, then cover and set aside.

Heat a cast-iron skillet or flat griddle over medium-high heat. If your pan is not well-seasoned, add a very small amount of butter to prevent sticking. Flour your workspace, then roll one dough ball in the flour to coat it. Press the dough into a flat disk, and then roll with a well-floured rolling pin until the dough is very thin (6 to 8 inches in diameter for small, 10 to 12 inches for large). Work from the center and rotate the dough 45 degrees every so often to keep from sticking. Add flour as needed.

Transfer the rolled-out lefse to the pan. Cook for 1 to 2 minutes on each side until the lefse rises slightly and starts to brown in spots. Transfer to a plate and cover to keep warm. Continue rolling and cooking your lefse until complete. Top with a bit of soft cheese, gravlax, and dill, and serve with a lemon wedge.

Cooking tip

Gravlax, a salt-cured salmon, is just one traditional topping for *lefse*, but you can also pair these with cheese, jam, butter, or cinnamon-sugar… it's up to you!

Norwegian fjord

Norwegian fjord

◄ While the specific dishes can vary between smörgåsbords, herring is the hallmark first-course ingredient.

▲ This mustard-dill sauce called *gravlaxsas* is a must-have condiment.

Breaking down the smörgåsbord

Rye bread is the traditional choice for the open-face sandwiches.

Smoked salmon is another signature dish, and the sweet dill flavors of marinated *gravlax* is a popular take.

Making a case for courses

The tongue-twisting Swedish word translates to a board of open-faced sandwiches—and you'll find plenty of those in the traditional Nordic spread. And while it may look like a jumble of fishy dishes thrown together, there's a definite rhyme and reason to a smörgåsbord.

1

Course one
Herring, cold potatoes, cheeses

2

Course two
Shellfish, more pickled and smoked fish

3

Course three
Sliced roasted meats, pâtés, egg salad, cucumber salad

4

Course four
Hot dishes, including meatballs, ham, and casseroles

5

Course five
Desserts

Take your time

Don't treat a smörgåsbord like an all-you-can-eat buffet. Rather than loading up your plate from the start, diners are expected to go up to the table five different times to sample each course individually.

Did you know?

Root vegetable casseroles—like this nutmeg-spiced carrot dish— are a classic part of a Finnish Christmas feast.

TOTAL TIME:

50 minutes

SERVINGS:
8–10

RECIPE ORIGIN:
Finland

INGREDIENTS:

2 cups rice

2 cups whole milk

5 medium carrots, peeled and shredded

2 eggs, beaten

1/2 tsp salt

1 Tbsp dark brown sugar

1 tsp nutmeg

3 Tbsp butter

1/2 cup plain bread crumbs

Porkkanalaatikko

Carrot casserole

DIRECTIONS:

Preheat oven to 375˚F. Cook the rice according to package directions.

Butter a 1- to 1 1/2-qt casserole dish. In a large bowl, combine cooked rice, milk, carrots, eggs, salt, sugar, and nutmeg, and pour into prepared casserole.

In a small saucepan, melt butter. Stir in breadcrumbs, then sprinkle evenly over the carrot mixture. Bake the casserole for 40 minutes until the top is lightly browned.

This healthier take on comfort food calls to mind the simple, fresh meals I grew up eating in Scandinavia.

—**Per**, *Go Ahead Tours*

Swedish meatballs

TOTAL TIME:

40 minutes

SERVINGS:
18 meatballs

RECIPE ORIGIN:
Sweden

INGREDIENTS:

1 baking potato, peeled and cut into 2-in cubes

1 large egg, beaten

1/3 cup plus 1 Tbsp whole milk

1/3 cup plus 1 Tbsp heavy cream

3/4 cup plus 2 Tbsp plain breadcrumbs

12 oz ground beef

12 oz ground pork

1 small white onion, finely chopped

2 tsp kosher salt

1/2 tsp ground white pepper

4 Tbsp unsalted butter, divided

DIRECTIONS:

Cook the potato in a small pot of boiling water, about 12 minutes or until easily pierced with a fork. Pat dry, then grate on the large holes of a box grater. Set aside to cool. Meanwhile, preheat oven to 425°F.

In a large bowl, whisk together egg, milk, and cream until combined. Stir in the breadcrumbs and let stand for 5 minutes to soften. Add the beef, pork, onion, salt, pepper, and grated potato and mix to combine. Shape into 2-in meatballs.

In a large, nonstick, ovenproof pan, melt 2 Tbsp of the butter. Add half of the meatballs and cook over moderate heat, turning until all sides are browned, about 8 minutes. Repeat with remaining meatballs and 2 Tbsp of butter.

Return all of the meatballs to the skillet and bake until cooked through, about 10 minutes. Serve on a platter alongside mashed potatoes and lingonberry jam.

RECIPE RECOMMENDED BY

Amanda
Go Ahead Tours

Lingonberry jam

TOTAL TIME:
15 minutes

MAKES:
3 cups

RECIPE ORIGIN:
Finland

INGREDIENTS:

4 cups lingonberries

1/2 cup water

1 cup sugar

DIRECTIONS:

Rinse and drain lingonberries in a colander, picking out any leaves. Place berries in a medium saucepan and add water, then heat until boiling. Add sugar and stir until dissolved. Lower heat to medium-high and simmer for 10 minutes.

Remove from heat and stir for 1 to 2 minutes. Chill before serving with meatballs, or serve warm as a topping for pancakes.

Sweden or Denmark: Who did it first?

The Swedish variety may be more famous, but meatballs are also a favorite snack in neighboring Denmark—though who made them first (and better) is a sore subject in Scandinavia.

But what's the difference between the two countries' recipes? In Sweden, meatballs are called *köttbullar* and are usually made with pork and beef. Pork and veal are a popular combo in Denmark, where the meatballs are called *frikadeller*. The Danish version also tends to be flattened out a bit—more of a patty than a ball—and Danes love their meatballs served *boller i karry*, which means topped with a curry gravy.

As for which country can claim to be the first in Scandinavia to bring meatballs to the table, it's hard to say. It's thought that meatballs were introduced to the region by Sweden's King Charles XII after returning to Europe from exile in Istanbul. So, while the Swedes might've tried them first, they likely originated in the Middle East and Mediterranean, where spiced meatballs called *kofta* made for a popular snack.

TOTAL TIME:

3 hours

SERVINGS:

14

RECIPE ORIGIN:

Finland

INGREDIENTS:

For the pastry

1 cup milk, lukewarm

4 Tbsp unsalted butter, melted and cooled to room temperature

2 1/4 tsp dry yeast

1/2 cup sugar

1 tsp salt

1 tsp cardamom

2 eggs, divided

4 to 5 cups bread flour

Nib sugar, for dusting

For the filling

1/4 cup unsalted butter, melted

3/4 cup light brown sugar

2 Tbsp cinnamon

Korvapuusti

Cinnamon rolls

DIRECTIONS:

In a small bowl, combine milk, butter, yeast, and sugar. Stir, then let sit for about 10 minutes until yeast begins to bubble and mixture becomes lightly foamy. In a large mixing bowl, combine salt, cardamom, and 1 beaten egg. Add yeast mixture and stir to combine.

If using a stand mixer, switch to the dough hook. Then, gradually add half the flour, kneading at slow speed until combined. Continue adding the remaining flour, kneading until the dough clears the sides of the bowl and is tacky, but not sticky. If kneading by hand, work the dough until it is smooth and does not stick to your hands.

Shape the dough into a ball and place in a lightly greased bowl. Cover with a cotton kitchen towel and let rise for about 1 hour, until the dough doubles in size. In a small bowl, mix together butter, sugar, and cinnamon for the filling, and set aside.

Next, shape and prepare the rolls. Line two 11x13-in baking sheets with parchment paper. Punch down dough and divide into 2 equal halves. Dust your workspace lightly with flour and roll out half of the dough into an 8x14-in rectangle. Spread half of the filling evenly over the top of your dough. Starting from the long side, roll the dough into a tight tube and place seam-side down. Make diagonal cuts in alternating angles to create 7 triangular pieces.

Place each roll on the baking sheets. Using your finger, press down through the center of each triangle to curve up the ends slightly. Cover the rolls with a cotton kitchen towel and let rise 1 hour until doubled.

Preheat oven to 400°F. Beat the second egg with water to create an egg wash, and using a pastry brush, cover each roll. Generously sprinkle each roll with nib sugar. Bake on the center rack for 10 to 15 minutes or until rolls are golden brown.

TOTAL TIME:

1 hour
+ 4 hours chilling

SERVINGS:
48

RECIPE ORIGIN:
Iceland

INGREDIENTS:

2 1/3 cups all-purpose flour

1/2 tsp baking soda

2 1/2 tsp ground ginger

1/2 tsp ground cinnamon

1/4 tsp nutmeg

1/8 tsp ground cloves

1/8 tsp white pepper

1/2 cup unsalted butter, softened

3/4 cup dark brown sugar

1/4 cup molasses

1/2 tsp fine sea salt

1 large egg yolk

4 oz whole milk yogurt

Piparkökur

Gingersnap cookies

DIRECTIONS:

In a large mixing bowl, sift together flour, baking soda, and other dry ingredients except for salt. In a separate bowl, use a stand mixer fitted with the paddle attachment or a hand mixer to beat the butter and brown sugar until creamed, with a light and fluffy texture. Add the molasses, salt, and egg, and beat until just combined.

Add half of the dry ingredients a little bit at a time, blending on low speed. Add the yogurt and mix until combined. Continue slowly adding remaining dry ingredients until thoroughly blended. Gather the dough into a ball and transfer to a clean work surface.

Press the dough into a disk and cover with plastic wrap. Refrigerate until chilled, about 4 hours or overnight. When ready, remove dough from the refrigerator and let soften until pliable, about 15 minutes. Position oven rack in the center of the oven and preheat to 350°F. Line 2 large baking sheets with parchment.

Lightly flour a work surface, then roll out dough to 1/8-in thickness. With a round glass or cookie cutter, punch out as many cookies as possible. Set cutout cookies on the prepared baking sheets about 1 to 2 in apart. Re-roll remaining scraps and continue rolling and cutting out cookies until complete.

Bake cookies until the edges are lightly browned, about 12 minutes. Remove baking sheets from the oven and let cookies cool for about 10 minutes before transferring to a wire rack to cool completely.

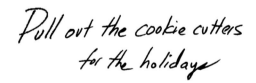

Pull out the cookie cutters for the holidays

Did you know?

A close cousin to the cookies, gingerbread houses first appeared in 16th-century Germany and became very popular after Hansel and Gretel stumbled upon the sugary structure in the Grimm brothers' fairytale.

There are so many layers baked into the flavors of our country—family recipes passed down through generations, mixed with ever-changing global influences. Far away or right at home, I love seeking out food with stories behind it!

—Heidi
President of EF Go Ahead Tours

Classic dishes to bring you home

Taste the world at the table in the U.S. and Canada.

From Cajun crawfish in Louisiana to Mexican enchiladas in Arizona to French Tourtière in Quebec, North America's "melting pot" nickname rings particularly true in terms of the cuisine. Here, multicultural influences can be seen, felt, and tasted in a big way. From restaurants that serve fusion cuisine to home-cooked meals that celebrate global flavors, there's a little bit of the world in every bite.

Global influence you can taste

1

Little Havana in Miami

An enclave for Cuban-Americans (as well as expats from various Latin American countries), Little Havana captures the spirit of the Caribbean island with its food, music, street art, and local neighborhood feel. Calle Ocho (or 8th Street) is at the center of the action. Stroll through for a *mojito*, *croquetas*, or just a *cafecito* (a sugary-sweet coffee).

2

Little Italy in New York City

Immigrants from Southern Italy settled here decades ago, bringing with them Grandma's recipes for classic Italian dishes. Over the years, the neighborhood has shrunk down to the blocks surrounding Mulberry Street and a fair share of touristy eateries have popped up, but visitors who venture off the beaten path will find what they're after.

3

Chinatown in San Francisco

The oldest and largest Chinatown in North America is located in the heart of San Fran. With the majority of households run by Mandarin-speakers, the neighborhood's residences, shops, restaurants, and small businesses evoke the feeling that you've stepped into a different country. A popular tourist destination for visitors who want to experience the culture (without the transglobal flight), the neighborhood attracts more visitors than the Golden Gate Bridge.

4

Koreatown in Los Angeles

Home to more Koreans than anywhere else in the world outside of Korea, this neighborhood boasts some seriously authentic and delicious eats. Not sure where to start? A Korean barbecue joint is a can't-miss. For a twist on the traditional fare, seek out a fusion restaurant or food truck. Los Angeles in general is a hub of fusion foods, with Latino and Asian influences melding together to form interesting new creations.

Get caught up on the freshest catch

If mouthwatering seafood is what you're after, you'll find it in any city and town along North America's coast. In New England, a good meal can be as simple as a bowl of creamy clam chowder, Lowcountry dishes like Atlantic shrimp and grits are favorites in the south, and San Francisco's oysters on the half shell are worth writing home about. And in the Canadian Maritimes, everything from lobster dishes and Nova Scotian scallops nod to the region's proud seafaring traditions.

Maple

From cookies to coffee and even candied salmon, you'll find maple-flavored everything on a trip to Canada.

Lobster

Legend has it that the largest lobster ever caught was off the coast of Cape Cod in Massachusetts in 1974. "Big George" weighed in at more than 37 pounds.

A NYC slice

Lombardi's in Nolita (which stands for North of Little Italy) holds the claim to fame as America's first pizzeria. After opening in 1905, Gennaro Lombardi went on to become a mentor within the city's Italian food scene. Though the wait can be long, locals and visitors still flock to the old-timey restaurant for its delicious, oven-crisp pies.

Wheat

As a major U.S. food source and export, wheat is grown in almost all 50 states, with Kansas and North Dakota leading the way.

Avocado

California produces about 90% of the country's avocados, and the crop—which is technically a fruit not a veggie—has come to symbolize the residents' healthy-eating reputation.

New England clam chowder

TOTAL TIME:

1 hour

SERVINGS:

6

RECIPE ORIGIN:

New England, U.S.

INGREDIENTS:

8 lbs cherrystone clams, scrubbed

2 Tbsp unsalted butter

1/2 lb bacon, cut into 1/2-in pieces

2 celery stalks, finely chopped

1 onion, finely chopped

1 garlic clove, minced

3 Tbsp all-purpose flour

1 qt whole milk

2 1/2 lbs Russet or Yukon Gold potatoes, peeled and cut into 1/2-in pieces

5 sprigs fresh thyme

2 bay leaves

Kosher salt and pepper, to taste

2 cups heavy cream

Fresh chives, chopped

Oyster crackers, to serve

DIRECTIONS:

In a large, heavy pot over high heat, combine clams and 4 cups water. Bring to a boil. Cover and cook until clams just open, about 8 to 10 minutes, stirring occasionally. Using a large slotted spoon, transfer clams onto a baking sheet to cool slightly. Then, pull clam meat from the shells and chop into bite-size pieces. Strain broth through a fine-mesh sieve set over a large bowl and set aside.

In a large pot, melt butter over medium heat. Add bacon and cook until the bacon begins to brown and crisp, about 8 minutes, stirring occasionally. Add celery, onion, and garlic, and stir often until onion is soft and translucent, but not browned, about 5 minutes. Sprinkle with flour and mix to coat. Add reserved clam broth, milk, potatoes, thyme, and bay leaves, and season with salt and pepper. Bring to a simmer and cook until potatoes are tender, 20 to 25 minutes.

Discard thyme stems and bay leaves, and add chopped clams back to the large pot. Add the heavy cream and bring to a simmer over medium heat. Remove from heat, season with salt and pepper, and garnish with chives. Serve with oyster crackers.

RECIPE RECOMMENDED BY

Linda
Traveler

Portland Head Light, Maine

TOTAL TIME:

25 minutes

SERVINGS:

4

RECIPE ORIGIN:
New England, U.S.

INGREDIENTS:

2 cups lobster meat, cooked and
chopped into bite-size pieces

2 Tbsp unsalted butter

4 hotdog buns

2 Tbsp mayonnaise

1 celery stalk, finely diced

1 Tbsp fresh tarragon leaves, chopped

Juice of 1 lemon

Kosher salt and pepper, to taste

Lobster roll

DIRECTIONS:

In a large bowl, combine lobster meat, mayonnaise, celery, and tarragon.
Add lemon juice and toss to combine. Season with salt and pepper.

Heat butter in a large skillet over medium heat. Add hotdog buns and toast until
golden brown, about 1 to 1 1/2 minutes on each side. Divide lobster salad into
4 helpings and heap into hotdog buns.

Did you know?

Lobster roll aficionados are split
between team mayo (like this recipe)
and team butter. Butter purists
usually skip the added veggies and
herbs and keep things simple.

RECIPE RECOMMENDED BY

Danielle
Go Ahead Tours

Poutine

TOTAL TIME:

20 minutes

SERVINGS:

4–6

RECIPE ORIGIN:

Canada

INGREDIENTS:

Baked or fried matchstick potatoes, cooked separately

1 Tbsp vegetable oil

1 shallot, minced

1 garlic clove, minced

2 cups beef stock

2 cups Canadian stout beer (or substitute additional 2 cups beef stock)

2 Tbsp ketchup

1 Tbsp apple cider vinegar

1 Tbsp whole green peppercorns

1/2 tsp Worcestershire sauce

2 Tbsp unsalted butter

2 Tbsp all-purpose flour

Salt and pepper, to taste

2 cups cheddar cheese curds

Fresh parsley, chopped, to garnish (optional)

DIRECTIONS:

In a saucepan, heat oil over medium heat. Add the shallot and garlic, and sauté until soft and translucent, about 5 minutes. Add the beef stock, beer, ketchup, vinegar, peppercorns, and Worcestershire sauce, and bring to a boil.

In a separate saucepan, melt the butter over medium-high heat. Add the flour and stir continuously to make a roux. Cook for about 2 to 3 minutes, until roux thickens and turns golden brown. Whisk the stock mixture into the roux and simmer until reduced by half, about 20 minutes. Season with salt and pepper, and strain the gravy. Drizzle gravy over potatoes and top with cheese curds and parsley.

Cooking tip

Don't worry if your poutine isn't particularly pretty. In fact, the name itself roughly translates to "mess" in Québécois slang.

Fried green tomatoes with feta

TOTAL TIME:

30 minutes

SERVINGS:

6

RECIPE ORIGIN:

The Southern U.S.

INGREDIENTS:

4 green heirloom tomatoes

2 eggs

1/2 cup milk

1 cup flour

3/4 cup plain breadcrumbs

3/4 cup yellow corn meal

2 1/2 tsp sea salt

1/4 tsp pepper

Vegetable oil, for frying

6 oz feta cheese

2 oz cream cheese, at room temperature

1/3 cup olive oil, divided

Juice of 1 lemon

2 bunches of fresh basil

DIRECTIONS:

Slice the tomatoes into 1/2-in discs and set aside. Pour the flour on a plate. In a mixing bowl, combine the eggs and milk and gently stir. In a second mixing bowl, combine the breadcrumbs, corn meal, salt, and pepper. Set up a tomato-breading assembly line with the dishes of flour, egg mixture, and breadcrumb mixture.

Coat the tomatoes in flour, then dip them in the egg mixture, then dredge them in the breadcrumb mixture to cover completely. Set the breaded tomatoes aside.

In a skillet with sides at least 1 inch high, heat vegetable oil over medium-high heat. In batches, add in tomato slices, leaving space between each one, and fry until golden brown on each side. Using a slotted spoon, remove tomatoes and place on paper towels to drain oil.

To make the whipped feta, combine feta and cream cheese in a food processor and pulse to mix. Add the olive oil, lemon juice, and basil, and salt and pepper if desired. Pulse until smooth. Spoon the whipped feta onto tomatoes and serve warm.

My mom is from Florida and this sophisticated take on a Southern classic always reminds me of late summer family get-togethers.

—**Brittany**, *Go Ahead Tours*

213

Good old-fashioned barbecue

Though many destinations claim the title as their own, Memphis, Tennessee, is often considered the king of American barbecue. The rival contenders? The Carolinas, Texas, and Kansas City, all of which boast seriously mouthwatering barbecue joints. Known for pulled pork sandwiches and your choice of either "wet" or "dry" ribs, Memphis-style barbecue is all about big heat and big flavor—we're talking recipes with 10, 20, even 30 different types of seasonings mixed with the condiment's usual vinegar, tomato paste, and molasses. And while the pork may be the main event, these side dishes don't play second fiddle.

Cast-iron cornbread

TOTAL TIME:
45 minutes

RECIPE ORIGIN:
Tennessee, U.S.

INGREDIENTS:

1 tbsp shortening

1 cup white cornmeal

4 Tbsp flour

1/2 tsp baking soda

1 tsp salt

1 egg

1 cup buttermilk

DIRECTIONS:

Preheat oven to 425°F. Place a 6-in cast-iron pan on your stovetop and melt the shortening (this is the pan you'll bake the cornbread in).

Sift cornmeal, flour, baking soda, and salt into a mixing bowl. In a separate mixing bowl, crack the egg, beat it, and add in the buttermilk. Pour the buttermilk mixture into the dry ingredients and stir until well-mixed but not overly smooth. Add the melted shortening and stir thoroughly. Pour batter into the greased pan and bake for 30 to 35 minutes until golden brown.

Mustard coleslaw

TOTAL TIME:
10 minutes
+ 2 hours chilling

RECIPE ORIGIN:
Tennessee, U.S.

INGREDIENTS:
For the salad
1 small cabbage
4 carrots
1 onion

For the dressing
1/2 cup mayonnaise
1/4 cup mustard
2 tsp apple cider vinegar
1/2 cup sugar
1/2 tsp cayenne pepper
1 tsp celery seeds
2 tsp salt
1 1/2 tsp pepper

DIRECTIONS:

Prep your veggies: Core the cabbage and peel the carrots and onion. If you're using a food processor, use the grater attachment and grate the cabbage, carrots, and onions, and combine in a large bowl. If you're not using a food processor, slice the vegetables into shreds (buying pre-cut veggies works too!).

Combine all the wet ingredients for the dressing and whisk together. Add in the dry ingredients for the dressing and whisk again. Pour the dressing on the cabbage salad, toss to coat, and cover. Allow coleslaw to chill for at least 2 hours before serving.

TOTAL TIME:

20 minutes

SERVINGS:

2

RECIPE ORIGIN:

Alaska, U.S.

INGREDIENTS:

1 lb skin-on salmon filets

2 Tbsp olive oil

Salt and pepper, to taste

1 lemon

1 Tbsp parsley, chopped

1/2 Tbsp fresh dill

Baked Alaskan salmon

DIRECTIONS:

Preheat oven to 425°F and line a roasting pan with foil. Prep the salmon by patting it dry with a paper towel. Using your hands, coat the filets with oil and season with salt and pepper. Cut your lemon in half and squeeze the juice of one half onto the fish. Sprinkle your herbs on each filet.

Place the salmon skin-side down in a roasting pan and transfer to the middle rack in the oven. Cooking time depends on both the thickness of your salmon and your preference. For rare, roast your salmon 4 minutes for every half-inch; to cook thoroughly, roast for 6 minutes for every half-inch. Remove from the oven and serve with sliced lemon on the side.

Did you know?

Salmon are born in rivers, migrate to the ocean, and return to their home river to reproduce. Every fall, this homecoming, dubbed the salmon run, offers opportunities to spot grizzly bears, eagles, and other wildlife at the river's edge.

The more avocado, the better!

California cobb salad

DIRECTIONS:

Lay a foundation of salad greens on your platter (or individual plates). Creating strips of color, place individual salad contents in rows. For the dressing, combine all vinaigrette ingredients, mix thoroughly, and drizzle over salad.

INGREDIENTS:

For the salad

1 lb chicken breasts, grilled and cut into strips

1 head of iceberg lettuce, chopped (or substitute salad greens of your choice)

1 avocado, cut into bite-size pieces

10 green beans, steamed

6 slices bacon, fried until crisp

2 radishes, chopped

Half an onion, finely chopped

2 tomatoes, cut into wedges

3 eggs, hard-boiled and cut into wedges

6 oz crumbled blue cheese

For the dressing

Juice of half a lemon

2 tsp red wine vinegar

2 tsp Dijon mustard

1/3 cup olive oil

Salt and pepper, to taste

Did you know?

Legend holds that this salad was invented at Brown Derby restaurant on the Hollywood Walk of Fame when owner Bob Cobb pulled together late-night leftovers for Sid Grauman, of the famous Grauman's Chinese Theater.

TOTAL TIME:

50 minutes

SERVINGS:

8

RECIPE ORIGIN:
United States

INGREDIENTS:

1 lb penne (or substitute noodles of your choice)

4 cups whole milk

4 Tbsp butter

6 Tbsp flour

1 tsp paprika, divided

Salt and pepper, to taste

12 oz cheddar cheese, shredded and divided

6 oz gruyère cheese, shredded

Classic mac & cheese

DIRECTIONS:

Preheat oven to 350°F. Cook noodles according to the package instructions, but remove from heat while noodles are still al dente. Drain, rinse, and set aside.

Add milk to a saucepan and bring to a slow boil so the milk is foamy but not bubbly. In another saucepan, melt the butter. Once the butter has liquefied, add in flour and whisk for 5 minutes over low heat, careful not to let the butter mixture brown. Remove from heat.

Pour the hot milk into the butter-and-flour mixture and whisk well. Add 1/2 tsp of paprika, plus salt and pepper to taste. Return the mixture to heat and cook over medium heat, whisking constantly until the sauce thickens, about 5 minutes.

Add the sauce to the penne and toss to coat. Butter a 13x9-in baking dish and fill with the pasta mixture. Set aside 1/3 of the cheddar cheese; pour the other 2/3 of the cheddar and all the gruyère into the pasta mixture and stir thoroughly. Sprinkle the rest of the cheese and paprika over the top. Bake 20 to 30 minutes, until the mac and cheese is bubbly and lightly browned.

Give it your own spin

The only thing better than fresh-from-the-oven mac and cheese? Fresh-from-the-oven mac and cheese packed with your favorite add-ons. For a springtime spin, peas and corn make a great combination. Or for autumnal flavors, add in butternut squash and sage. Throwing a summer party? Pull out all the stops with fresh lobster meat. And no matter the occasion, buffalo mac and cheese is always a crowd favorite.

Take it up a notch

Pancetta

Pesto

Lobster meat

Peas

Broccoli

Shaved truffles

Goat cheese

Butternut squash

Katie
Go Ahead Tours

TOTAL TIME:

1 hour, 15 minutes

SERVINGS:

1 pie

RECIPE ORIGIN:

United States

INGREDIENTS:

For the apple filling

6 to 7 apples, pared, cored, and thinly sliced

1/2 cup all-purpose flour

1 cup white sugar

1 cup brown sugar

1 tsp cinnamon

1/8 tsp nutmeg

Juice of half a lemon

For the pie crust

2 cups all-purpose flour

1 tsp salt

2/3 cup shortening

4 Tbsp butter, chilled and divided

Ice water

1 egg

A pinch of cinnamon

A pinch of white sugar

Apple pie

DIRECTIONS:

Start by making the apple filling. Combine all the ingredients and mix until the apple pieces are well-coated. Set aside.

Preheat oven to 375°F. In a mixing bowl, sift the flour and salt. In a separate mixing bowl, combine the shortening and 2 Tbsp butter. Cut the shortening mixture into the dry ingredients by hand until it's the consistency of cornmeal. Working in stages, sprinkle 1 Tbsp of ice water over the mixture and continue working the dough so it's moistened. Repeat 4 to 7 times until all the dough is just moist and pea-sized grains begin to form.

Being careful not to handle the dough too much, divide it into halves and roll to create 2 even balls of dough. Roll the first ball out into a circle, slightly larger than a 9-in pie plate. Transfer the dough into the pie plate, lay flat, and trim to the edge of the dish. Add the apple filling in flat layers, and dot with small pieces of the remaining butter on top.

Roll out the second half of the dough into a 12-in circle. Place on top of the apple filling and fold along edges to seal together. Trim edges and decorate border with fork imprints or your desired design. To create a glossy finish to your pie crust, beat an egg yolk in a small mixing bowl and using a pastry brush, lightly glaze the top of the pie. Sprinkle with cinnamon and sugar, and prick the top with fork prongs a few times to allow steam to release when baking.

Wrap the circular edges with foil and bake for 25 minutes. Remove the foil border and continue baking until the top-layer crust is golden brown, about 20 to 25 minutes.

After growing up in New England, nothing says autumn to me like homemade pie made with freshly picked apples.

—**Katie**, *Go Ahead Tours*

"

I am a self-proclaimed foodie, and I was in heaven sampling the many culinary delights in Peru. The many varieties of corn and potatoes alone make Peru special, but there is also ceviche, causa, empanadas, tamales, lomo saltado, pollo a la brasa, chicha morada, and, of course, cuy!

—Scott,
5th-time traveler
Ancient Peru & Machu Picchu

Juicy fruits, spicy stews & a bounty of beans

Latin America

Latin America's cuisine celebrates the basics in the very best way.

Staples like corn, beans, and rice form the base of many dishes—but it's the colorful and powerful combination of spices that brings pizzaz to your plate. With such varied landscapes throughout the region, everyone from cattle farmers in Argentina and fisherman off the coast of Chile to families in Cuba and chefs in Costa Rica have left their mark on local traditions.

How to cut a pineapple

1
Twist off the green crown.

2
Cut in half lengthwise and then repeat, so that you've quartered the pineapple.

3
Slice off the core along the pointed center line of each quarter.

4
Cut off the skin, and set aside.

5
Lay the skin underneath the pieces like a cutting board and slice into triangles.

6
Serve pineapple using the skin as a tray and enjoy!

Navigating the maize

Maize, or corn, is a versatile ingredient that's native to Latin America and found in many modern-day dishes.

Head to pg. 237 to try a corn pie.

The perfect roast

▲

Brazil is the world's top coffee producer. If you want to taste the full breadth of flavor in the country's coffee, pick up a bag of peaberry beans. Circular and smaller than the average coffee bean, peaberries have a stronger, richer taste than arabica and robusta beans.

All about beans

It doesn't matter if you just rolled out of bed and want some *desayuno* or if it's supper time and you're serving up *cena*, beans are a staple ingredient in many Latin American meals. Brazil favors black beans, Mexico opts for pinto beans, and in Peru you'll find lima beans—of course!

What are plantains?

While similar to bananas, plantains are not meant to be eaten raw and are instead cooked and served in a variety of ways. Throughout Latin America, you'll find them baked and covered with cheese, sautéed with sugar, or fried into crunchy chips.

Spice it up

No Latin American dish is complete unless the beef or chicken has been coated with *adobo*. This spice rub only takes 5 minutes to make, but will have your family and friends thinking you're a certified chef.

2 Tbsp salt

1 Tbsp paprika

2 tsp ground black pepper

1 1/2 tsp onion powder

1 1/2 tsp dried oregano

1 1/2 tsp ground cumin

1 tsp garlic powder

1 tsp chili powder

Wine, lime & cocktail time

Sip, stir, and shake your way through Latin America with these four classic cocktails.

Peruvian pisco sour

3 oz pisco brandy

1 oz simple syrup

1 oz key lime juice

1 egg white

Ice cubes

A few dashes of Angostura bitters

1 lime, sliced into wedges

Mix the pisco, simple syrup, lime juice, and egg white in a cocktail shaker. Add ice to fill, and shake. Strain into an old-fashioned glass and sprinkle the Angostura bitters on top of the foam. Garnish with a lime wedge.

Mexican margarita

2 oz tequila

1 oz lime juice

3/4 oz agave nectar (or substitute 1/2 oz simple syrup)

3/4 oz cold water

Ice cubes

1 lime, sliced into wedges

Salt, to rim

Shake the tequila, lime juice, agave nectar, and water vigorously with ice and strain into a chilled rocks glass filled with ice. Garnish with a lime wedge and salt rim.

Argentinian red splash

1 1/2 oz Malbec wine

1 1/2 oz white tequila

2 oz club soda

1/2 oz lime juice

1 lime, sliced into wedges

Ice cubes

Combine all ingredients in a cocktail shaker filled with ice. Shake and strain into a glass over fresh ice. Garnish with a lime wedge and serve.

Cuban mojito

1 lime, sliced

8 mint leaves

2 tsp sugar

2 oz white rum

Ice cubes

Soda water

Cut lime and squeeze 3/4 of it into a highball glass. Add mint leaves and sugar. Blend the ingredients together by pushing and twisting with a muddler. Add rum and ice. Mix to dissolve the sugar, keeping the mint leaves on the bottom of the glass. Add soda water and garnish with lime cut into wedges or rounds.

TOTAL TIME:
25 minutes

SERVINGS:
6

RECIPE ORIGIN:
Costa Rica

INGREDIENTS:

Olive oil, to sauté

1 red bell pepper, diced

1 onion, finely diced

3 garlic cloves, crushed

Two 15-oz cans black beans, with liquid

2 Tbsp Lizano or Worcestershire sauce

2 cups brown rice, cooked

Salt and pepper, to taste

A small bunch of fresh cilantro, chopped, to garnish

Gallo pinto

Costa Rican rice and beans

DIRECTIONS:

In a skillet with a little oil, sauté the bell pepper and onion until they are soft and onion is translucent, about 5 minutes. Add the garlic and continue to sauté for 1 to 2 more minutes.

Add the black beans with their liquid and at least 2 Tbsp of Lizano or Worcestershire sauce. After 3 minutes, add the rice and stir gently. Continue to cook for about 3 minutes. Season with salt and pepper, and garnish with cilantro.

To the untrained eye, gallo pinto is just rice and beans, but it is bursting with flavor. In Costa Rica, it's cooked with peppers, onions, and cilantro. It comes with every meal, so no traveler will miss out!

—**Miriam**, *Go Ahead Tours*

Did you know?

Gallo pinto literally translates to "spotted rooster," which may come from the appearance of the dish as the beans give a spotted look to the rice that is similar to the plumage of a rooster.

Guacamole

Pebre

Chili pepper salsa

TOTAL TIME:
15 minutes

TOTAL TIME:
10 minutes

SERVINGS:
4

SERVINGS:
4–6

RECIPE ORIGIN:
Mexico

RECIPE ORIGIN:
Chile

INGREDIENTS:

3 ripe avocados

3/4 cup Roma tomato, finely chopped

2 serrano chilies, seeded, deveined, and very finely chopped

3 to 4 Tbsp onion, finely chopped

3 Tbsp fresh cilantro, minced

Salt, to taste

INGREDIENTS:

1 large onion, finely chopped

3 garlic cloves, minced

1/2 cup fresh cilantro, finely chopped

3 Tbsp red chili pepper paste (or 2–3 Tbsp fresh chili peppers, finely minced)

2 Tbsp olive oil

1 Tbsp red wine (or substitute red wine vinegar)

Salt and pepper, to taste

Juice of half a lime

DIRECTIONS:

Remove the flesh of the avocados and mash them in a bowl with the back of a fork. Fold in the other ingredients to incorporate evenly. Season with salt.

The guacamole should be served at room temperature as soon as you make it. Don't prepare it in advance as it will turn brown very quickly.

DIRECTIONS:

Combine onion, garlic, and cilantro in a small bowl. Stir the red chili pepper paste or chili peppers into the same bowl. Add the oil and red wine. Season mixture with salt and pepper, and add lime juice.

Store salsa in the refrigerator for up to 1 week. It will taste spicier the day after you make it.

RECIPE RECOMMENDED BY

Scott
Traveler

Peruvian fish ceviche

TOTAL TIME:

2 hours, 30 minutes

SERVINGS:
8

RECIPE ORIGIN:
Peru

INGREDIENTS:

1 lb high-quality, sushi-grade white fish like halibut

Juice of 8 limes

Juice of 4 lemons

Juice of 2 oranges

1 Tbsp salt

1 onion, very thinly sliced

1 rocoto or habanero chili, seeded

1 pt cherry tomatoes, chopped (optional)

4 Tbsp cilantro, chopped

DIRECTIONS:

To prepare the ceviche, cut very fresh fish into small cubes and place in a non-reactive glass or plastic container with a lid. Mix in citrus juice, salt, onion, chili, and tomatoes if desired, and cover. Refrigerate for at least 2 hours, or leave to chill longer if you have larger cubes of fish. Garnish with cilantro and serve.

Did you know?

One of the most authentic ways to eat Peruvian ceviche? With sweet potato! This native veggie cuts the dish's acidity, and is traditionally boiled and served in thick slices alongside the fish—but is just as good baked into crunchy chips.

TOTAL TIME:
10 minutes

SERVINGS:
2

RECIPE ORIGIN:
Chile

INGREDIENTS:

1 avocado

4.5-oz can of tuna, drained

1/4 cup red bell pepper, diced

1/2 cup cooked green peas

1/2 cup cooked corn

1 Tbsp jalapeño, minced

1/4 cup fresh cilantro leaves, roughly chopped

Juice of half a lime

Salt and pepper, to taste

Scallions, to garnish

Palta rellena

Tuna-stuffed avocado

DIRECTIONS:

Cut avocado in half and remove the pit. Scoop out some of the avocado from the pitted area to widen the hole. Place the scooped avocado into a medium mixing bowl and mash it with a fork.

Add the tuna and vegetables to the mixing bowl along with mashed avocado—feel free to substitute in fresh veggies of your choice. Pour lime juice over and stir until everything is well mixed. Scoop the tuna into the avocado. Season with salt and pepper, and garnish with cilantro and scallions.

TOTAL TIME:
45 minutes

SERVINGS:
4

RECIPE ORIGIN:
Peru

INGREDIENTS:

4 Tbsp vegetable oil, for frying

3 eggs

2 skinless, boneless chicken breasts, cooked and cut into bite-size pieces

4 oz cooked ham

2 garlic cloves, minced

1 Tbsp grated ginger

3/4 cup sugar snap peas, diagonally cut

1 red bell pepper, diced

1 1/2 carrots, thickly grated

3 cups long-grain rice, cooked and cold

4 Tbsp light soy sauce

2 tsp sesame oil

Small bunch of cilantro, chopped, to garnish

2 scallions, chopped, to garnish (optional)

Arroz chaufa

Peruvian fried rice

DIRECTIONS:

Coat a skillet in oil and warm over medium-high heat. Beat the eggs and pour into the skillet, making a thin omelet. Transfer the cooked egg to a cutting surface and cut into small squares, then set aside.

In that same skillet over medium heat, warm the remainder of the oil. Then, sauté chicken and ham for about 3 minutes until they begin to brown. Add garlic and ginger, and stir for 30 seconds. Add the snap peas, pepper, and carrots, and stir well. Finally, add the egg and cold rice, and fry to heat thoroughly. Stir in soy sauce and sesame oil, and remove from heat. Serve warm and garnish with cilantro and scallions if desired.

Did you know?

In 1849, the first Chinese immigrants arrived in Peru during the Gold Rush period. *Arroz chaufa* draws heavily on the culinary elements that the Chinese brought to the country—specifically soy sauce and ginger. When you're in Peru, head to a *chifa*, a Chinese-Peruvian fusion restaurant, to enjoy the cuisine.

TOTAL TIME:

1 hour
+ 2 hours chilling

SERVINGS:
24

RECIPE ORIGIN:
Argentina

INGREDIENTS:

For the dough

1 cup water

3/4 cup butter

2 3/4 cups flour

2 tsp salt

A pinch of paprika

For the filling

3 Tbsp olive oil

1 yellow onion, peeled and minced

1/2 red bell pepper, cored, seeded,
and finely diced

1/2 chicken bouillon cube

1/2 tsp paprika

1/2 tsp red pepper flakes

1/2 tsp ground white pepper

1/2 tsp ground cumin

3/4 lb boneless beef shoulder, finely diced
(or substitute ground beef)

Salt, to taste

1 Russet potato, peeled, finely diced,
and boiled

1/3 cup raisins (optional)

8 green Spanish olives, pitted and chopped

3 scallions, trimmed and chopped

1 hard-boiled egg, peeled and chopped

Baked empanadas

DIRECTIONS:

For the dough, heat water and butter in a saucepan over medium heat until butter has melted. Mix flour and salt in a large mixing bowl, make a well in the center, and sprinkle in a pinch of paprika. Pour a little of the warm liquid in and stir with fingertips to make a wet paste. Pour in remaining liquid and work the flour with your hands until you get a wet dough. Gather into a ball, then wrap the dough in plastic and refrigerate for at least 2 hours.

For the filling, heat oil in a large skillet over medium heat. Add onions, bell pepper, bouillon cube, paprika, red pepper flakes, white pepper, and cumin, and cook until onions are soft and translucent, about 5 minutes. Add beef, season with salt, and cook until beef is browned. Place filling in a large bowl and let cool. Mix in potatoes, raisins, olives, scallions, and egg.

Preheat oven to 400°F. Tear off pieces of dough, rolling into about 24 golf ball-sized balls. Using a rolling pin, roll out dough balls on lightly floured surface into 5-in circles. Place 3 Tbsp of filling in the center of each dough circle. Fold dough over and press edges down to create a seal, then go back over edges pressing with the tines of a fork to close any gaps. Place empanadas on a cookie sheet and bake until golden brown, about 15 to 20 minutes.

RECIPE RECOMMENDED BY

Scott
Traveler

Sautéed sweet plantains

TOTAL TIME:
10 minutes

SERVINGS:
6

RECIPE ORIGIN:
Cuba

INGREDIENTS:

1/4 cup peanut oil, for frying

2 Tbsp butter

3 very ripe yellow plantains,
peeled and cut into 1-in-thick slices

3 Tbsp brown sugar

Salt, to taste

Confectioners' sugar, to serve (optional)

DIRECTIONS:

Heat oil and butter in a large skillet over medium-high heat until the butter begins to sizzle. Gently toss plantain slices with brown sugar, then place into hot oil. Fry until the plantains begin to turn golden brown. Continue frying until they have caramelized, about 2 minutes per side. Place plantains on a paper towel-lined plate and sprinkle with salt before serving. Top with confectioners' sugar if desired.

Patagonia, Chile

1 hour, 30 minutes

SERVINGS:
12

RECIPE ORIGIN:
Chile

INGREDIENTS:

For the beef and onion filling

1 lb ground beef

2 large onions, chopped

2 tsp olive oil

2 garlic cloves, finely chopped

1 Tbsp beef bouillon powder

1/2 tsp garlic salt

1 1/2 tsp paprika

1/2 tsp ground cumin

1/2 tsp dried oregano

Salt, to taste

For the corn topping

40 oz corn kernels, thawed if frozen

14.75-oz can creamed corn

3/4 tsp dried basil

3 Tbsp vegetable shortening

1 1/2 tsp beef bouillon powder

1/2 tsp fine-grain sea salt

2 Tbsp raisins, soaked in warm water

2 large hard-boiled eggs, cut into thin slices

3 oz black olives, sliced

Sugar, to taste

Pastel de choclo

Chilean corn pie

DIRECTIONS:

Preheat oven to 350°F. Lightly grease a baking dish (a 13x9-in baking dish works well for this recipe).

For the filling, sauté the ground beef and onions in oil over medium-high heat in a large sauté pan. When the beef has browned, add garlic, beef bouillon powder, garlic salt, paprika, cumin, and oregano. Continue to cook until the meat is cooked through, and season with salt. Reduce the heat to medium-low and simmer until onions are very soft and no crunch remains, then remove the pan from the heat.

For the topping, put the corn kernels, creamed corn, and basil in a blender in batches and pulse until the corn is puréed but not completely smooth. Pour the corn purée into a large pot and add the shortening, beef bouillon powder, and salt. Cook the corn mixture over medium-high heat until it comes to a boil. Once it comes to a boil, continue letting it cook for 5 more minutes, stirring constantly to prevent it from burning. Then, remove the pot from the heat.

Cover the bottom of the greased baking dish with a thin layer of corn topping. Spread all of the beef filling over the corn layer. Drain the raisins soaking in the warm water. Scatter the hard-boiled eggs, olives, and raisins over the meat filling. Finish by covering everything with the remaining corn topping. Use the tines of a fork to make grooves in the corn topping, then sprinkle a light layer of sugar over the top.

Bake for 30 minutes or until bubbles are breaking the surface on the sides of the baking dish. Then, change the oven to high broil and cook until the top is golden brown. Remove the baking dish from the oven and let it sit for 10 minutes before serving.

TOTAL TIME:

15 minutes
+ overnight marinating

SERVINGS:
6–8

RECIPE ORIGIN:
Cuba

INGREDIENTS:

10 garlic cloves

2 tsp salt

1 tsp black peppercorn

1 cup orange juice

Juice of 4 lemons

Juice of 4 limes

1/2 cup onion, minced

1 tsp ground oregano

1 cup olive oil

4 lbs top sirloin, cubed for kebabs

Cuban pinchos de carne

Cuban beef kebabs

DIRECTIONS:

Mash garlic, salt, and peppercorn into a paste with a mortar and pestle. Stir in the citrus juices, onion, and oregano. Let sit at room temperature for 30 minutes. Heat the oil in a 2-qt saucepan until hot, around 300°F. Remove oil from heat and quickly whisk in the garlic-orange juice mixture until well blended. Let cool.

Place the sirloin cubes in a non-reactive bowl. Pour the marinade over the meat, cover the bowl with plastic wrap, and refrigerate at least 4 hours, but preferably overnight. If you are using wooden skewers, soak them in water before using. Skewer the meat and arrange on a heated grill. Cook for 8 to 10 minutes or until cooked to your liking, turning occasionally.

TOTAL TIME:

30 minutes

TOTAL TIME:
30 minutes

SERVINGS:
4

RECIPE ORIGIN:
Mexico

INGREDIENTS:

1/4 cup mayonnaise

1/4 cup sour cream

1/2 cup finely crumbled Cotija or feta cheese,
plus more for serving

1/2 tsp chili powder, plus more for serving

1 garlic clove, finely minced

1/4 cup fresh cilantro, finely chopped

4 ears of corn, shucked

1 lime, cut into wedges

Elotes

Mexican street corn

DIRECTIONS:

Clean and oil a grill. Set half the burners to high heat. Cover grill and preheat for 5 minutes. While grill heats, combine mayonnaise, sour cream, cheese, chili powder, garlic, and cilantro in a large bowl. Stir until combined and set aside.

Once grill is hot, cook corn, rotating occasionally until cooked and charred in spots on all sides, about 8 minutes total. Transfer corn to a plate and top with cheese mixture. Sprinkle with extra cheese, chili powder, and cilantro. Serve with lime wedges.

Did you know?

If street corn, or *elotes*, is what you're after, late-night snack stands are the places to go—the nosh is most often served after hours in Mexico. Want a similar dish but don't want to eat the corn off the cob? Spring for *esquites*, made only from the kernels.

239

Argentinian Asado

Asado isn't just Argentina's signature meal—it's a cultural experience. Simply put, asado is the Latin American take on a barbecue where flank steak, ribs, lamb, pork, sausage, and other meats are cooked over an open fire or large grill called a *parrilla*.

This tradition was formed by the 19th-century gauchos who supported their nomadic lifestyle by basing their diet around the wild cows that roamed the area. Over the decades, asado has become a way for friends and family to meet up and spend time together while celebrating their culture.

The meats are never marinated and they cook on the grill or over the fire for around 2 hours. Once they're done, they're cut into large pieces, and served with chimichurri sauce. The most authentic way to take part in an asado is by going to a local's house and spending the day preparing, cooking, and eating the various meats—but if you only find yourself in the country for a short period of time, check out these restaurants.

3 spots in Buenos Aires to savor asado

La Cabrera

José Antonio Cabrera 5099

Don't be distracted by the bread and sides—the real star of the menu here is the asado section (try the ribeye). For fewer crowds and lower prices, stop by for happy hour between 7 and 8:30pm. Otherwise, be sure to secure a reservation.

Parrilla Peña

Rodríguez Peña 682

Buenos Aires may be a booming tourist destination, but Parrilla Peña still maintains its traditional charm. If you're looking to chow down on a standout steak dinner at an authentic, quaint locale, this is your place.

La Estancia

Calle Lavalle 941

The *asadors* at La Estancia have been serving up delicious dishes since they welcomed their first customers in 1962. Watch as the meat is cooked around a circular fire pit before dining on hearty helpings of steak, pork, chicken, and more.

TOTAL TIME:
30 minutes

SERVINGS:
3/4 cup

RECIPE ORIGIN:
Argentina

INGREDIENTS:
1/4 cup fresh, flat-leaf parsley, coarsely chopped
3 Tbsp red wine vinegar
4 large garlic cloves
2 Tbsp fresh oregano leaves
2 tsp red pepper flakes
Kosher salt and pepper, to taste
1/2 cup olive oil

Chimichurri sauce

DIRECTIONS:

In a food processor, combine parsley, vinegar, garlic, oregano, and red pepper flakes. Process until smooth, then season with salt and pepper. Transfer the sauce to a bowl and pour oil over the mixture. Let stand for at least 20 minutes. If refrigerating overnight, bring to room temperature before serving.

TOTAL TIME:
30 minutes
+ overnight marinating

SERVINGS:
4

RECIPE ORIGIN:
Brazil

INGREDIENTS:

Juice of 3 limes

5 garlic cloves, minced

Salt and pepper, to taste

2 lbs chicken wings

1/2 cup flour

Vegetable oil, for frying

1/4 cup olive oil

5 garlic cloves, sliced

Fresh, flat-leaf parsley, chopped, to garnish (optional)

Red pepper flakes (optional)

Lime wedges, to serve

Frango à passarinho

Brazilian-style chicken wings

DIRECTIONS:

In a large bowl, combine lime juice and garlic, and season with salt and pepper. Add the chicken wings and toss them with the marinade, making sure every piece is coated. Cover and let sit in the fridge overnight. The next day, add flour and wings to a sealable sandwich bag. Close the bag and shake it to coat evenly.

Fill a saucepan with enough vegetable oil to cover the wings. Heat the oil on medium-high and, when the oil reaches 375°F, lower to medium-low and start frying wings in batches of 5 or 6 at a time.

When the wings begin to gain some color, turn the heat up to high and fry until golden brown. Set fried wings on a paper towel to absorb excess oil. Turn the heat back to low and proceed to fry remaining wings.

While wings cook, heat olive oil in a sauté pan and sauté garlic for about 3 minutes. Once all wings are fried, transfer to a serving dish and pour garlic oil over the top. Garnish with parsley and red pepper flakes, and serve with lime wedges if desired.

Did you know?

Meat-lovers will feel right at home in Brazil, where all-you-can-eat barbecue eateries known as *churrascarias* abound. Waiters in these traditional restaurants slice various cuts of meat off of giant skewers right at your table, and large buffets offer authentic side dishes and hearty salads.

TOTAL TIME:
45 minutes
+ 4 hours cooking

SERVINGS:
6–8

RECIPE ORIGIN:
Cuba

INGREDIENTS:

Olive oil, as needed

2 lb flank steak

2 tsp kosher salt, plus more to taste

1/2 tsp pepper, plus more to taste

1 large yellow onion, thinly sliced

1 large green bell pepper, thinly sliced

1 large red bell pepper, thinly sliced

1 large yellow bell pepper, thinly sliced

4 garlic cloves, minced

2 tsp dried oregano

2 tsp ground cumin

2 tsp sweet paprika

1 tsp smoked paprika

1/8 tsp ground allspice

1/8 tsp ground cloves

1/2 cup dry white wine

1 cup chicken broth

16-oz can crushed tomatoes

6-oz can tomato paste

2 bay leaves

1 large carrot, cut in half

1 large celery stalk, cut in half

1 cup pitted green olives, rinsed and drained

1/2 cup roasted red peppers, drained and thinly sliced

1/4 cup pimientos, drained

2 Tbsp capers, rinsed and drained

1/3 cup fresh, flat-leaf parsley, chopped

Ropa vieja

Stewed beef & vegetables

DIRECTIONS:

Heat a splash of oil in a Dutch oven or heavy-bottomed skillet over high heat. Pat the beef dry and sprinkle with salt and pepper. Once pan is very hot, add the beef and brown on all sides. Transfer the beef to a plate, leaving drippings and blackened bits in the pan.

Add vegetables to the same pan and cook over medium heat until caramelized, about 15 to 20 minutes. Mix in the garlic and spices, and cook for another minute. Add the wine and bring to a rapid boil, deglazing the bottom of the pan and scraping up the browned bits. Add the broth, crushed tomatoes, tomato paste, and bay leaves. Simmer for 5 minutes.

Return the roast to the pot along with the carrot and celery. Bring to a boil, reduce heat to low, cover, and simmer until beef is tender and falls apart easily, about 3 to 4 hours. Once beef is cooked, transfer it to a plate and shred it, then put it back into the sauce. Discard celery, carrots, and bay leaves.

Stir in the olives, roasted red peppers, capers, and pimientos. Simmer uncovered to thicken the sauce for 30 minutes. Stir in the parsley and season with salt and pepper.

RECIPE RECOMMENDED BY
Gustavo
Go Ahead Tours

Meals hosted by locals!

Paladares

Imagine enjoying a home-cooked meal abroad—in Cuba, you can.

In Cuba, the most authentic food isn't being cooked inside a fancy restaurant, it's down the street just behind a local's front door at a *paladar*.

Paladares are Cuban restaurants that run out of locals' homes, though the culinary style and complexity varies. Some are as simple as a couple cooking for a few groups of people. Others feature a variety of meals being served throughout the whole house, with each room representing a different type of cuisine. More recently, there's been an increase in trained chefs opening and running their own paladares that closely resemble traditional restaurants.

These authentic eateries used to be illegal under Cuba's strict, state-run business regulations. It wasn't until 2011 that these laws fully shifted and business owners gained control over the size of the paladar, what foods are on the menu, and the amount of employees. With the changes in regulation, there's been a boom in the amount and popularity of these restaurants, especially within Havana.

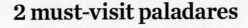

2 must-visit paladares

San Cristobal

Calle San Rafael #469, between Lealtad and Campanario, Havana

Known for its Creole-influenced Cuban fare and eclectic décor, this popular spot treats guests to tasty dishes in an early 20th-century mansion.

La Carboncita

Calle 3ra #3804 between Calles 38 and 40, Havana

Aside from traditional Caribbean cuisine, Italian food is well-loved on the island, and this is the best place for a slice of pizza or plate of pasta.

▲

Chefs are always finding innovative ways to create meals since they must work with whatever ingredients are available in stores. This means that not only do paladar menus frequently change, but you can find everything from ropa vieja and paella to risotto and duck.

TOTAL TIME:

10 minutes

SERVINGS:

24

RECIPE ORIGIN:

Brazil

INGREDIENTS:

14-oz can sweetened condensed milk

4 Tbsp cocoa powder, sifted

A pinch of salt

2 Tbsp butter, plus more for rolling balls

Chocolate or rainbow sprinkles, as needed

Add in colored sprinkles for the holidays

Brigadeiros

Brazilian fudge balls

DIRECTIONS:

In a small sauce pan, combine sweetened condensed milk, cocoa powder, salt, and butter. Set pan on the stovetop and heat it over medium-low, stirring constantly to allow mixture to thicken and prevent it from burning. When a spoon run through the chocolate creates a well, remove from heat and let cool to room temperature.

Spread sprinkles on a plate or pour into a wide bowl. Once the chocolate is cool, roll into tablespoon-sized balls using lightly greased palms. Then, roll the balls in the sprinkles until they're evenly covered and place them in paper or foil candy cups.

Brigadeiros are the perfect dessert for chocolate lovers! They're like what we think of as fudge but even creamier and perfectly bite-size. You'll want to eat a whole plate of them, but they're so rich you'll be full before you can.

—**Lauren**, *Go Ahead Tours*

TOTAL TIME:

15 minutes

+ 12 hours freezing

SERVINGS:

8

RECIPE ORIGIN:

Cuba

INGREDIENTS:

2 1/2 cups club soda, chilled

Juice of 4 large limes

1/2 cup fresh mint leaves

1/2 cup sugar

2 Tbsp white rum

2 limes, sliced into thin rounds

2 oranges, sliced into thin rounds

Mojito ice pops

DIRECTIONS:

In a small bowl, combine the club soda and lime juice. Add the mint leaves, sugar, rum, and lime slices. Muddle the ingredients together until well mixed.

Place orange pieces and additional mint leaves into popsicle molds. Pour the liquid into molds, evenly distributing muddled ingredients from the mixture. Freeze for 1 1/2 hours, remove from freezer to insert popsicle sticks, and continue to freeze overnight. To remove popsicles from the molds, dip the molds in warm water and gently pull on the sticks.

Did you know?

The history of the mojito is full of mystery and intrigue. While its roots are undeniably tied to Cuba, everyone from Sir Francis Drake, African slaves, Ernest Hemingway, and James Bond have influenced its creation and place within the modern bar scene.

TOTAL TIME:
1 hour, 30 minutes

SERVINGS:
36 cookies

RECIPE ORIGIN:
Argentina

INGREDIENTS:

1 2/3 cups all-purpose flour

2 1/2 cups corn starch

1/2 tsp baking soda

2 tsp baking powder

1 cup unsalted butter, softened

3/4 cup white sugar

3 egg yolks

1 tsp vanilla rum

1/2 tsp vanilla extract

1/2 tsp lemon extract

2 tsp lemon zest

11.5-oz jar dulce de leche

1/2 cup unsweetened shredded coconut (optional)

Confectioners' sugar, to serve (optional)

Alfajores

Caramel sandwich cookies

DIRECTIONS:

Preheat oven to 350°F. Line baking sheets with parchment paper. Whisk together flour, corn starch, baking soda, and baking powder; set aside.

In a separate, large bowl, beat the butter and white sugar with an electric mixer until light and fluffy. Add the egg yolks one at a time, allowing each one to blend into the butter mixture before adding the next. Beat in the rum, vanilla extract, lemon extract, and lemon zest with the last egg. Gently fold in the flour mixture with a spoon, making a crumbly dough. When the dough begins to stick together, press it together into a ball with your hands. Wrap with plastic wrap and chill for 30 minutes to 1 hour.

Roll out the dough, using as little flour as possible, about 1/4 in thick. Cut out cookies with a small round cookie cutter. Continue pressing the dough together, rolling it out, and cutting until you have used it all.

Place cookies 1/2 in apart on the prepared cookie sheets. Bake in the oven until set, but not browned, 7 to 10 minutes. Remove the cookies immediately to cool on a wire rack.

Spread the underside of a cooled cookie with 1 tsp of dulce de leche, then sandwich together with another cookie until the caramel oozes out the sides. Roll the sides in shredded coconut if desired and top with confectioners' sugar.

TOTAL TIME:

2 hours

+ 4 hours chilling

SERVINGS:

1 cake

RECIPE ORIGIN:

Mexico

INGREDIENTS:

Unsalted butter, for coating a baking dish

1 cup all-purpose flour

6 large eggs

1 cup white sugar

1 Tbsp dark rum, such as Myers's, plus more as needed

14-oz can sweetened condensed milk

2/3 cup evaporated milk (not nonfat)

1/2 cup unsweetened canned coconut milk

1 cup sweetened flaked coconut

1 1/2 cup heavy cream

1 Tbsp confectioners' sugar

Coconut tres leches cake

DIRECTIONS:

Preheat oven to 325°F and arrange a rack in the middle. Coat a baking dish with butter (a 13x9-in glass baking dish works well for this recipe). Place the flour in a small bowl and whisk to break up any lumps. Set greased baking dish and bowl of flour aside.

Separate the eggs, placing the yolks in the bowl of a stand mixer. Reserve the whites in a separate, medium-sized bowl. Add the white sugar to the yolks and, using the paddle attachment, beat on high speed until pale yellow, about 5 minutes. Transfer the mixture to a large bowl and set aside. Thoroughly clean and dry the stand mixer bowl. Place the egg whites in the clean bowl and, using the whisk attachment, whip on high speed until peaks form, about 1 1/2 minutes.

Using a rubber spatula, stir about 1/3 of the egg whites into the yolk mixture to lighten it. Then gently fold in the remaining whites. Sprinkle the flour over the egg mixture and gently fold it in, until flour is just combined. Do not overmix.

Pour the batter into the prepared baking dish and bake until the cake is puffed, golden, and the edges pull away from the sides of the pan, about 20 to 25 minutes. Meanwhile, place the rum and condensed, evaporated, and coconut milks in a large bowl and whisk until combined, then set aside.

Remove the cake from the oven and place on a wire cooling rack. Using a toothpick or wooden skewer, poke holes all over the cake and allow to cool for 15 minutes. Pour the milk mixture evenly over the cake and continue cooling, about 45 minutes more. Tightly cover with plastic wrap and refrigerate at least 4 hours or overnight.

When the cake is ready to serve, spread the coconut in an even layer in a large frying pan. Toast over medium heat, stirring often, until lightly browned and fragrant, about 5 minutes—if the coconut begins to burn, reduce the heat. Immediately transfer from the pan to a small bowl.

Place the heavy cream and confectioners' sugar in a large bowl and whisk until medium peaks form—if you like, flavor it with a tsp of dark rum. Spread the whipped cream over the cake, top with toasted coconut, and serve.

Did you know?

While we love this coconut twist on a Mexican classic, you can make your cake even more authentic by swapping the coconut milk with heavy cream.

Mexico

66

The waterways in Bangkok were incredible. A highlight? Heading through a canal toward the Damnoen Saduak Floating Market, where locals sell produce from their boats.

—Eugene
58th-time traveler
Thailand: The Golden Kingdom

Eats from the Far East

Asia

Asia's cuisine is inextricably tied to the continent's diverse cultures.

Here, culinary traditions draw on age-old cooking techniques, local ingredients, and long-standing customs. Each country, and even city, on the world's largest continent has its own specialties—you won't find the same dishes at dinner in Beijing and Bangkok. Colorful and bold, the cuisine of this region showcases the perfect balance of all things sweet, spicy, and savory.

Asian ingredients: the usual culprits

Recipes run the gamut across Asia, but these staples are used in many countries.

Rice

From Basmati rice in India to Jasmine rice in Thailand, this grain comes in many types, with each variety's length, color, and texture lending itself to a particular style of cooking.

Soy

This protein-filled bean has been used in Asian cooking for many years in the form of edamame, tofu, miso, and, of course, soy sauce.

Noodles

Whether they're made with ground rice, flour, or egg, noodles never disappoint. Try Udon and Soba in Japan, and glass noodles in China and Vietnam.

Spices

Adding aroma, flavor, or heat to a dish, spices play a big role in the region's cuisine. Cassia, chili, ginger, tamarind, and turmeric are just a few you may pick up on.

Floating markets, Thailand

Authentic cooking tools

a staple in Asian cooking

Wok

This piece of cookware is prized for its versatility. Traditionally round-bottomed and made of cast iron or carbon steel, a wok can be used to prepare an entire meal according to a wide range of techniques. Steaming, boiling, deep frying, or stir frying? You can use your wok to try any of those cooking methods.

Works with the wok

Wok spatula

Rice paddle

Wok ladle

Chopsticks

Invented by the ancient Chinese, chopsticks are typically long and thin with blunt ends. These utensils can be made of everything from bamboo to wood to plastic.

Outside of China, other countries including Cambodia, Thailand, and Vietnam, have also adopted similar types of chopsticks for enjoying some, but not all, dishes.

In Japan, chopsticks are slightly shorter and rounder with a pointed end, and in Korea, they're often made of metal and paired with a spoon.

Did you know?

Etiquette rules for handling chopsticks vary by culture, but one rule is common: Never leave them sticking vertically out of your bowl of food. This is symbolic of a funeral ritual, so always remember to place them on the provided chopstick rest.

TOTAL TIME:
1 hour

SERVINGS:
4

RECIPE ORIGIN:
Vietnam

INGREDIENTS:

For the wok mixture

1 tsp vegetable oil

10 medium shrimp, peeled

A pinch of sugar

A pinch of salt

For the salad mixture

Half of 1 green papaya, grated (or substitue green mango or bean sprouts)

Half of 1 cucumber, grated

1 carrot, grated

1/2 tsp ginger, finely chopped

2 tsp white vinegar or lime juice

A pinch of sugar

A pinch of salt

For assembly

4 pieces rice paper

10 medium lettuce leaves, sliced

2 Tbsp fresh coriander, mint, and basil, chopped

Fresh shrimp rolls

DIRECTIONS:

Prep the wok contents. Pour oil into a wok or pan at medium heat. Add shrimp, pinches of sugar and salt, and cook for 1 minute.

In a separate bowl, prep the salad mixture by combining the papaya, cucumber, carrot, ginger, white vinegar or lime juice, and pinches of both sugar and salt. Mix well.

To assemble, lay out rice paper. If using dried rice paper, soften each sheet by immersing it in water for a few seconds. (Tip: Place a leaf of lettuce between each piece of paper to prevent them from sticking.)

Place a helping of wok contents, salad mixture, lettuce, and fresh herbs on the rice paper. Roll up each piece of paper, tucking the edges of the paper in as you go.

Our cooking lesson at the Red Bridge Cooking School in Hôi An began with a market tour led by the chef instructor— that was a phenomenal way to start, sourcing the local foods we'd later cook.

—**Margaret & Chris**,
2nd-time travelers
Vietnam & Angkor Wat

A taste of Thailand

Cooking like a local on tour

SEE POM'S RECIPES ON PG. 261, 268 & 27

261 - Tom Yum Goong

268 - Phad Thai

271 - Sticky rice with mango

Essential ingredients in the Land of Smiles

Lemongrass

This herb, popular throughout Asia, can be used to bring fresh citrus flavor to soups, salads, and teas.

Fish sauce

A condiment made with fermented anchovies, this staple in Thai cooking gives dishes a distinctive salty taste.

Learning to cook with local ingredients was the highlight of my Thailand trip. The lesson was a perfect introduction to Thai flavors and culinary traditions, and I left feeling ready to make a few dishes for my friends back home!

—**Sherry**,
2nd-time traveler
Thailand: The Golden
Kingdom

The best way to get a taste of a destination's culture? Learning to cook traditional dishes using fresh ingredients from a local chef. You'll do just this at Cooking at Home Thai Culinary School during an excursion on our *Thailand: The Golden Kingdom* tour.

The dynamic duo behind this culinary school situated on the outskirts of Chiang Mai is Pom, who leads the lessons, and her husband Vatsin. From an early age, Pom spent a lot of time in the kitchen with her mother. Now, she shares her family's recipes with visitors from around the world in a large kitchen attached to their home.

During a typical class, travelers create a four-course meal under Pom's instruction. She leads demonstrations, carefully describing each ingredient—from lemongrass to galangal to Thai eggplants—and explaining how to prepare it. Each traveler-turned-chef has their own station to work on their dishes (with help from Pom and her assistants, of course!). The finished dishes are enjoyed in a covered dining area, looking out to beautiful views of the surrounding greenery.

Pea eggplant

Much smaller than traditional nightshades, these tiny aubergines burst with bitterness when raw, but become less bitter when cooked.

TOTAL TIME:

1 hour

SERVINGS:

6–8

RECIPE ORIGIN:

Japan

INGREDIENTS:

1 lb cabbage, finely minced

1 Tbsp kosher salt, divided

1 lb ground pork

1 tsp white pepper

3 garlic cloves, minced

1 tsp fresh ginger, minced

3 scallions, minced

2 tsp sugar

1 package gyoza wrappers
(40 to 50 wrappers)

4 Tbsp vegetable oil

1/2 cup rice vinegar

1/4 cup soy sauce

2 Tbsp chili oil (optional)

Pork & cabbage gyoza

DIRECTIONS:

In a large bowl, combine cabbage and 2 tsp of salt. Toss, then transfer to a fine mesh strainer and set it over the bowl for 15 minutes. Squeeze out any excess liquid using a clean dish towel. Then, add cabbage, pork, remaining salt, pepper, garlic, ginger, scallions, and sugar to a large bowl. Knead until mixture is well combined.

Line a baking sheet with parchment paper and fill a small bowl with water, then prepare your gyoza. Drop 1 Tbsp of filling in the middle of each wrapper. Dip your fingertips in water to moisten the edge of the wrapper, then fold it in half and seal. As each crescent-shaped dumpling is formed, place it on the baking sheet.

Place a medium, nonstick skillet over medium heat and warm 1 Tbsp of oil. Arrange 10 to 12 gyoza in a single layer in the pan and cook about 1 1/2 minutes, or until the bottoms are evenly golden brown. Add 1/2 cup of water and increase heat to medium-high. Cover the skillet with a lid and allow gyoza to steam for 3 minutes. Remove lid and cook, swirling pan frequently, for another 2 minutes or until water has fully evaporated. Remove from pan and repeat with remaining gyoza.

In a small bowl, combine rice vinegar, soy sauce, and chili oil. Place gyoza on a plate browned side up and serve with the sauce.

RECIPE RECOMMENDED BY

Diana
Traveler

Did you know?

Gyoza are Japanese dumplings.
While they're very similar to
Chinese potstickers, it's the
extra garlic, extra vegetables,
and thinner wrappers that set
them apart.

TOTAL TIME:
30 minutes

SERVINGS:
2

RECIPE ORIGIN:
Thailand

INGREDIENTS:

2 cups stock or water

2 stalks lemongrass

4 kaffir lime leaves, destemmed
and torn into large pieces

5 slices of galangal

2 garlic cloves, halved and smashed

2 shallots, halved and smashed

5 shiitake or button mushrooms

1/2 cup shrimp, washed, shelled,
and deveined

2 large tomatoes, diced

1/4 tsp salt, plus more to taste

1 Tbsp fish sauce

1 Tbsp lime juice

2 to 6 green and red Thai chilies, crushed

A couple coriander leaf stems,
roughly chopped

FROM AN EXPERT'S KITCHEN:

Tom yum goong

Sour & spicy shrimp lemongrass soup

DIRECTIONS:

Pour stock into a pot and bring to a boil over medium heat. Prepare the lemongrass by removing each stalk's loose outer layer and 1/4 in from the bottom. Lightly smash each stalk and slice diagonally into 1-in pieces. When stock starts to boil, place lemongrass, lime leaves, galangal, garlic, and shallots into the pot. Boil for about 10 minutes to draw out flavors.

Add mushrooms and let water return to a boil. Then, add shrimp, tomatoes, salt, fish sauce, and lime juice. Stir to combine and cook until prawns turn pink, about 8 minutes. Add as many chilies as you'd like (the longer you cook them, the more their heat will come out in the soup). Adjust seasoning to taste—soup should be sour, spicy, and salty. Turn off the heat and toss in coriander leaves. Then, transfer soup to bowls and serve.

Your guide to ramen noodles

In a country where food is meticulously prepared using tried-and-true techniques, it could be said that ramen is a culinary rogue. This nuanced noodle dish known the world over only took off in Japan about 100 years ago, but has since become an everyday staple prepared in thousands of different ramen shops. While particular ingredients, a chef's creative touch, and more contribute to the layered flavors in each bowl, here are four must-have elements that culminate in a balanced, harmonious meal.

Broth

Japanese chefs often seek out ways to put their own stamp on their particular ramen broth (incorporating seafood is just one way, for example). But, the most common elements include chicken or pork bones and *dashi*, a stock made from kelp and dried fish flakes.

Tare

In search of umami? This hard-to-define savory element is infused into ramen with one of the four types of *tare*, or sauce: *shio*, *shoyu*, *miso*, and *tonkotsu*. These main broth bases set each style of ramen apart.

Noodles

Ramen noodles may have gotten their start in China as *lo mein*, but have since become a Japanese staple. They get their chewy texture and yellow color from an alkaline water known as *kansui*, and are traditionally made with wheat flour, hand-pulled, and serve al dente.

Toppings

While extras such as sweet corn and butter can make their way to the top of a bowl of noodles (looking at you, Sapporo ramen), more classic accoutrements include roasted pork, egg, scallions, fish cakes, bean sprouts, bamboo shoots, and *nori* (seaweed paper).

Tare 101: Uncover your umami

1

Shio

Meaning "salt," this is one of the oldest ramen bases, and the golden broth is the one we have come to know most often in North America.

2

Shoyu

This tare's soy sauce base creates a light-brown broth with a rich, tangy flavor, and is one of the most popular ramen styles in Tokyo.

3

Miso

This version made with fermented bean paste was invented in the northern city of Sapporo, and has become one of the most popular styles throughout the country.

4

Tonkotsu

Boiling ground-up pork bones results in this very distinct broth base, which lends a cloudy appearance to the soup.

A short history of instant ramen

If your college days were synonymous with countless packages of instant ramen, you can thank Momofuku Ando. This businessman and inventor dreamt up the pre-packaged meal as a response to Japan's food crisis following World War II. At the time, bread made from flour supplied by the U.S. was easier to come by than noodles, but Ando wanted his countrymen to stick to their roots. In 1958, he discovered that he could preserve noodles and their unique texture by flash-frying them in tempura oil. And just like that, one of Japan's culinary staples became readily available and one of the world's most revolutionary food products was born.

While there may be no way to substitute actually sitting down in a ramen shop in Japan, here are a few ways to punch up your pre-packaged ramen at home.

- *Top it off with a halved, soft-boiled egg*
- *Infuse freshness with scallions and bok choy*
- *Make it a meal with sliced pork or chicken*
- *Bring out umami with sautéed mushrooms*
- *Replace the flavor packet with miso paste*
- *Mix in a kick with hot chili oil or Sriracha*

Know your ramen rules

While it's usually impolite to slurp your food, that's not the case with ramen. You want to eat it quickly so the noodles don't get too soft in the hot broth, while being careful not to burn your mouth. So, those patrons who don't even really look up from their bowl while they rush through their dish? Yes, they are doing it the right way—and you should disregard all you know about *politesse* and follow suit.

RECIPE RECOMMENDED BY

Achala
Go Ahead Tours

TOTAL TIME:
30 minutes

SERVINGS:
4

RECIPE ORIGIN:
Southern India

INGREDIENTS:

3 Tbsp olive oil

1 tsp whole brown mustard seeds

2 whole dried, hot red chilies (optional)

15 to 20 fresh curry leaves (or substitute 10 fresh basil leaves), torn

1/2 onion, chopped

1 tomato, chopped

2 tsp ground coriander

1/4 tsp cayenne pepper

1 tsp garam masala

7 to 9 red potatoes, peeled and cubed

8 oz water

1 tsp salt

4 oz coconut milk, well-shaken

4 Tbsp fresh coriander, chopped

Classic potato curry

DIRECTIONS:

Heat oil in a pan over medium-high heat. Add the mustard seeds and chilies. When the seeds begin to pop, add the curry or basil leaves and onion. Reduce heat to medium and cook for about 3 minutes, stirring well. Add tomato, coriander, cayenne pepper, and garam masala, and stir for 1 minute. Add the potatoes and stir for 1 more minute.

Pour water into the pan and add salt, then bring to a boil. Reduce heat, cover, and cook until potatoes are tender, about 15 to 20 minutes. To finish, add the coconut milk and coriander. Stir well before serving.

This is a very versatile curry that's really common in Southern India. It's typically eaten with one of our main carb dishes for brunch, like *dosa*, which is similar to a crêpe, or *idli*, a savory cake made with soaked rice. I have lots of memories of waking up on weekend mornings and eating this as a family!

—**Achala**, *Go Ahead Tours*

20 minutes

SERVINGS:
4

RECIPE ORIGIN:
Laos

INGREDIENTS:

1 garlic clove

2 to 4 chilies

1 Tbsp shrimp paste

1/4 Tbsp crab paste

2 cups green papaya, peeled and sliced into long, thin strips

1 Tbsp fish sauce

1 Tbsp padek (fermented fish sauce)

3 Tbsp sugar

2 Tbsp lime juice

6 cherry tomatoes, halved

4 yardlong or green beans, cut into small pieces

Tam maak hoong

Papaya salad

DIRECTIONS:

Use a mortar and pestle to grind the garlic and chilies together. Add the shrimp and crab pastes to the mixture and continue grinding. Once mixture is combined, toss in papaya, fish sauce, padek, sugar, and lime juice, and mix with a spoon. Finish by mixing in the tomatoes and beans, then serve.

Cooking tip

When it comes to the papaya you use for this dish, choosing an unripe one with a tangy flavor and crunchy texture is key! While green papaya is a must, anchovy paste can be substituted for the *padek* if you can't find the specialty ingredient (or if fermented fish sauce isn't your thing).

TOTAL TIME:
1 hour, 30 minutes

SERVINGS:
1

RECIPE ORIGIN:
Vietnam

INGREDIENTS:

For the carrot and daikon pickle

1 large carrot, peeled and cut into matchsticks

1 lb daikons, peeled and cut into matchsticks

1 tsp salt

2 tsp plus 1/2 cup sugar

1 1/4 cups distilled white vinegar

1 cup lukewarm water

For the sandwich

1 baguette, cut to about 7 in

1 to 2 Tbsp mayonnaise

A drizzle of Maggi seasoning sauce
(or substitute soy sauce)

4 oz pork, grilled and sliced

4 slices of cucumber

A few sprigs of fresh cilantro, roughly chopped

3 slices of jalapeño pepper

Bánh mì

Traditional Vietnamese sandwich

DIRECTIONS:

First, prepare your *do chua*, or pickled carrot and daikon. Place the carrot and daikon matchsticks in a medium bowl. Add a tsp of salt and 2 tsp of sugar. Knead the vegetables for several minutes until they've softened and excess water begins to collect in the bowl. Drain and rinse under cold water, then dry well.

In a separate bowl, combine the remaining sugar, vinegar, and water, and stir. Pour the brine over the carrot-and-daikon mixture, fully covering the vegetables. Marinate for at least 1 hour.

To prepare your sandwich, slice the baguette lengthwise and remove the inside of each half. If desired, toast the bread until crispy. Once the baguette has cooled, spread mayonnaise on each side, then drizzle with Maggi seasoning sauce (or soy sauce). On the bottom half of the bread, pile the pork, cucumber, cilantro, jalapeño, and a generous helping of the pickled carrot and daikon. Close the sandwich and slice in half before serving.

Did you know?

The name of this classic Vietnamese sandwich nods to its French colonial roots. Meaning "wheat bread," *bánh mì* came about when the French controlled Indochina and introduced the baguette to the region.

Nicole
Go Ahead Tours

TOTAL TIME:
1 hour, 30 minutes

SERVINGS:
2

RECIPE ORIGIN:
Japan

INGREDIENTS:

1 tsp olive oil

1 onion, sliced

1/2 lb beef, thinly sliced

3 Tbsp soy sauce

2 Tbsp sake

1 tsp ginger, grated

1 Tbsp sugar

2 tsp dashi powder

1/2 cup water

3 eggs, beaten

2 cups brown rice, steamed

2 tsp sesame seeds

Scallions, to garnish (optional)

Gyūdon

Beef & rice bowl

DIRECTIONS:

In a medium pan over medium-high heat, warm the oil. Add the onion and cook until caramelized, about 20 to 45 minutes depending on heat, stirring frequently.

Add beef, soy sauce, sake, ginger, and sugar. Cook until beef has absorbed the flavors, about 3 minutes. Then, add the dashi and water. Let mixture boil for about 3 minutes, then reduce to medium heat and simmer for 5 minutes.

Pour beaten eggs over the contents of the pan and stir for about 3 more minutes, until the egg is fully cooked. Divide brown rice into two bowls, top with beef mixture, and garnish with sesame seeds and scallions if desired.

RECIPE RECOMMENDED BY

Pom
Local expert

TOTAL TIME:

25 minutes

SERVINGS:

2

RECIPE ORIGIN:

Thailand

INGREDIENTS:

1 Tbsp fish sauce

1 1/2 Tbsp tamarind juice or tamarind concentrate

2 Tbsp water

1 1/2 Tbsp raw white sugar

1 tsp chili powder (optional)

4 tsp ground roasted peanuts, plus more for serving

2 Tbsp vegetable oil

3 shallots, crushed and chopped

1 oz firm tofu, diced

8 oz chicken, diced

1 egg

1/4 cup fresh rice noodles

1/4 cup chives, cut into 1-in pieces

1/4 cup bean sprouts, washed and drained, plus more for serving

1 lime, cut into wedges

A sprig of fresh cilantro, to garnish (optional)

Shredded carrot, to garnish (optional)

FROM AN EXPERT'S KITCHEN:

Phad Thai

Fried noodles with chicken

DIRECTIONS:

In a small bowl, combine fish sauce, tamarind juice, water, sugar, chili powder, and peanuts. Mix thoroughly. Adjust flavors to your desired taste, then set aside.

In a medium wok, heat the oil. Add shallots and tofu, and cook until shallots are fragrant and tofu is golden. Add the chicken and cook until it starts to brown.

Push the shallot, tofu, and chicken mixture up along one side of the wok. Crack the egg in the cleared area and use your spatula to scramble lightly. Once eggs set, fold chicken mixture in.

Add the rice noodles and sauce mixture. Stir well and frequently until the noodles are evenly coated and have absorbed most of the sauce. (If the noodles are still too firm, add some water to help soften them as they cook.)

Toss chives and bean sprouts into the wok and stir. When vegetables are partially wilted, transfer to two individual plates. Serve with a wedge of lime, and garnish with peanuts, bean sprouts, cilantro, and carrots if desired.

I was shocked by how easy it was to make during our cooking lesson, and it really turned out to be the best Phad Thai I had during the whole tour. It gave me the confidence to know I could cook with Thai flavors at home!

—Nicole, *Go Ahead Tours*

Did you know?

This sweet, salty, sour, and spicy
dish is one of the most popular and
traditional quick meals in Thailand.
It can be made with prawns instead
of chicken, or vegetarian-style with
additional tofu.

269

TOTAL TIME:

45 minutes
+ 4 hours chilling

SERVINGS:
30 cookies

RECIPE ORIGIN:
China

INGREDIENTS:

2 cups all-purpose flour

3/4 tsp baking powder

1/2 tsp baking soda

1/4 tsp salt

1/2 cup butter, softened

1/2 cup shortening

3/4 cup white sugar

1/4 cup brown sugar

1 egg

1 tsp almond extract

1/2 cup white sesame seeds

Sesame cookies

DIRECTIONS:

Sift flour into a medium bowl. Mix in the baking powder, baking soda, and salt. In a separate large bowl, combine the butter, shortening, white sugar, and brown sugar. Add the egg and almond extract, and beat well. Pour in the flour mixture and stir until everything is well combined.

Form the dough into 2 rolls, each about 1 ft long. Cover them with plastic wrap and place in the refrigerator for at least 4 hours, or overnight. When ready to prepare cookies, remove the dough rolls from the refrigerator and preheat oven to 325°F. Lightly grease a baking sheet.

Fill a bowl with sesame seeds, then cut each roll of dough into 15 even pieces. Roll each slice into a ball, then dip into the bowl to coat evenly with sesame seeds. Place each ball on the prepared baking sheet. Bake the cookies for about 15 to 17 minutes, or until edges are golden and a toothpick inserted into the center comes out clear.

TOTAL TIME:

45 minutes
+ 3 hours soaking

SERVINGS:
4

RECIPE ORIGIN:
Thailand

INGREDIENTS:

1 cup uncooked white sticky rice

Water, as needed

1 1/2 cup thick coconut milk, divided

1 1/2 tsp salt, divided

1/2 cup sugar

1 to 2 ripe mangoes, peeled and sliced

1 Tbsp white sesame seeds

FROM AN EXPERT'S KITCHEN:

Sticky rice with mango

DIRECTIONS:

Rinse the rice. Then, place in a bowl and cover with water, up to 3 in above the rice. Soak for at least 3 hours, or overnight. When ready to cook, drain the sticky rice through a fine sieve. Fill a pot with 6 to 10 in of water, then place the rice in a sieve or steamer basket. Cover and steam over medium-high heat for 30 minutes, stirring halfway through to ensure rice cooks evenly.

While the rice cooks, combine 1/2 cup of coconut milk and 1/2 tsp of salt in a medium saucepan over low heat until salt dissolves. Transfer to a bowl and reserve as a salty cream topping. Using the same saucepan, combine 1 cup of thick coconut milk, 1 tsp salt, and sugar over medium heat. Bring to a boil, stirring frequently.

Once the rice has finished cooking, transfer to a large bowl. Pour the warm coconut sauce over the rice and mix well. Let the mixture stand for 30 minutes so the flavors can be absorbed. Scoop the rice evenly onto 4 dishes with mango slices. Drizzle the salty cream on top and sprinkle with sesame seeds to serve.

More matcha, please!

This bamboo whisk, or "chasen," is key to preparing matcha

China

In the country that boasts the title of the world's top tea producer, there is a mind-boggling variety of options to try. Two of our picks? Longjing, a green tea cultivated in the Zhejiang Province, and Dianhong, a black tea from the Yunnan Province.

Vietnam

Lotus tea, made for special events and celebrations, is one of the country's most unique drinks. In a complex and time-consuming process, lotus flower is mixed with green tea to give *trà sen* a fragrant scent.

India

There are many types of tea cultivated across the subcontinent, including black tea. When paired with honey, milk, and a blend of spices like cinnamon, cloves, and cardamom, it forms the tasty concoction known as *masala chai*.

Myanmar

Green tea is cultivated at plantations in the eastern part of the country. Besides being used as a drink, the leaves are sometimes pickled and served on top of salad, called *lahpet*.

Matcha is having a moment in North America. While the powdered, antioxidant-filled substance has gained popularity here in recent years, it has been enjoyed for centuries in Japan. Made from dried green tea leaves that have been ground into a fine powder, matcha plays a big role in the traditional Japanese tea ceremony.

A host carefully prepares and serves tea according to particular procedures during this ritual, which is an art form in itself. Each step in the time-honored process calls for specific tools. After being sifted through a sieve, matcha is scooped into a bowl. Then, it's whipped with a *chasen*, or bamboo whisk, until it begins to foam. The host serves it to those who have witnessed its preparation and can appreciate it with all the senses.

Guests are expected to follow certain etiquette guidelines, such as turning the bowl slightly before drinking and remaining quiet throughout the practice. Matcha is not prepared with any milk or sugar, but served with small sweets instead. Savor each drink and treat that you're presented with—it's a sign of respect to finish everything.

Sipping on sake

What to know about Japan's signature drink

1

Learn the basics

While we think of sake as rice wine here in the West, it's actually a brewed beverage closer to beer. In fact, the word sake translates to alcohol in general; the sake we think of is called *nihonshu* in Japan.

2

Serve your neighbor

When drinking sake with others, it's customary to fill your neighbor's cup and to let them do the same for you. In fact, it can be considered rude to pour your own sake, hinting that you don't trust your host to take care of you.

3

Say *kanpai*, or cheers

Sake is a social drink that's meant to be shared. Once everyone's ceramic cups are filled, raise a glass with a friendly *kanpai*. To show respect to an elder or coworker when you toast, make sure that the rim of your cup clinks below the rim of their cup.

Celebrate the little things

While sake is a part of big moments like weddings and New Year's Day, it's also a way to sit back and enjoy life's simple pleasures too—so much so, that the Japanese have specific names for these universally happy moments:

My first taste of sake in Japan was at a tiny soba restaurant in Tokyo, where the waiter helped me select a bottle that paired perfectly with my noodles.

I'll always remember that meal and enjoying sake in a traditional cup—its small size made me sip slowly and appreciate all the flavors of the drink.

–Courtney, *Go Ahead Tours*

Hanami-zake

Sake that you drink while admiring the *hanami*, or springtime's colorful cherry blossom season

Tsukimi-zake

Sake that you drink while celebrating a full moon in autumn—considered an offering for a good harvest

Yukimi-zake

Sake you drink while peacefully watching the snow fall outside your window

Set the stage

In traditional settings, sake is poured from a decorative flask called a *tokkuri* into small cups. Usually ceramic and delicately painted, the small cup, called an *ochoko*, likely got its name from a derivative of the Japanese saying for "just a little," making it the perfect vessel for slowly sipping sake.

Some sake varieties, like *junmai* and *honjozo*, are best served warm; while others like *ginjo* and *daiginjo* are best moderately chilled. To warm sake up, place the entire flask into a pot of water and bring to a boil.

"

One night we had the opportunity to have dinner at the home
of a local family. They were very generous and gracious, and
sitting down to a meal at their table was a real highlight.
As we enjoyed the lamb dinner they'd prepared, they spoke
about what it's like to live in New Zealand. I could tell that
the most important thing in their life is family. It's rare to
connect with local people and it was just a magical evening.

—Rick
3rd-time traveler
New Zealand: Untamed Landscapes

Top-notch cuisine Down Under

Australia & New Zealand

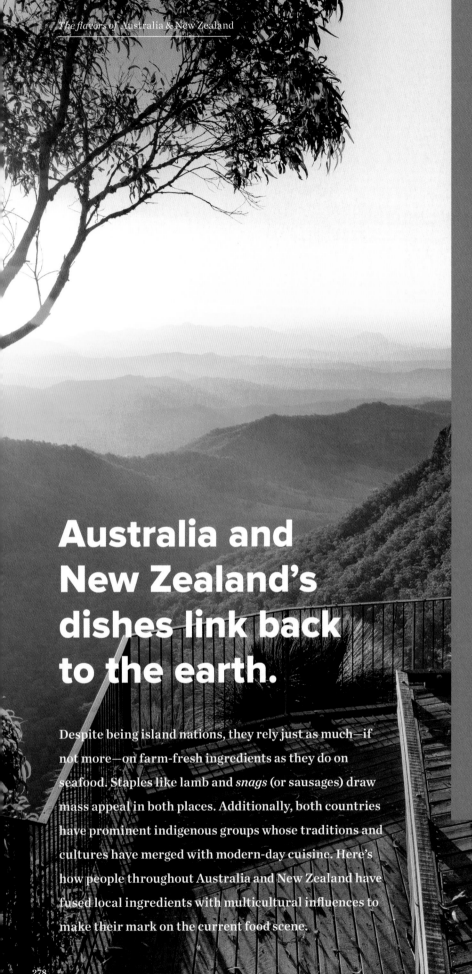

Australia and New Zealand's dishes link back to the earth.

Despite being island nations, they rely just as much—if not more—on farm-fresh ingredients as they do on seafood. Staples like lamb and *snags* (or sausages) draw mass appeal in both places. Additionally, both countries have prominent indigenous groups whose traditions and cultures have merged with modern-day cuisine. Here's how people throughout Australia and New Zealand have fused local ingredients with multicultural influences to make their mark on the current food scene.

Speak the foodie slang

Native Aussies and Kiwis may be the only ones able to get those charming accents down pat, but you don't need to talk like a local to order traditional eats like one. Here are a few popular slang terms to know for different types of *tucker*, or food.

Adam's ale

This is Australia's colloquial term for water, and is said to be a silly reference to the only thing Adam had to drink when he was in Eden.

Spag bol

Short for "spaghetti bolognese," this Aussie term refers to the classic Italian dish.

Dagwood dog

Most commonly eaten at Australia's annual festival called the Royal Show, these are battered, deep-fried hotdogs served on a stick and dipped in ketchup.

Hot chips

You'd order a piping plate of these if you happened to catch a craving for french fries in New Zealand.

Greasies

New Zealanders love their fish and chips, and this is the term you'd use to order a plate for yourself.

Anzac biscuits

These sweet biscuits became popular in New Zealand during WWI because they don't require eggs and keep well.

Shrimp on the barbie

It may seem like just a playful phrase, but barbecues hold a special place in Australian life. Reminiscent of picnics that took place as part of the 1900s bush culture, modern-day barbecue has been a mainstay Down Under since the 1950s. So do as the Aussies do and gather with friends and family as you throw some prawns, chops, and snags on the grill.

The lamb down under

Australia is almost the same size as the continental U.S. and around half of the country's land is used for farming and grazing— so it's no surprise that dishes like grilled and roasted lamb are popular no matter which region you're visiting.

Aboriginal culture

For thousands of years, Australian Aboriginals utilized more than 5,000 different native foods, including kangaroo, emu, and macadamia nuts. In New Zealand, the Māori are an indigenous group of Polynesian descent who are known for *hangi*, a method that uses steam, hot rocks, and cloth to cook food inside a manmade hole in the soil.

Kiwis

The word "kiwi" is more than just the name of the fuzzy green fruit you'll find at the grocery store—it's also used to refer to people from New Zealand. The nickname is seen as a source of pride for New Zealanders and comes from the country's native, flightless bird of the same name.

Raise a glass to easy living

If your idea of relaxation is kicking back with a glass of wine in hand, Australia and New Zealand have just what you're after. Life is as laid back as it comes in these South Pacific spots. And one of the many things they have in common is a reputation for up-and-coming wines. The wines produced in each destination are both fresh and award-winning, with styles that span crisp, spicy, and aromatic—it just depends which region you visit.

Viticulture by the numbers

400K+	60	1819	80
The amount of Australia's wine vineyard acreage, which is mostly clustered in the southeastern corner of the continent.	The number of wine regions in Australia, which collectively produce all the major wine styles, thanks to a wide variety of climates.	The year Anglican Reverend Samuel Marsden planted New Zealand's first grape vines on the North Island in Kerikeri.	As in 80 miles—on the island of New Zealand, wines thrive in cooler temps because no vineyard is planted more than this distance away from the coast.

Wine regions to know

Hunter Valley

If you head just north of Sydney, you'll hit Hunter Valley, Australia's oldest wine-growing region. Of all the varieties the warm, humid destination gets right (and yes, medium-bodied Shiraz and Chardonnays full of minerality are among them), its real claim to fame is the dry white called Sémillon. This unique wine hails from France and ranges from clean and citrusy to complex and nutty the more it ages—and pairs perfectly with the region's abundant seafood.

Yarra Valley

Foodies will feel right at home in the Yarra Valley. It's in this southern Australian region that the state of Victoria's wine industry came to fruition, and today, good wine and good food are hallmarks of the area. With winemaking roots that date back more than 170 years and upwards of 80 wineries that churn out innovative varietals, there's most certainly something for every palate. Pinot Noir, Chardonnay, and sparkling wines thrive in the region's cooler temps, and can be served with locally sourced products like fresh-caught salmon, organic fruit, and handmade cheese.

Marlborough

New Zealand has this large wine-growing region to thank for putting it on the map as a wine hub to watch. Here on the top tip of the South Island, the days are sunny and the nights are cool, and growers have perfected the production of New Zealand's most important varietal: Sauvignon Blanc. This white wine started winning critics over in the 1980s, and of all the Sauvignon Blanc produced around the world, Marlborough's could arguably be classified as some of the best and most distinct.

Central Otago

Sitting pretty as the world's southernmost wine-making region, Central Otago is the place to go to both drink good wine and marvel at breathtaking landscapes. Here, soaring mountains rise up alongside picturesque lakes, and it's on this varied terrain that New Zealand grows some of its best varietals. One type to seek out? Pinot Noir. The grapes grow well in the region's mica-rich soil and varied climate, which includes warm, cold, and dry seasons. While Pinot Noir is Central Otago's standout, aromatic Chardonnays and crisp Sauvignon Blancs certainly hold their own.

Sips to tip back in the South Pacific

Australia: Shiraz

Robust and fruity are two defining features of a typical Shiraz. This red wine, called Syrah in most other locations, was brought to Australia in 1830 by James Busby. He is often called "the father of the Australian wine industry" since he introduced many varieties of Spanish and French grape vines into Australia. This was the beginning of Australia's viticulture and today, Shiraz is among Australia's top-produced and most popular wines. Try pairing this rich wine with a hearty stew or roast beef.

New Zealand: Sauvignon Blanc

Fresh, tropical, and crisp—New Zealand's most popular wine goes best with a summer salad, herbed fish, or light seafood. Sauvignon Blanc skyrocketed New Zealand into the wine industry's spotlight and continues to be the country's most highly produced white variety. Along with being refreshing and acidic, the strong herbal notes and citrus undertones of grapefruit, passion fruit, and lime help differentiate a New Zealand Sauvignon Blanc from other regions'.

RECIPE RECOMMENDED BY

Richard
Traveler

TOTAL TIME:
15 minutes
+ overnight marinating

SERVINGS:
4

RECIPE ORIGIN:
Australia

INGREDIENTS:

2 1/2 tsp red wine vinegar

1 Tbsp extra-virgin olive oil

1 Tbsp honey

3 garlic cloves, minced

1 1/4 tsp fresh rosemary, finely chopped

1/2 tsp dried thyme

3/4 to 1 tsp sea salt

Pepper, to taste

8 lamb chops

Great for summertime!

Rosemary grilled lamb chops

DIRECTIONS:

Mix vinegar, oil, honey, garlic, rosemary, thyme, salt, and pepper in a large bowl until salt dissolves. Add lamb and mix to coat. Cover and marinate in the refrigerator overnight.

Heat grill to medium-high. Cook lamb about 3 minutes on each side, or to your preference.

Transfer lamb to a plate, cover loosely with foil, and let it rest for 5 minutes before serving.

Highlights on our New Zealand trip were many, but the traditional lamb dinner cooked by and served in the home of a New Zealand family stands out for me.

–Rick,
3rd-time traveler
New Zealand: Untamed Landscapes

TOTAL TIME:

3 hours

SERVINGS:

8

RECIPE ORIGIN:

New Zealand

INGREDIENTS:

For the filling

1 Tbsp olive oil

2 tsp brown sugar

1 onion, finely diced

1 Tbsp balsamic vinegar

2 tsp salt

1/2 cup pumpkin, diced

1/4 cup carrot, diced

1/4 cup parsnip, diced

1/2 cup green beans, diced

3 tsp fresh thyme

3/4 cup blue cheese

Pepper, to taste

For the dough

2 tsp lemon juice

1/2 cup ice water

1 cup flour

2 tsp salt

1 1/3 cups butter, cold and cut into cubes

2 eggs

Fall vegetable pie

DIRECTIONS:

To make the dough, add lemon juice to water. Mix the lemon water, flour, and salt into a dough. Knead until it builds elasticity, then refrigerate for 30 minutes.

To make the filling, heat oil in a sauté pan. Add all filling ingredients except blue cheese to the pan. Sauté mixture on medium heat for 30 minutes or until vegetables are golden and soft. Season with pepper and set aside.

Remove the dough from the fridge and roll out into a rectangle. Place cubes of butter onto the pastry, then fold and roll. Repeat this process three times before letting the pastry rest for 1 hour.

Preheat oven to 400°F. Make an egg wash for dough by beating eggs with a splash of cold water. Line a pie tin with the dough, stretching the dough up over the edges. Place filling in the center, top with cheese, then brush with egg wash. Fold dough 2 to 3 inches inward over the filling. Brush again, then bake for 25 minutes or until golden.

I visited an amazing little cafe on the South Island that was very farm-to-table. It had all sorts of delicious-looking meat pies, sausage rolls, quiches, scones, and more, but since it was dipping into the fall season, I couldn't resist trying their famous vegetable pie! New Zealanders are known for their pies and it was clear why. The crust was flaky and I could tell the vegetables were straight from the garden.

—**Brittany**, *Go Ahead Tours*

Did you know?

Contrary to popular belief, shrimp and prawns are not the same. They're both crustaceans but differ in size and anatomy— prawns are more closely related to lobsters. The good part? They can easily be substituted for each other in recipes.

TOTAL TIME:
30 minutes

SERVINGS:
4

RECIPE ORIGIN:
Australia

INGREDIENTS:

For the aioli

3 egg yolks

2 garlic cloves, finely chopped

1/2 tsp dijon mustard

Juice of half a lemon

A pinch of salt

1 cup extra-virgin olive oil

For the shrimp

1/3 cup butter

1 garlic clove, finely chopped

Juice and zest of 2 limes, divided

1 long red chili, seeded and finely chopped

2 Tbsp fresh, flat-leaf parsley, chopped

1 1/2 lbs uncooked shrimp, deveined in shell (or substitute prawns)

Salt and pepper, to taste

Grilled lime & chili shrimp

with garlic aioli

DIRECTIONS:

Place the egg yolks, garlic, mustard, lemon juice, and a pinch of salt in a food processor, and blitz to combine. With the motor running, slowly drizzle in the oil and blend until thick. Transfer aioli to a bowl and set aside.

Melt butter in a small saucepan over low heat. Once melted, remove the pan from heat and stir in the garlic, lime juice, zest of 1 lime, chili, and parsley. Drizzle the butter mixture over the shrimp and sprinkle with zest of the second lime. Season with salt and pepper.

Preheat grill to high heat, and once hot enough, place shrimp on grill. Cook for 3 to 5 minutes or until the flesh is just cooked through. Arrange on a serving platter alongside the bowl of garlic aioli.

SERVINGS:

4

RECIPE ORIGIN:

Australia

INGREDIENTS:

2 pontiac potatoes, peeled and coarsely chopped

2 cups peas

1/4 cup sour cream

Salt and pepper, to taste

1 Tbsp butter

1 leek, white parts only, thickly sliced

1 Tbsp caster sugar

1 Tbsp white wine vinegar

2 tsp fresh thyme

8 beef sausages

Sausages with leeks & mashed peas

DIRECTIONS:

Fill a saucepan with water, add a pinch of salt, and bring to a boil. Add potatoes and cook for 15 minutes. Drain potatoes, return them to the pan, and add sour cream and peas. Use a fork to mash until almost smooth. Season with salt and pepper.

Melt butter in a nonstick frying pan over medium heat until foaming. Add the leek and cook, stirring occasionally, for 5 minutes or until brown. Add the sugar, vinegar, and thyme. Cook, stirring occasionally, for 5 minutes. Season with salt and pepper.

While leek is cooking, heat a frying pan over high heat. Add sausages and cook for 5 to 7 minutes or until cooked.

Divide the mash among serving plates and top with sausages. Spoon on the leek mixture and serve immediately.

Did you know?

While the Brits call sausages *bangers*, the Aussies call them *snags*, which is thought to have originated from the British slang for a light meal. Regardless of what you call them, you'll find these savory snacks everywhere in Australia.

Add your favorites

Pavlova is named after Russian ballerina Anna Pavlova, and both Australia and New Zealand claim to be the place of its creation. The best part of this dish is not its mysterious origin, but rather that it's so easy to customize the type and amount of toppings. Tart fruits make the best garnish since they balance out the sweetness of the meringue—here are our eight favorites!

Mix & match

Blackberries

Strawberries

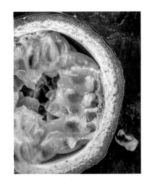

Passion fruit

Raspberries

Pomegranate seeds

Blueberries

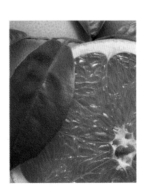

Grapefruit

Kiwi

Pavlova

TOTAL TIME:
2 hours, 45 minutes

SERVINGS:
1 pavlova

RECIPE ORIGIN:
New Zealand

INGREDIENTS:

Butter, to coat baking surface

2 tsp cornstarch, plus more for dusting

6 egg whites

1 1/4 cups caster sugar

1 tsp white vinegar

1/2 tsp vanilla extract

1 1/2 cups heavy cream

2 Tbsp confectioners' sugar

Zest and juice of 2 limes

2 bananas, thinly sliced diagonally

3 kiwis, peeled and thinly sliced

2 cups strawberries

Fresh mint, to garnish

DIRECTIONS:

Preheat oven to 250°F. Line an oven tray with foil. Brush with melted butter and dust with cornstarch, shaking off excess. Mark a 9.5 in-diameter circle on foil.

Use an electric mixer to whisk egg whites until soft peaks form. Gradually add sugar, 1 Tbsp at a time, beating well after each addition, until meringue is thick and glossy, and sugar dissolves. Rub a little meringue between fingers. If gritty with sugar, continue to whisk until sugar dissolves. Add cornstarch, vinegar, and vanilla and whisk until just combined.

Spoon meringue onto the foil, using the marked circle as a guide. Smooth sides and top of pavlova. Use a small spatula to form little peaks around pavlova's edge. Bake in the oven for 1 1/2 hours or until pavlova is dry to the touch. Turn off oven. Leave pavlova in oven with the door ajar to cool completely. When completely cold, transfer to a serving plate or cake stand, or store in an airtight container until ready to serve.

Use an electric mixer to whisk the cream and confectioners' sugar in a medium bowl until firm peaks form. Spoon cream onto the top of pavlova. Pour lime juice into a ceramic or glass bowl. Add banana slices and toss to coat with juice. Drain. Decorate pavlova with banana, kiwis, strawberries, and lime zest, and garnish with mint. If desired, swap out or combine these toppings with the fruit of your choice. Star fruit and passion fruit are authentic alternatives.

"

Jerash and Petra are among the most interesting

places we have ever visited. The food was excellent,

and the opportunity to have several meals in Bedouin

settings helped us to experience their way of life.

—Robert
6th-time traveler
The Wonders of Ancient Israel

Flavors from the deserts & the souks

Africa & the Middle East

Africa and the Middle East boast a bold mosaic of unique flavors.

When it comes to each destinations' cuisines, it's safe to say that there's a link between the diversity of the cultures and the complex flavors of the food. Mediterranean influences shine through in Israel and Egypt, while Indian immigrants in Kenya, Tanzania, and beyond have brought with them rich curry dishes, coconut-milk-infused sauces, and more. Bright spices, savory stews, fresh vegetables and fruits—the memorable fare here calls to mind each country's colors and warmth.

A new take on classic flavors

The drinks and dishes of Africa and the Middle East are often characterized by layered flavor profiles—and some unexpected ingredients. Here are a few of the most delicious bites with a twist.

Avocado ice cream

In South Africa, this classic salad accompaniment is often used to make ice cream, and avocado-mint shakes are a favorite in Cape Town.

Cardamom coffee

Ever had a cup of Arabic or Turkish coffee? That unique, unexpected flavor is from cardamom, a spice that usually lends a savory element to main courses.

Baobab lemonade

From the leaves to the superfruit, every part of a baobab tree is put to good use in Africa. Even the fruit pulp is used to create a drink likened to lemonade.

Baklava with rose water

In this twist on the flaky Middle Eastern dessert (often called *baklawa*), the floral, sweet notes come from added rose or orange blossom water.

Africa's culinary roots go deep

Africa's wide expanses of open land have fostered deep-rooted farming and herding traditions, which play a major part in the cuisine of the continent. Almost every dish revolves around filling starches like maize or rice, as well as fresh vegetables and fruits. In the east, that means filling root vegetables, bananas, watermelon, and coconut grown along the coast. While meat and fish aren't commonly enjoyed as main dishes by locals, they're often added to stews for extra heartiness. No matter the meal, locally sourced ingredients lend themselves to earthy flavors and protein-rich dishes.

This reliance on the land isn't just delicious to taste in traditional fare, but it's just as beautiful and intriguing to witness. Keep your eyes peeled as you drive through Tanzania and Kenya, where you're sure to spot members of the Maasai tribe herding cows, sheep, and more. Or marvel at small, family-run farms that dot the landscape while passing through rural villages, where locals grow most of their own food.

Tagine

This term does double duty in both the Middle East and North Africa. It refers to conical, earthenware pots as well as the slow-cooked meat or vegetable dishes prepared in them.

Biltong

A snack staple in South Africa, this cured meat is made from beef, chicken, fish, or game such as wildebeest or springbok antelope. To prepare it, thick, flat strips are air dried using vinegar, salt, and spices.

Dolma

This word refers to stuffed vegetable dishes and is most often used to describe leaves stuffed with rice, meats, and herbs in the Middle East. In Istanbul, shared taxis packed with commuters are often nicknamed *dolmas*.

Dig in the right way

Forget the fork, because eating with your hands is a common and acceptable way to enjoy many meals in both Africa and the Middle East (think pita bread dipped in hummus or *fufu*, a type of spongy starch used to scoop West African stews). But there are still some universal rules shared by the two destinations that dictate the proper way to do it. Be sure to wash your hands before your meal, and when popping each morsel into your mouth, use only your fingers and only your right hand—the left is considered unclean.

293

At the heart of South African wine

From miles of picturesque coastline to cosmopolitan cities to world-class animal viewing, just about everything in South Africa is sublime. It's no wonder, then, that the destination's wines have made their way onto the list of amazing things the country has to offer. Get to the core of "the Rainbow Nation's" wine scene along the Western Cape. Bounded by roaring ocean and soaring mountains, the area experiences cool, rainy winters and warm, dry summers—and creates wines that bridge the gap between Old- and New-World styles.

Viticulture by the numbers

62

As in Route 62, the longest wine route in the world, which meanders through South Africa's most fertile valleys for more than 500 miles from Cape Town to Port Elizabeth.

1925

The year Pinot Noir and Cinsault grapes were first blended to create South Africa's now-famous Pinotage.

30%

Although sometimes disputed, 30% is widely regarded as the minimum percentage of Pinotage required for a blend to be granted status as a "Cape Blend."

100M+

With more than 100 million gallons of wine exported annually, South Africa has earned a spot on the list of the world's top 10 wine producers—among other greats like Italy and France.

Where to go for the best sips

The year 1973 brought about South Africa's *Wyn van Oorsprong* (Wine of Origin) act, which defined the country's different wine regions. If you're looking for authenticity and quality, keep an eye out for a WO seal to ensure that the wine you're sipping is made only from grapes from its region. Here's a handful of the country's many WO production areas and the vintages that make each unforgettable.

Stellenbosch:
a showstopper in the Winelands

This historic region in the center of the Western Cape's Winelands has boasted a winemaking tradition since the 17th century, and still wears the crown as South Africa's winemaking epicenter. The reds thrive off of cool ocean breezes and have the sandstone and granite soils to thank for their bold minerality. Of the area's many top-notch vinos, Pinotage (which was first created in Stellenbosch in 1925), Cabernet Sauvignon, Sauvignon Blanc, and Chenin Blanc are must-tries.

Franschhoek:
a sparkling town for sparkling

With a name that means "French Corner," a climate similar to France's, and the title of South Africa's culinary capital, it comes as no surprise that Franschhoek holds its own in wine production. The town's wheelhouse? White grape varieties such as Sauvignon Blanc, Chenin Blanc, and Semillon. While each wine has a certain *je ne sais quoi*, the region's real gem is sparkling wine made using South Africa's traditional method, *Méthode Cap Classique*— similar to the process used to make French Champagne!

Paarl:
the pearl of the Cape

Sitting pretty just north of Stellenbosch is Paarl, a region where hot summers balance out high rainfall, and rich, fruity red grapes abound. While Paarl's wine route has come to be called the "red route" (think Shiraz and Cabernet), there's certainly something to be said for the region's award-winning Chenin Blanc and Chardonnay. As for Paarl's varied terroir? It's ideal for growing a variety of different grapes, which results in unique, robust blends.

Two wines to win you over

Pinotage

Of all the varietals South Africa is known for, indigenous Pinotage is the country's indisputable standout. This bold hybrid of Pinot Noir and Cinsault has come to be known as the country's national grape, and the fruity, spicy taste of the deep red, tannic wine it produces is a favorite for blends in particular.

Chenin Blanc

Whether you prefer crisp, fruity wines, always opt for an unoaked Chard, or are looking for a good blend, the Chenin Blanc grape can deliver. It's distinguished as South Africa's most widely cultivated grape, and sipping the bright, acidic white wine it creates is the perfect way to round out an adventure-filled day on a game drive.

RECIPE RECOMMENDED BY

Rebecca
Go Ahead Tours

TOTAL TIME:
20 minutes

SERVINGS:
4

RECIPE ORIGIN:
Morocco

INGREDIENTS:

For the salad

1/2 lb soft, log-shaped goat cheese

8 fresh figs

2 handfuls arugula

4 leaves red-leaf lettuce, chopped

16 fresh basil leaves, cut in ribbons

For the dressing

1/2 cup extra-virgin olive oil

1 Tbsp balsamic vinegar

2 tsp lemon juice

2 tsp honey

2 pinches of salt

1 pinch of pepper

Goat cheese & fig salad

DIRECTIONS:

For this French-influenced salad, spread the red-leaf lettuce and arugula on a medium plate. Then, cut the log of goat cheese into 12 slices, quarter the figs lengthwise, and arrange both ingredients on the top of the salad.

For the dressing, whisk together all ingredients and drizzle over the top of the salad. Finish the plate off with basil and serve.

My group and I ordered this salad in Casablanca and shared it. The fresh figs and goat cheese in Morocco are amazing, especially in the summer!"

—**Rebecca**, *Go Ahead Tours*

Cooking tip

Prefer to use dried figs for your salad? You can! Simmer them in a mixture of 4 parts water, 2 parts balsamic vinegar, and 1 part honey until they're soft, about 30 minutes. The liquid will rehydrate and flavor them, making them the perfect consistency for your dish.

TOTAL TIME:
1 hour
+ overnight soaking

SERVINGS:
4

RECIPE ORIGIN:
Israel

INGREDIENTS:

1/2 pound dried chickpeas, rinsed

Water, as needed

2 oz fresh cilantro, parsley, or mint leaves, or preferably a mixture of all three

6 scallions, white and pale-green parts only, sliced

2 garlic cloves, minced

1 tsp ground cumin

1/2 tsp ground coriander seed

2 tsp kosher salt

2 to 3 cups vegetable oil, for frying

3 Tbsp harissa paste

3 oz pitted black olives, roughly chopped

Tahini sauce, hummus, and/or zhug (Yemenite hot sauce), to serve

Falafel with harissa & black olives

DIRECTIONS:

Place chickpeas in a large bowl of cold water and cover. Let soak at room temperature overnight. Once they have tripled in volume, drain, rinse, and dry them using a salad spinner or a clean dish towel.

In a food processor, pulse chickpeas, fresh herbs, scallions, garlic, cumin, coriander, and salt until the chickpeas are finely minced. Once you think you've reached a good consistency, try this test: Squeeze a handful of the mixture into a ball. If it barely holds together, you're ready to fold in harissa and black olives with a spatula.

Spoon the mixture into a separate bowl and refrigerate covered for about 15 minutes. Then, 1 Tbsp at a time, scoop heaping portions into your hands and form into balls.

Place a deep cast-iron pan or nonstick skillet over high heat and warm 3/4 in vegetable oil until it's 375°F. Gently place chickpea balls into the hot oil and cook until the bottoms are browned. Flip the balls and allow the other side to brown for about 4 minutes, then place on a paper towel and season with salt. Serve with tahini, hummus, or zhug.

Hummus

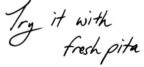

Try it with fresh pita

TOTAL TIME:

2 hours

+ overnight soaking

SERVINGS:

4

RECIPE ORIGIN:

Israel

INGREDIENTS:

1 cup dried chickpeas, rinsed

Water, as needed

1/4 cup tahini

2 garlic cloves

1/2 cup lemon juice

1 tsp salt

Pepper, to taste

1/2 tsp ground cumin

3 Tbsp extra-virgin olive oil

2 Tbsp pine nuts, to garnish

Paprika, to garnish

2 Tbsp fresh herbs like parsley or rosemary, to serve (optional)

DIRECTIONS:

Place chickpeas in a large bowl of cold water and cover. Let soak at room temperature overnight. Once they have tripled in volume, drain and rinse. Add chickpeas along with just enough cold water to cover them to a pot and place on high heat. Once the water starts to boil, turn the heat down and allow to simmer. Cook on low for about 1 hour, ensuring there's always enough water in the pan to cover the chickpeas. Remove pan of chickpeas from heat once they're soft and skin has begun to separate. Ladle out 1 1/2 cups of water to put aside before draining.

Scoop out 1/4 cup of chickpeas to use as a garnish and pour the remaining into a food processor. Add tahini, garlic, lemon juice, salt, pepper, cumin, and 1/2 cup of the water you saved to the processor, and purée until you achieve the ideal consistency: smooth and paste-like. If you have a hummus that's still too thick, go ahead and add more water as needed. Once you reach your desired consistency, spoon the hummus onto a plate or into a bowl and create a well in the center.

Place a medium frying pan on medium heat and toast pine nuts in 1 Tbsp oil. Drizzle oil into the indentation you created in the center of your hummus dish and sprinkle browned pine nuts, extra chickpeas, paprika, and fresh herbs if desired over the top. Serve with pita bread, raw vegetables, or your snack of choice.

TOTAL TIME:
45 minutes

SERVINGS:
6–8

RECIPE ORIGIN:
Egypt

INGREDIENTS:

For the dressing

Juice of 1 1/2 lemons

2 Tbsp pomegranate molasses

2 tsp white wine vinegar

3/4 cup extra-virgin olive oil

2 small garlic cloves, minced

1/2 tsp dried mint

4 tsp ground sumac, soaked in 4 tsp warm water for 15 minutes

Kosher salt, to taste

For the salad

3 ripe tomatoes, chopped

2 cucumbers, chopped

5 small radishes, thinly sliced

1 small head romaine lettuce, sliced

2 cups purslane leaves

6 scallions, thinly sliced

2 cups fresh, flat-leaf parsley, chopped

1 cup fresh mint leaves

Two 8-in-diameter pita breads, toasted and cut into bite-size pieces

1/4 cup extra-virgin olive oil

Kosher salt, to taste

Ground sumac, to garnish (optional)

Fattoush salad

DIRECTIONS:

First, whisk together your dressing in a small bowl, starting with your liquids. Mix up lemon juice, molasses, and vinegar before gradually stirring in oil. Once everything is well-blended, mix in garlic, mint, and sumac (including any water the spice didn't soak up). Season with salt.

Next, prepare the salad. Place your chopped veggies in a large bowl and combine with the majority of the dressing. Then, add in scallions, parsley, and mint leaves.

In a medium bowl, toss pita slices in olive oil and a pinch of salt. Add pita to your salad and combine. Finish salad with a sprinkle of ground sumac, and drizzle on remaining dressing if you desire.

Fantastic is the only way I can describe our tour of Egypt. The pyramids, desert, camels, trip on the Nile, Egyptians we met on the cruise, and food were truly amazing.

—Diane,
2nd-time traveler
Egypt & the Nile

Herbs, spices & souks

In the Middle East, spices and herbs are the real heroes of traditional cuisine, bringing bold flavors and bright colors to each dish. Here's what you might find if you were to peek inside a local's kitchen cabinet or wander through one of the region's bustling bazaars, where dazzling piles of colorful spices beckon.

What is a souk?

Walking through a traditional Middle Eastern souk is an unmatched sensory experience. These bustling open-air marketplaces are the spots to rub elbows with locals as you shop for a variety of authentic goods including exotic spices, gold jewelry, hand-woven fabrics, and earthenware *tagines*.

The spice trade's ancient roots

In antiquity, spices were as synonymous with fortune as they were with flavor, and they served as Arab merchants' instant ticket to wealth. Their use in the Middle East dates as far back as the 15th century, when cinnamon, pepper, cloves, nutmeg, and more flowed along a trade route known as "the Silk Road." The route stretched from the Far East to Europe—and Middle Eastern traders sitting smack dab in between the two destinations monopolized the market thanks to their prime location.

A sprinkle of spice mixtures

Baharat

Each Middle Eastern country has its own take on this blend, which translates to "mixed spices" in Arabic, and is commonly used to season meat and poultry. In stores, you can find flavorful combinations called *sebah baharat*, or seven spices.

Ras El Hanout

Up to 30 of the best spices go into this strong blend, which originated in the North African county of Morocco and translates to "top of the shop" in Arabic. Merchants in the Middle East put their own spin on their mixtures, and each finished product adds a punch to soups, roasted vegetables, curried rice, and more.

Za'atar

In this versatile, flavorful blend, thyme is balanced out by the nutty flavor of sesame seeds, the lemon-like taste of sumac, and a pinch of salt. Marjoram and oregano are commonly included, and the mixture is added to everything from pita bread to fresh fish dishes.

Mint

Aromatic and fresh, mint is a versatile herb that can bring more flavor to sweet desserts and hearty meat dishes alike.

Sumac

Often used as a substitute for lemons, sumac's tart tanginess lends acidic undertones to everything from fish dishes to spice mixes.

Cumin

Fragrant and warm, cumin adds a savory, spicy, and slightly bitter element to meats, couscous, hummus, falafel, and more.

Anise

Native to the Middle East, this star-shaped seed is often ground up and incorporated into cookies, breads, and cakes for a sweet taste reminiscent of black licorice.

Turmeric

The bright yellow color and mild flavor of this classic spice adds a pop to dishes such as curries, stews, rices, and soups.

Cardamom

The aromatic essence of cardamom brings a level of complexity to any dish, and is popularly added to coffee for a unique kick.

Saffron

Commonly referred to as "red gold," this expensive spice resembling delicate threads brings a honey-like flavor to rice dishes, kebabs, and beyond.

Caraway

Strong, earthy, and reminiscent of cumin, caraway can be used to add a touch of spice to Middle Eastern dishes, including the popular sauce known as *harissa*.

Nutmeg

Nutmeg's nutty, earthy taste infuses baked goods, confections, and savory dishes alike with a subtle sweetness similar to cinnamon.

TOTAL TIME:
1 hour, 40 minutes

SERVINGS:
6

RECIPE ORIGIN:
Turkey

INGREDIENTS:

1 lb 2 oz ground lamb

2 tsp Kosher salt, divided

2 tsp ground cumin, divided

6 tsp ground sumac, divided

2 Tbsp ground Urfa pepper flakes, divided

2 Tbsp ice-cold water

1 cup fresh, flat-leaf parsley, to garnish

1 red onion, thinly sliced, to serve (optional)

6 pieces lavash or pita bread, to serve (optional)

Adana kebab

Ground lamb kebab

DIRECTIONS:

In a large bowl, combine lamb with 1 tsp salt, 1 tsp cumin, 2 tsp sumac, and 1 Tbsp pepper flakes. Using your hands or a mixer, knead the ingredients together until the mixture starts to stick to the side of the bowl. Knead in water and refrigerate for about 1 hour. While the meat is chilling, combine the rest of the cumin, sumac, pepper flakes, and salt in a separate small bowl.

Create 12 balls of the lamb mixture by dividing it with damp hands and rolling between your palms. Then, mold each ball into a long, flat shape around a skewer. Heat your grill and arrange kebabs on the surface. Turn each with tongs and sprinkle with the spice mixture occasionally until all sides are slightly charred and the meat is cooked, about 12 minutes.

Top kebabs with parsley and serve with warm bread and your choice of fresh vegetables, such as onion, for crispness.

TOTAL TIME:

2 hours, 40 minutes

SERVINGS:

4

RECIPE ORIGIN:

Turkey

INGREDIENTS:

1 cup plain yogurt

10 garlic cloves, mashed into a paste, divided

1⁄2 cup lemon juice, divided

1⁄4 cup olive oil, divided

2 Tbsp Aleppo pepper, divided

1 Tbsp ground cumin

1 Tbsp ground coriander

1⁄2 Tbsp dried mint leaves

Kosher salt and black pepper, to taste

1 lb boneless, skinless chicken thighs, cut into 2-in pieces

10 fresh mint leaves, finely chopped

Shish taouk

Spiced chicken kebabs with garlic yogurt sauce

DIRECTIONS:

In a small bowl, whisk together yogurt, half of the garlic, a third of the lemon juice, 2 Tbsp oil, and 1/2 Tbsp Aleppo pepper. Put aside until you're ready to serve skewers.

In a separate, large bowl, combine the rest of the garlic, lemon juice, oil, and Aleppo pepper with cumin, coriander, mint, salt, and black pepper. Toss chicken in the mixture and chill for 2 hours. Skewer chicken on about 8 skewers, then heat grill and arrange kebabs on the surface. Turn each skewer with tongs occasionally until chicken is slightly charred and cooked through, about 10 to 12 minutes.

Serve with yogurt sauce.

Did you know?

While the origins are up for debate, it's been said that kebabs got their official start in Turkey. Turkish soldiers would skewer meat using their swords and roast it over open fires in fields, and it's believed that's how the traditional *kebab*, which means "to roast," came about.

TOTAL TIME:
45 minutes

SERVINGS:
6

RECIPE ORIGIN:
Morocco

INGREDIENTS:

2 Tbsp water (for dressing)

1/2 cup thawed orange juice concentrate, undiluted

1/3 cup lemon juice

2 Tbsp olive oil

2 tsp ground cumin

1/2 tsp salt

1/4 tsp pepper

3 cups chicken breasts, chopped, skinned, and cooked

2 cups cucumber, peeled and chopped

1 cup red bell pepper, chopped

1/4 cup green onions, thinly sliced

2 cups water (to cook couscous)

1 1/2 cups uncooked couscous

1/2 cup golden raisins

1/2 cup fresh cilantro, chopped, to serve (optional)

North African chicken with couscous

DIRECTIONS:

In a large bowl, whisk together water, orange juice, lemon juice, and oil for the base of the dressing. Then, stir in cumin, salt, and pepper. Add chicken, cucumber, bell pepper, and green onions to the bowl, and toss with the dressing.

Next, place a medium saucepan on high heat and bring 2 cups of water to a boil. Add couscous and raisins, remove mixture from the heat, and cover. Allow couscous to stand and soak up liquid for 5 minutes, then fluff with a fork. Add couscous into the bowl with the dressing, chicken, and vegetables, and fold in so that everything is well-mixed. Plate and garnish with fresh cilantro if desired.

Did you know?

Couscous is a culinary staple in North Africa—in fact, it's Morocco's national dish—and it's usually handmade by sprinkling water on semolina flour and rubbing the mixture to roll it into small balls.

TOTAL TIME:
40 minutes

SERVINGS:
4

RECIPE ORIGIN:
Morocco

INGREDIENTS:

A generous pinch of saffron

20 oz fish or chicken stock

1 Tbsp olive oil

1 onion, chopped

2 garlic cloves, chopped

A small piece of ginger (thumb-sized), peeled and grated

1/2 green chili, finely sliced, plus more to garnish (optional)

1 Tbsp tomato purée

2 tsp ground cumin

1 tsp ground coriander

1 tsp cinnamon

10 cherry tomatoes, halved

2 Tbsp ground almonds

Zest of 1 orange

Juice of half an orange

1 Tbsp honey

1 1/2 lbs white fish, cut into large chunks

1/2 red bell pepper, sliced into rings

1 lemon, sliced into rounds

A handful of flaked almonds, toasted, to garnish (optional)

A small bunch of cilantro, chopped, to garnish (optional)

Couscous and yogurt, to serve (optional)

Fish tagine with saffron & almonds

DIRECTIONS:

Put saffron threads in your choice of hot stock and allow to steep. Then, place a separate large pan on medium heat and warm up oil. Sauté onion in heated oil until it's soft and translucent, about 5 minutes, before mixing in garlic, ginger, and sliced chili. Cook for a few minutes, then stir in tomato purée, cumin, coriander, and cinnamon. Cook for about 3 minutes before incorporating halved tomatoes, ground almonds, orange zest and juice, honey, and saffron-infused stock. Allow the mixture to simmer uncovered until tomatoes break down, about 10 minutes.

Once tomatoes have broken down, immerse fish in the sauce and top with bell pepper and lemon. Turn heat to low, cover, and simmer until the fish is cooked, 2 to 3 minutes. Serve in cooking dish with almonds, cilantro, chili, couscous, and yogurt if desired.

RECIPE RECOMMENDED BY

Leonore
Tour Director

RECIPE RECOMMENDED BY

Jamie
Go Ahead Tours

Pumpkin & sweet potato soup

TOTAL TIME:

2 hours

SERVINGS:

6

RECIPE ORIGIN:

Tanzania

INGREDIENTS:

2 Tbsp vegetable oil

1 onion, chopped

1 leek, chopped

1 pumpkin, peeled and chopped

2 large sweet potatoes, peeled and chopped

1 tsp fresh ginger, grated

2 garlic cloves, chopped

1 tsp ground cinnamon

4 cups chicken stock

2 to 3 cups water, plus more as needed

Salt and pepper, to taste

3/4 cup cream

A small bunch of fresh, flat-leaf parsley, finely chopped, to ganish

DIRECTIONS:

Heat oil in a large soup pan over medium heat, and sauté onion and leek until soft and translucent, about 5 minutes. Then, mix in pumpkin, sweet potato, ginger, garlic, and cinnamon. Let the mixture cook for about 5 minutes before adding chicken stock and water. If needed, add more water to the pot to completely cover the vegetables.

Turn the heat to high and bring mixture to a boil. Then, reduce to low heat and allow soup to simmer until pumpkin and sweet potato are soft, about 1 hour. Stir occasionally, and season with salt and pepper. Gently mash by hand, then transfer soup to a blender and purée until smooth. If mixture is too thick, add water as needed. Mix in cream before serving and top with chopped parsley.

Did you know?

It's common for locals in Africa to enjoy fresh vegetables in their own daily meals, and chefs in the national park lodges use these same ingredients in soups, stews, and more. Keep an eye out for dishes made with seasonal vegetables while on safari!

INGREDIENTS:

For the filling

1 Tbsp butter

2 Tbsp vegetable oil

2 onions, chopped

1/2 tsp garlic, chopped

1 Tbsp curry powder

1 tsp ground turmeric

1 1/2 lbs minced lamb or beef

2 slices bread, crumbled

1 tsp salt

1 tsp pepper

3 oz dried apricots, chopped

1 Granny Smith apple, peeled and chopped

1/4 cup sultanas (golden raisins)

1 1/2 oz slivered, roasted almonds

1/4 cup milk

1 egg

Zest of half a lemon, finely grated

Juice of half a lemon

6 lemon, orange, or bay leaves

Yellow rice, to serve

For the topping

1 cup milk

2 eggs

1/2 tsp salt

Bobotie

Minced meat pie

DIRECTIONS:

Preheat oven to 325°F.

For the pie filling, place a medium saucepan over medium heat and warm up butter and oil. Add onion and garlic, and sauté until onion is soft and translucent, about 5 minutes. Mix in curry and turmeric and cook for about 1 minute before adding meat, cooking until golden brown, about 7 minutes. Spread mixture into a large, greased casserole dish.

In a separate bowl, combine bread, salt, and pepper. Then, fold in apricots, apple, sultanas, and almonds before whisking in milk, egg, and lemon zest and juice. Spread the mixture evenly over your casserole, arrange lemon, orange, or bay leaves on top, and cover with foil. Place dish in the oven.

While bobotie cooks, whisk together milk, eggs, and salt for the topping. Once your dish has been baking for 1 hour and 15 minutes, cover with topping mixture and increase the temperature to 400°F. Allow the dish to bake until the top is lightly browned, about 15 more minutes. Serve with yellow rice.

SERVINGS:
6

RECIPE ORIGIN:
Israel

INGREDIENTS:

1/4 cup vegetable oil

2 lbs fresh tomatoes, quartered

2 tsp tomato paste

6 garlic cloves, roughly chopped

1 tsp sweet paprika

Salt, to taste

6 eggs

1/4 cup fresh, flat-leaf parsley, chopped, to garnish

Red onion, sliced, to serve (optional)

1 cup feta cheese or cubed tofu (optional)

Shakshuka

Stewed tomatoes with poached eggs

DIRECTIONS:

Place a small saucepan over low heat and warm up oil. Add tomatoes, tomato paste, garlic, paprika, and salt, and thicken the mixture by simmering uncovered for about 30 minutes.

Grease a 12-in frying pan and transfer the sauce to the pan to simmer. Once the sauce has reached a simmer, crack the eggs in and top with parsley. Add onion, feta, and tofu if desired and cover until eggs are set, about 4 minutes. Scoop the finished dish directly out of the pan and onto individual plates at the table to serve.

One of my favorite memories? My first lunch in Israel. The table was suddenly ablaze with colors; savory dips, roasted and pickled vegetables, glistening olives, fresh salads, and a seemingly infinite selection of sauces lay before us. The mainstays of Middle Eastern condiments—hummus, baba ganoush, tahini, and tabouleh—were all there, too.

—Emily,
1st-time traveler
The Wonders of Ancient Israel

TOTAL TIME:
30 minutes

SERVINGS:
6

RECIPE ORIGIN:
Kenya

INGREDIENTS:

1 cup fresh ground coconut

1 1/2 cups sweet potatoes, boiled or mashed

3/4 cup sugar

1/2 tsp cinnamon

1/2 tsp mixed spices

3/4 cup milk

1/2 cup water

4 Tbsp melted butter

2 eggs

Coconut & sweet potato pudding

DIRECTIONS:

Heat oven to 350°F. In a medium bowl, thoroughly combine coconut and sweet potato. Then, incorporate sugar, cinnamon, and spices, blending well. Pour in milk, water, and melted butter, and beat until the consistency is smooth. In a separate bowl, lightly whisk eggs before mixing them into coconut and sweet potato mixture. Whisk everything together until there are no lumps.

Grease a cooking dish and bake mixture until the top of the pudding is golden brown, about 30 minutes. Plate dessert while it's hot or let it cool and serve.

Did you know?

Coconut trees grow abundantly along Africa's eastern coast, and coconut is a common ingredient in both sweet and savory dishes in Kenya, Tanzania, and beyond.

"

Food is our common ground, a universal experience.

—James Beard

Recipes by region

Latin America

(continued)

Asia

Australia & New Zealand

Africa & The Middle East

Trying your hand at one of these dishes?

Snap a picture of your masterpiece and share it with **#goaheadtours** on Facebook and Instagram!

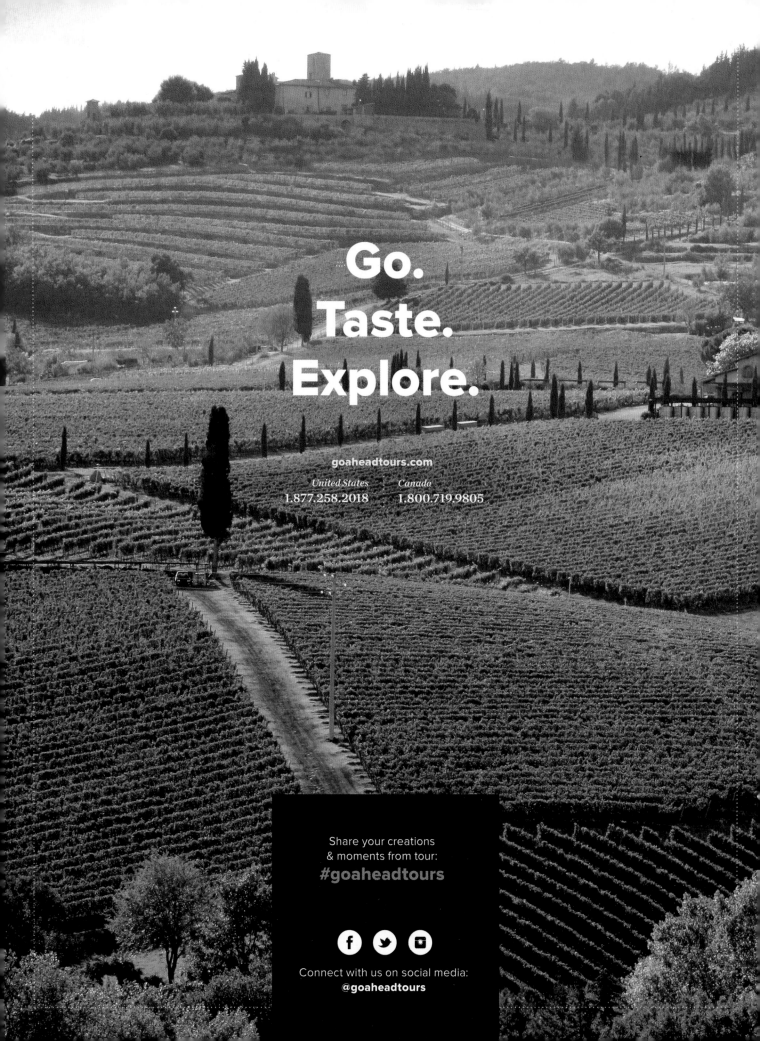

Go.
Taste.
Explore.

goaheadtours.com

United States
1.877.258.2018

Canada
1.800.719.9805

Share your creations
& moments from tour:
#goaheadtours

Connect with us on social media:
@goaheadtours